The RUGGED LIFE

THE MODERN GUIDE TO Self-Reliance

Clint Emerson

ILLUSTRATIONS BY DAVID REGONE

Rodale • New York

Library of Congress Cataloging-in-Publication Data
is available.

ISBN 978-0-593-23519-5
Ebook ISBN 978-0-593-23520-1

Printed in the United States of America

Book design by Jan Derevjanik
Cover design and illustration by Jim Tierney

1st Printing

First Edition

"It is easy to see that a greater self-reliance must work a revolution in all the offices and relations of men; in their religion; in their education; in their pursuits; their modes of living; their association; in their property; in their speculative views."

—Ralph Waldo Emerson

CONTENTS

INTRODUCTION: Who is the RUGGED LIFE For? 8

1 | BE YOUR OWN Builder 014

2 | BE YOUR OWN Power Grid 036

3 | BE YOUR OWN Farmer 052

4 | BE YOUR OWN Butcher 092

5 | BE YOUR OWN Hunter 130

6 | BE YOUR OWN Home-maker 166

7 | BE YOUR OWN Protector 186

8 | BE YOUR OWN RTO 200

9 | BE YOUR OWN First Responder 212

10 | BE YOUR OWN Handyman 232

AFTERWORD: Be Your Own Homesteader 262
ACKNOWLEDGMENTS 266 • INDEX 267

INTRODUCTION | WHO IS THE RUGGED LIFE FOR?

The Rugged Life is for everyone who feels they can use more adventure, freedom, and choice in their lives and who's ready to get out of their comfort zone and try new hard things.

Taking on the Rugged Life means actually thinking with purpose about how you want to live and what you want for your family. And then being curious, confident, and committed enough to take on the skills and know-how to handle whatever is thrown at you.

In my *100 Deadly Skills* books, I explored the first minutes, hours, and days of a crisis. And how to maintain a baseline of being alive—still breathing, having most of your blood still in your body, with no other threats in sight. Now in *The Rugged Life* I'm moving beyond survival to how to thrive over the long term, for months, years, even a lifetime, by being self-reliant. And that starts with learning how to be a modern homesteader.

If that conjures up visions of log cabins, covered wagons, and bonnets, don't worry; that's definitely not what we're talking about. Modern homesteading takes that same level of pioneer spirit and brings it forward to the needs and expectations of today. No bonnets necessary, and plenty of variability in how far you choose to go with it.

At its most basic level, homesteading is farming, but instead of raising and growing things to sell, you're doing all that work to feed yourself and your family. It's about doing as much for yourself as you can (or as you choose to), with the intention of living life more simply and with more self-sufficiency. That can mean that you never go to the grocery store, period, or it can mean that you go once a month for dry goods. You get to choose.

Now, I have to tell you, I'm incorporating many of the ideas in this book into my own life, but homesteading is not something they taught at BUD/S (that's a Navy SEALs joke). But I do know from my years in the military that with the right guidance you can learn to do anything. So for the past year I've been traveling the country seeking out experts in self-sufficient living and homesteading.

Everyone I spoke to was kind enough to share their why and their how. And each interestingly had their own individual specialty. Some were focused on producing their own power, knowing that if they're off-grid, they are more in control and less reliant on power companies. Some figure, "If I can just get enough eggs for my breakfast, that's all I need," while others grow their own hay to feed their livestock.

From the Trayers, who cut and milled their own wood to build their house (which runs on only 300 watts harvested from the sun); to the Rapiers, who have six kids—and one more on the way—helping out with raising their sheep, goats, chickens, quail, and horse; to the Norrises, who can preserve enough of the food they grow themselves to feed themselves for a year, these folks know what they're doing, and they learned it by doing it.

Deciding What You Are Ready For

In *The Rugged Life* you get to choose to step back a little or a lot. Whether you decide to move your family off-grid to the middle of God-Knows-Where or you're gathering the salad for your dinner from your windowsill garden in a city, it's up to you. That's the Rugged Life. It can be whatever you want to make of it—because you are in charge of your own choices and your own level of commitment. You can live the Rugged Life while farming your own food and using the waste from your toilet for compost or you can live the Rugged Life while keeping a chicken coop in your backyard and watching Netflix with your dog. You can homestead in a suburb or in the middle of your twenty-acre sanctuary. It's all on the same spectrum.

But whether you're on- or off-grid, you want to be able to support yourself, and I don't necessarily mean financially. Being truly self-reliant means that you are able to be anything you need yourself to be. Be Your Own Farmer. Be Your Own Handyman. Be Your Own First Responder. Be Your Own _____.

True off-the-grid living takes incredible commitment to spend every hour of every day in service of subsistence. Even if that's for you, it might not be for everyone else in your household. So before we go further, take a moment to ponder the following questions from the off-the-gridders profiled in the book to see what level of the Rugged Life is right for you (and for your family).

THE TOP 10 *ARE YOU SURE ABOUT THIS?*

1. Do you have the right mind-set?
Things are going to go wrong, and when
they do, you have to know what to do. Are
you the sort of person who will work the
problem, or will you give up?

**2. Do you like the people you'll be
living with?** Sure, you probably love them,
but we're talking every day, all day, just you
and them. If they're not enough for you and
you need outside contact, consider how
off-grid you want to go. Seriously, if your
family drives you crazy, make sure you've
got friends and neighbors around.

3. Do you like research? 'Cause you're
going to be doing a lot of it. You will make
mistakes, but you'll make fewer of them
if you study up on how to do it right the
first time.

**4. Do you like traveling and taking
vacation?** Because if you have livestock,
you won't really get to leave home.

5. Do you have a strong stomach?
Slaughtering is one thing, but consider
having to deal with the carcass of your dead
livestock.

6. Do you commit? If you're the sort of
person who signs up for a 30-day diet or
exercise program and gives up after a week,
this may not be the life for you.

7. Do you have the money? If you're in
this to live more cheaply, you're always
going to be able to get cheaper eggs at the
store. Equipment, feed, land, it all adds up.
Your eggs are going to be more healthful
and way more delicious, but they are going
to cost more.

8. Do you have time? In order to afford all
of this, you'll likely still have a day job, at
least at the beginning. What does your job
allow you to be able to do in the remaining
hours of the day?

9. Do you like hard work? When you've
got the flu, you've still got to feed the
chickens and milk the goats.

10. Do you have a Why? Everybody has to
have one, something to get them to keep
at it when the crops fail or the sheep gets
bloat or the barn collapses in a tornado.
What is the Why that will keep you going?

Three Basic Skills

Don't worry if you are not ready for full off-the-grid living. Not many are. There is still plenty you can and should learn, though, from the principles of modern homesteading, which relies on three skills that apply to whatever level you are ready for:

⊗ **Knowing How to Build**

👑 **Knowing How to Farm**

🦌 **Knowing How to Hunt**

You could *maybe* skip out on the hunting if you're raising livestock, but honestly, it's a good thing to know how to do just in case. What if all your rabbits get sick and die?

Now, do you have to be an expert in all three of those things? Absolutely not. It helps, sure, but there's a whole lot of learning as you go in homesteading. There're also a lot of experimentation and creativity—both of which come from making mistakes and then learning from them.

You've got to just get out there and do it. You can fail once, twice, even three times, but after that, you not only know

how to do something, you know *why* it works for you, and therefore when it comes to doing the next thing—like building a house after you've successfully built a shed, or raising a sheep after you've successfully raised chickens—you'll know that much more about how to get it right the first time. All the information given here is meant to help you make *fewer* mistakes, but none of it is a substitute for paying attention to your surroundings and using common sense. You need to figure out what works best for you.

At the outset, living the Rugged Life doesn't require a specific set of skills so much as it requires a specific mind-set: you have to decide to be the kind of person who keeps trying and keeps improvising. What works for someone else may not work for you, and you have to be open to failing your way into figuring out what does work for you. I'm going to give you many suggestions and hints for ways to make things easier/cheaper/more effective, but the reality is that only you will be able to determine what your rugged life looks like, and what makes you love it and want to keep living it.

Choosing Your Own Adventure

Here's the thing: I never met a single person who is truly self-sufficient. Everyone relies on the outside world to a certain extent, whether it's going to the hardware store to buy a tool to build their chicken coop or ordering special yeast online to make their bread. Folks may be completely self-reliant in one way, and completely dependent in another. They chose what was important to them, and at what level of self-reliance they wanted to operate. One of the greatest changes since the hippie back-to-the-land movement of the 1960s and '70s is that technology allows us to incorporate many of the benefits of modern homesteading right into our tied-into-the-grid homes—solar power, energy-saving builds, gardens, chickens, bees, water catchment.

In every chapter, I will offer half steps and full steps, and you can pick and choose what works for you. Want to be full solar-power but still do most of your grocery shopping at the supermarket? Done. Want to farm but not give up your air-conditioning or internet? You got it. When you live the Rugged Life, you get to choose your own adventure. Each of the skills covered in this book stands on its own, and taken together, they can help you design the kind of life you want to live. Whatever level you choose, I'm going to give you the real picture. You want to keep chickens? Well, they don't just cluck and then boom, you've got an egg! There are steps involved, including setup, maintenance, anticipation of setbacks, and endgame. I'm not just going to tell you how to build a coop, I'm going to make sure you know what chicken poop smells like and what you can do with it (chicken manure makes the best fertilizer).

But when you're making those choices, consider pushing yourself a little. Yeah, this is rugged, but that doesn't mean it's impossible. It's just a different way of getting your food and living your life, though it does require some work (and depending how off-the-grid you go—a lot of work) from you. Every step toward self-reliance subtracts some convenience. You've got to be a little more patient, a little more willing to put in the work, and generally a little tougher. But the satisfaction you get from doing all of this yourself is completely worth it.

"I went to the woods because I wished to live deliberately, to front only the essential facts of life, and see if I could not learn what it had to teach, and not, when I came to die, discover that I had not lived."

—Henry David Thoreau

The first step of modern homesteading is knowing where you want to live and what kind of home you want to live in. If you read through the questions of other homesteaders and decide that you aren't ready to leave the grid, that's fine. You can still retrofit an existing home, spec out a new home, or build a weekend retreat (that's ready for a full move-in) incorporating many self-sufficient and energy-independent principles.

There's still cheap land to be found. If you are willing to put in the time and research and live off the beaten path you can still find affordable farmland. But you put a house on that land and the price quadruples. And here's the thing: that house is likely to be more than you need. If you want to live off-grid, you don't want a big house. You want something small that'll be easy to keep warm in the wintertime and easy(ish) to keep cool in the summer. The best part about building for yourself, though, is your ability to get creative. Choosing your site to allow you to build with south-facing windows, north-facing hay bales, and an exterior kitchen with a center courtyard? That might be just right. Or you can plant plenty of shade trees and think about sleeping in the basement in the summer. It's entirely what works for you.

Of course, "warm" and "cool" are relative terms, and are dependent on your thermal comfort zone. If you can't sleep unless you've got a blanket on you and it's a balmy 68°F, then you'll probably need to stay on the grid and get central air. But if you're able and willing to be more flexible with your comfort, there are some things you can do to build a house that suits you and your needs, and draws as little energy as possible.

So how flexible are you? What's important to you?

Aesthetics. Don't discount these! The most energy-efficient house is probably a hole in the ground, but that can get really depressing really fast. How do you want your home to feel? What materials are you happy being surrounded by?

Budget. You can make a great cheap house, but there are downsides, often including aesthetics and comfort. What can you afford?

DIY. How much of this can you do yourself, and what will you need to hire out?

Size. How many people are going to be living there with you? How much space do you really need?

Climate. What's the temperature like where you live, in both summer and winter? Build to suit where you live, accepting the realities of your local climate, rather than trying to battle the climate to suit your aesthetic. And take climate into account when you're deciding *where* to live in the first place! If you see some land that's $1,500 an acre, swell, but if it's in the desert, you're going to need a ton of water, and you'll probably have to buy it. So how cheap is that land, really?

Site. What's your building site like? Can you use vegetation or placement to offset energy usage?

Based on your answers to all those questions, you may decide you're better off with an existing house or updating an existing house. But if you're still into the idea of building your own homestead, let's talk some more about thermal comfort.

Thermal comfort in building materials is dependent on two things:

→ **Thermal mass,** which is a material's ability to absorb or release heat. Stone, adobe, earth, and concrete are all high in thermal mass, and will absorb heat when it's hot (making you feel cooler) and release heat when it's cold (making you feel warmer).

→ **Insulation,** which slows the passage of heat. Insulation is light and fluffy, and the more of it you have, the more it can trap air pockets of heat. Again, it will keep you warm in the winter and cool in the summer. Insulate everything—your home, your barn, your animal housing, all of it. It's worth it.

It all comes down to how comfortable you can make yourself and your home. Remember, you're going to be living and working your homestead all day every day. You want to be able to rest and relax so that you can get up and do it all again tomorrow.

HOT TIP
Put tarpaper between the house and the roof. It'll seal out moisture and act as a barrier to leaks. If you're in a really humid environment, consider putting tarpaper on your walls, too. You can also put in a ventilation fan on the roof, to pull out the heat and prevent the greenhouse effect. Not only will this keep you cooler, it'll prevent condensation, which can lead to black mold.

Building by Zone

It's helpful to think about the climate zones in the US to determine what kind of home you should build and where.

Given that, you have a few options for the type of home you can build.

EARTHEN HOMES

Earthen homes are by nature extremely high in thermal mass, and so don't require much insulation. Earth with decent clay content will absorb moisture and balance the humidity in your home. There's a reason people have been building them for thousands of years. And if you build them yourself, earthen homes can be—get it—dirt cheap. They tend to work best in the areas with low humidity such as the Southwest. There are several options for earthen homes:

Adobe, a mixture of sand, clay, and some sort of fiber (usually straw) that is dried and made into bricks, and then stacked and mortared to form walls.

Rammed earth, a mixture of earth, sand, gravel, and clay that is wet, compressed, and often mixed with cement. It's a little harder to work with, but when done right, creates a durable, stonelike wall.

Cob, a mixture of clay, sand, water, and straw, which is formed into walls. It's soft enough to mold into whatever form you like, whether you want to build a hobbit house or another fanciful shape that works for you.

STRAW HOMES

This can seem like an incredibly bad idea, given the story of the big bad wolf, but straw is actually a great form of insulation. It doesn't work all that well in high-moisture climates for obvious reasons, but if you've got a source and live in a dry environment, you've got a ready supply of eco-friendly and inexpensive building materials. Stack up some straw bales for walls with high insulation, and add thermal mass with a layer of earthen plaster.

You could also pack some loose, clay-coated straw into structural forms, as with cob. If you pay attention to the weather patterns, you can put more clay in the wall that needs more thermal mass (often the south wall), and more straw in the wall that needs more insulation (often the north wall).

COMPOSITE HOMES

If that's all a little too DIY for you—and if you're worried about building up to code—you can also purchase composite materials that are durable, easy to work with, and that create airtight, energy-efficient structures. Since they are airtight, you have to make sure you're creating proper ventilation, or you will have issues with mold.

BUILDING ZONES

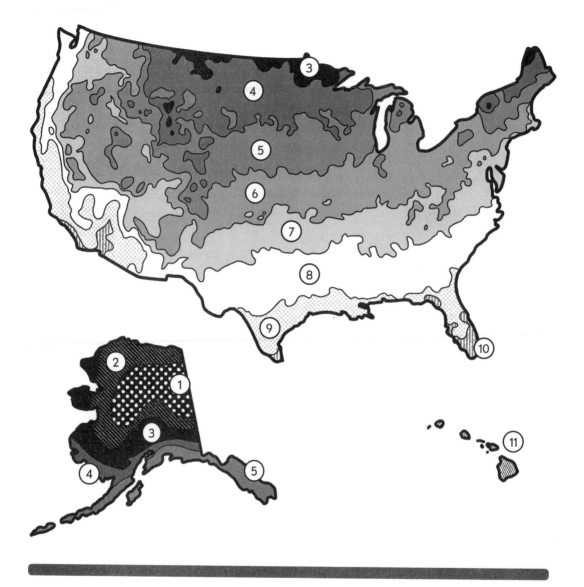

The building zones on this map match up in general with growing zones, and can help you think about where you live in relation to the weather—but that's not very specific and can vary widely within regions. For instance, Zone 7 is hot and dry in most places, but it goes up to Washington State, which is of course very rainy. As always, do your research. For more information on growing zones, check out Chapter 3.

BUILD FOR THE CLIMATE

COLD
Zones 1, 2, 3, 4

MODERATE
Zones 5, 6

HOT + HUMID
Zones 9, 10, 11

HOT + DRY
Zones 7, 8

ALTERNATIVE HOMES

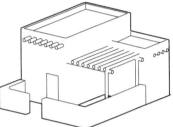
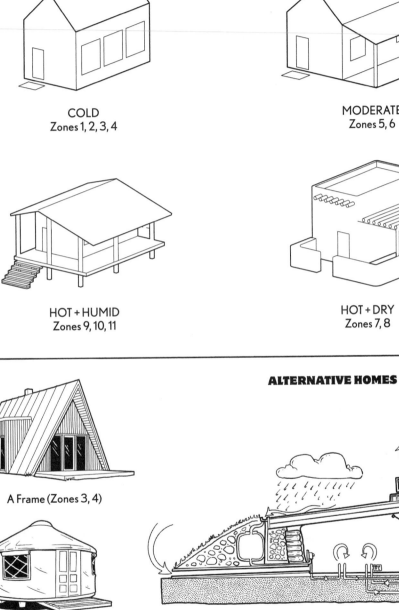

A Frame (Zones 3, 4)

Yurt (Zones 5, 6)

Earthship (Zones 7, 8)

Depending on where you live, some adjustments may need to be made for insulation, weatherproofing, etc.

Structural Insulated Panels. SIPs contain a core of rigid foam insulation that is surrounded by composite board. They arrive precut and provide insulation, but not thermal mass. They're expensive, but if you're paying a contractor, you may well end up saving money because they're incredibly easy and fast to work with.

Insulating Concrete Forms. ICFs are interlocking, hollow blocks or panels that can be stacked without mortar. There are cavities within these rigid foam structures that are reinforced with steel and then filled with concrete. They are thermally efficient and structurally sound, and their modular capabilities mean that you can be a little more creative with your structure.

HOT TIP

"Make sure you have a concrete block foundation. Wood will just rot."
—The Trayers

EARTHSHIPS

The name kind of says it all: these homes are pretty damn cool. They include natural materials, including earth and straw, as well as upcycled old tires or whatever else can be used that will still make the home energy-efficient. They are intended for off-grid living in nonhumid areas, incorporating sun and rainwater into the structure. They use thermal mass and cross-ventilation to maintain thermal comfort, and they are designed as simply as possible. That said, you'd probably want to purchase the plans since construction can get complex.

YURTS

These tentlike structures are durable, inexpensive, and shockingly livable. They're sold as kits and can be large enough to accommodate an entire family. They are extremely energy-efficient and ideal for off-grid living. They can be hot in the summer, but with proper ventilation, you'll stay cool enough. You can also build them on a raised platform to give you additional breeze and storage underneath.

HOT TIP

Whatever you build, make sure it's level. "Measure twice, cut once" is not a joke.

WOOD HOMES

What about wood? It's accessible, it's relatively inexpensive, we all basically know how to work with it. The trouble is, it's actually a terrible building material. It splits and shrinks, bugs eat it, and it's vulnerable to fire and rot. If you're like the Trayers and you can just cut down a tree and mill yourself some boards to build your house with, then hell yes, use wood. It always makes sense to use what you have. But if you're purchasing supplies, it's better to work with something more energy-efficient. If you do use wood, make sure you're using additional spray foam insulation to minimize air leakage, and add some rigid insulation on the exterior. If you're in an area with heavy rain or snowfall, an A-frame house will keep your roof from collapsing.

HOT TIP

If you generate a blueprint, you can take it to a home improvement store and they will get you the supplies you'll need to build it.

SPOTLIGHT

Tammy and Glenn Trayer • Tammy and Glenn are living the Rugged Life at its most extreme. They subsist in Northern Idaho on around 11 watts a day, treating their energy use like dollars. (This is essentially the equivalent of running one regular lightbulb in an on-the-grid home for 12 hours.) They built their house from wood they cut and milled themselves, and they hunt the majority of their meat, filling their freezer with turkey, deer, and elk during hunting season and living off of those stores until the next year. They use gravity-fed water for their sink, keeping a barrel of water upstairs in the bedroom. They built a clay fireplace for their greenhouse, which maintains and distributes the heat in place of grow lights, so they can grow (and harvest) all year long. They both feel like they were born two hundred years too late, but they live that way anyway! Their goal has always been to live on their own terms, with as little pull on society as possible. See more at trayerwildnernessacademy.com.

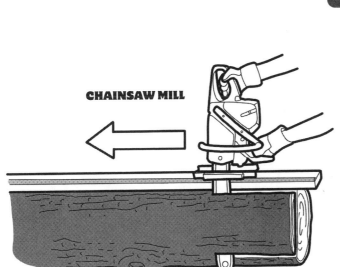

CHAINSAW MILL

HOT TIPS

The Trayers have a full sawmill, but you can cut your own planks out of felled trees for just a couple of hundred bucks. A chainsaw mill is a super-cool contraption. Say you've cut down a tree and you want to mill your own boards. All you have to do is affix this attachment to your chainsaw. Using a purchased board as a guide, you run the bracket of the mill along that flat board, giving you a straight clean cut all along the tree. Keep at it, layer after layer, and you can create several boards out of just one tree. There's a bit of a learning curve, of course, but you can get high-quality boards with just a little practice.

The locust tree is one amazing tree. If you can use that wood, your house won't rot, and no termite will be able to touch it.

Oak is another good strong wood, and cedar can handle most weather conditions.

Van Life

It's possible to homestead nomadically, and in fact it's become a doable and popular option for many people. Want to travel around seeing the country? Want the flexibility and transience of not being bound to a home address? Want to cast off all your stuff and live free and unencumbered? You can do that. Remember how folks used to drive around in VW buses in the '60s? Well, since then Van Life has become a lot more pleasant . . . and therefore a bit more complex.

Yeah, you can go full RV and drive a rig as big as a tour bus. Or you can be a little (or a lot) more rugged and fit up your van yourself. The kind of van you equip depends on a number of factors:

→ How big is your household . . . er, vanhold?

→ How tall are you? You want to be able to stand up comfortably.

→ How much storage space do you need? Think about items such as clothes, equipment, books, and things like bikes and surfboards.

→ Do you want natural light?

→ Will you be cooking inside the van? How about working?

→ Will you be putting in a bathroom?

That bathroom question is a big one. Yeah, of course you want one, but vans are *tiny* and even just a toilet will take up a lot of space. Depending on where you go, you may well have access to a public restroom. Most campgrounds where you'll park will have facilities. And if you're off in the woods, well, trees will do for liquid waste, but you don't want to leave your poop lying around. Scoop it up and pack it out.

If you're reading that and thinking, man, that is *not* for me, you can always DIY a composting toilet (see page 50).

Showering is definitely not going to happen in-van. But truck stops, state parks, and gyms have showers, and you can hook up a solar shower to rinse off outside if you've got the weather and the privacy for it. And look, it's just you and yours in your van. If you're all doing a sponge bath every other day or so, nobody's going to complain.

Speaking of weather, if you want to be able to drive your van *anywhere,* you're going to need to make sure you can regulate the temperature in there. After all, you're not going to be running the heat or air-conditioning all night. Put in some foam insulation—that'll keep you warm in the winter and cool in the summer—and make sure you can give yourself ventilation when you need it.

Once you determine your basic needs, sit down with some graph paper and sketch out how you would equip a small school bus or other high-top van (seriously, head space is important). Space will always be at a premium, so try to sketch to scale and make sure everything has more than one use—your bed will also function as a couch and your workspace will also be your eating space.

VAN DWELLING

Common Vehicle Choices

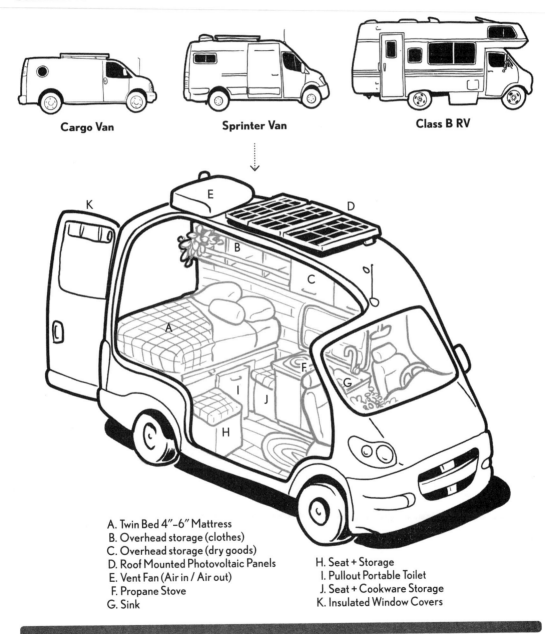

Cargo Van   Sprinter Van   Class B RV

A. Twin Bed 4"–6" Mattress
B. Overhead storage (clothes)
C. Overhead storage (dry goods)
D. Roof Mounted Photovoltaic Panels
E. Vent Fan (Air in / Air out)
F. Propane Stove
G. Sink

H. Seat + Storage
I. Pullout Portable Toilet
J. Seat + Cookware Storage
K. Insulated Window Covers

Staying Warm

The truth is that being hot is unpleasant but for the most part it won't kill you if you can stay hydrated and find some shade. If you don't do well in the heat, then consider living in areas that still have only a few uncomfortable summer days, like Zones 1 and 2. The thing you really have to worry about is staying warm in the winter. Freezing to death in your own house isn't a way anybody wants to go, and depending on where you live, that can be a real issue.

The classic homesteading method is a wood-burning fireplace or woodstove. The smaller your home, the less wood you need to keep it warm, which means less labor for you. There's a saying: when you cut your own firewood, you get warm four different times—while you're cutting it, while you're chopping it, while you're stacking it, and while you're burning it. If you have the land for it, you can take down trees, split the wood, and store enough to see you through the winter. Remember, though, your wood needs to dry out, so you have to cut enough wood for *next* winter. Anything you cut now will be too wet to burn.

Of course, not all wood is created equal. Hardwoods including maple, oak, ash, and most fruit trees will burn for a longer time at a higher temperature—but that may not be what you've got growing in your forest. If you're stuck with softer woods such as pine, spruce, or cedar, you're going to need even more. Tempting as it may be, especially if you're running out of fuel, don't burn salvaged construction wood inside your house. It's often treated with chemicals that can produce hazardous fumes, and it will clog up your chimney. It's probably okay for a bonfire, though, so long as it's not painted or varnished.

TROUBLESHOOTING

Say you need to fell a tree that's too close to a structure for comfort, but that thing's got to go. Look, it doesn't matter how many wedges you cut, the tree is going to fall in the direction it's leaning and that will typically mean whichever side has the most vegetation, i.e., the side that gets the most sun. What you need to do in this case is rig up a pulley system. Take some rope and wrap it around a nearby tree, making sure that it's big enough that it won't get pulled over, too. Use that tree as leverage, stringing up a pulley so you can haul the tree you want to fell in the direction you want it to go, without, you know, pulling it on top of you. Cut the tree as above, but have someone standing by tugging on that pulley, guiding the tree to fall where you want it to.

If you're okay with heights, you could also get a harness and some tree-climbing shoes and "top" the tree by lopping off the uppermost branches. The idea is to cut enough off the top that you can then fell it without damaging any nearby structures.

How to use an axe

You'll want to set aside a large stump as your splitting base, which will save your back some effort, and protect your axe in case you miss. Place the log on top of the base, keeping any knots near the bottom. Take aim and swing, letting your axe fall from above your head down into the log. Let the axe do the work. If the log stays on your axe when you lift it back up, simply slam it back down again. Slice your log like you would a pie, divvying it up into fairly equal pieces.

3 CORDS OF WOOD

1 season of heat for 1,000 sq ft house

HOT TIP

If you're not going to use the trees on your land to create lumber yourself, have a lumber mill come pick it up. Depending on the weight and type of your trees, that's cash in your pockets. People are always looking for lumber and/ or wood. You can also get a mobile sawmill to come to you—they will plane your wood and leave it on-site for you. Make sure you're keeping enough firewood to keep you warm for the winter, though.

HOW TO CHOP AND STORE WOOD

Hand-chopping wood is nature's gym. If you chop a full cord, you really won't need any other exercise. But far easier is to rent a splitter. Depending on where you live, you should even be able to get one dropped off and then picked up when you are done. They save a huge amount of time. But they are also a great way to get your hand crushed. So read all directions and don't drift off while using one.

HOW TO
FELL A TREE

STEP 1: Estimate Felling Zone

There's a trick you can do with an axe handle where you face the tree, hold an axe handle at arm's length, and then back away until the top of the axe is even with the treetop and the bottom is even with the base. Your feet should be just about where the top of the tree will land—but this is just an estimate, so allow for even more room.

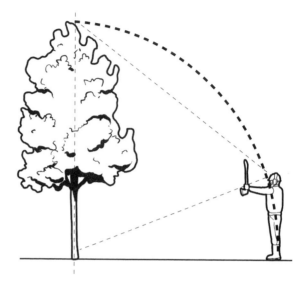

STEP 2: Clear Cutting Zone

Clear away any brush from around the trunk to make sure you have easy access, and check your escape routes. The tree may not fall exactly where you expect it to, so make sure you've got two clear paths to run away, each around 45 degrees away from each other in opposite directions.

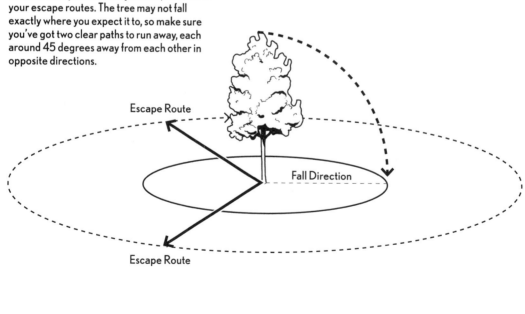

Escape Route

Fall Direction

Escape Route

STEP 3: Create Notch

You can do this with a chainsaw, and you want to place it on the side of the tree you want to hit the ground. Make the depth of the notch around one-fifth of the trunk's diameter, with reasonably sharp angles (see diagram). Make the top cut first, followed by the bottom, adjusting until the wedge falls out.

STEP 4: Make the Felling Cut

On the opposite side of the trunk from the notch, slice directly into the tree, aiming for the apex of the notch. The instant the tree begins leaning, pull the saw free, set the chain break, and walk away along your escape route—don't ever take your eyes off the tree.

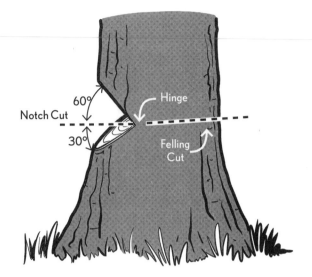

60°
Notch Cut
30°
Hinge
Felling Cut

STEP 5: Chop it Up

Use the chainsaw to remove the larger branches and to slice the trunk into the length that will fit in your woodstove.

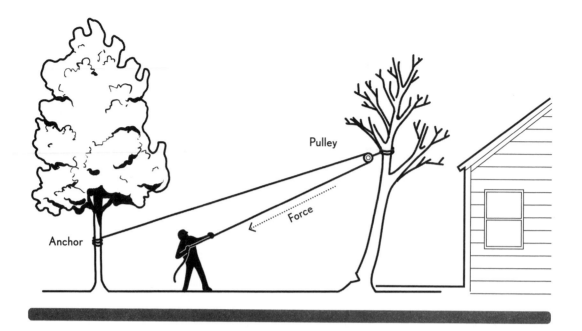

Pulley

Force

Anchor

Stack your logs where they can dry out, either in a shed or under your house, though that can attract rats and other rodents. You want some airflow, so keep them stacked off the ground on pallets. Make pillars in the four corners of your intended stack by crisscrossing to create more stability, then stack your remaining logs in a single row between them. Move carefully and with precision. There's nothing more annoying (and possibly dangerous) than seeing your hard work topple over. And remember, if you are stacking unseasoned wood, you won't be using it for a while, so create a system that places older wood in the front, closest to the furnace or woodstove.

To get through a northern US winter, you'll probably need three cords of wood to heat a 1,000-square-foot home (so obviously if your house is bigger than that, your supply of wood goes up—remember, the smaller your house, the easier it is to heat).

A cord of wood is defined as 128 cubic feet, which is a stack of wood that is 4 feet wide, 4 feet high, and 8 feet long.

So how many trees is that, exactly? Estimating based on a tree that has a 10-inch-diameter trunk, you're likely to need five trees for one cord of wood. You're looking at having to fell, chop up, and season fifteen trees for every winter. If it's available, you can always buy firewood, but that'll run you around $200 to $400 per cord delivered.

HOT TIP

Pellet Stoves. Pellet stoves are a cleaner option than your traditional woodstoves. They burn pellets made from compressed sawdust, bark, and other leftover materials from lumber mills, or from agricultural waste, so they're a reasonably green option. That said, while they are more cost-efficient than, say, a furnace, they aren't cheap—installation alone will run you at least $1,500, and they require professional maintenance. Heating a home for the winter requires an average of three tons of pellets, at about $200 per ton.

Understanding the physics of your fireplace or woodstove can help you build a more efficient fire. Chimneys operate on the principle that hot air rises above cold air, and so the movement of hot gases rising from the fire creates a pressure difference between the inside of the flue (the duct inside the chimney) and the room. This is called a draught and it forces air into the fireplace—air which then feeds the fire and keeps it burning.

The thing is, though, more air makes your fire burn more quickly, and it will result in some heat loss. So you want it to be as closed as possible to extend the life and heat of your firewood—but you may also need to add some airflow if your fire could use a little more life. Pay attention to how your fire is burning. If it's roaring, it's probably going through too much wood too quickly, and you should close the damper partway. But if it's smoldering and you can barely see any flame, it's not giving off enough heat, and you'll want to open the damper back up again. Keep adjusting throughout the day, paying attention to your needs and the needs of the fire.

FIREPLACE MAINTENANCE

The reason we don't burn unseasoned wood is that its high water content will build up creosote in your chimney. Creosote is a by-product of wood burning that consists mainly of tar, and as you might imagine, it's highly flammable. If there's too much of it, it will eventually catch fire—and trust me, you don't want this kind of high-heat chimney fire to happen while you're sleeping and miles and miles away from the fire department. Because you can't be sure everyone knows what they're doing when it comes to fire, always have your chimney checked by a professional when you're buying a house. You don't want someone else's mistakes to end up costing your life.

Even seasoned wood will cause creosote buildup eventually, particularly if your fire isn't burning hot enough. To check on your flue, peer up into it, shining a flashlight or maybe angling a mirror. You'll also want to peer in from above, climbing up on the roof, removing the chimney cap, and shining a flashlight down in there. If you see buildup of a flaky, black substance, you need a cleaning. You can do the cleaning yourself, but if you see damage, definitely get a professional in there to make any necessary repairs.

If you do want to try cleaning the chimney yourself, know that it's a little complicated and you need specific equipment, so it may be better to hire someone. You can't just use any old brush; you need a chimney brush that's sized and shaped to fit your flue, as well as enough extension rods to push that brush all the way down. If you have a brick flue, you can use a metal brush, but for a stainless steel flue, you'll need a poly brush.

You'll work from the top down, so start by closing the door to your stove, or if you have a fireplace, taping plastic across the opening—otherwise you'll get ash all over your living space. Open up the damper and then climb up your ladder. Remove the chimney cap and scrub your brush up and down, working from the top of the chimney down to the bottom, adding extension rods as you go.

Once you reach the bottom, check inside to see if you've scrubbed away all the creosote. If not, keep at it. Once the flue is clean, use a Shop-Vac to clean up all the soot and creosote that have fallen.

HOW TO
BUILD A FIRE IN A FIREPLACE

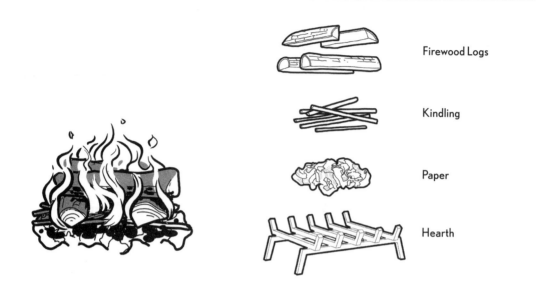

Firewood Logs

Kindling

Paper

Hearth

STEP 1: Clean It Out

You may or may not have a removable ash pan, but either way, make sure you clean out the ashes from the previous fire.

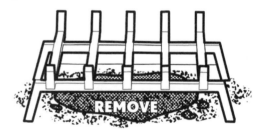

REMOVE

STEP 2: Open the Flue or Damper

Again, this will depend on your model, but make sure the airflow is wide open.

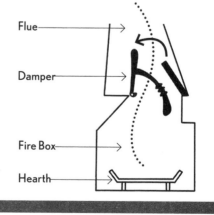

Flue

Damper

Fire Box

Hearth

STEP 3: Prepare the Kindling

Loosely crumple up a whole bunch of newspaper or other uncoated paper, then stack some kindling atop the paper. You want these to be your smallest, airiest, driest pieces of wood. Allow some space, as air is what is going to keep your fire burning.

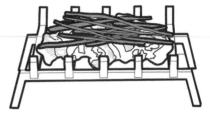

STEP 4: Light the Fire

Using a stick lighter or a long match, light the paper in multiple places and watch the kindling catch fire.

STEP 5: Feed the Fire

Add more kindling, then slightly larger pieces of wood, placing them perpendicular to each other, like Lincoln Logs. Feed it slowly but attentively, adding wood when a log is halfway burned. When the fire is burning well, you can add your regular-sized logs, but don't overwhelm it. Close the flue or damper if needed.

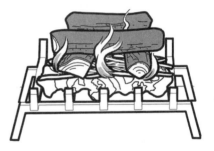

STEP 6: Enjoy the Warmth, but Monitor

From here on out, it's just a matter of paying attention. You may need to adjust the ventilation to keep more or less oxygen coming in (more will make the fire happier, but it will also burn through your fuel faster). Add logs before the logs in the stove are coming close to burning out.

GEOTHERMAL HEAT

About 6 to 8 feet underground, it's a balmy, consistent 50°F—year round. That is a wildly valuable—and free—source of temperature control, and with some effort and creativity, you can harness it in a variety of ways.

Dig yourself a big hole. We're talking 6 to 8 feet down, and wide enough so you've got around 160 square feet. Take some PVC pipe and lay it out, running it back and forth, covering as much area as possible. Fill the hole back up, leaving air intakes on either side. Using fans that run on solar, push the cold air down into the coil of PVC you've created underground. That air will get warmed there, and then it'll work its way back up, and with the help of another solar-powered fan, it will flow into your home, your chicken coop, your barn, your greenhouse—anything that needs temperature regulation. This system is known as a geothermal loop.

GEOTHERMAL LOOP

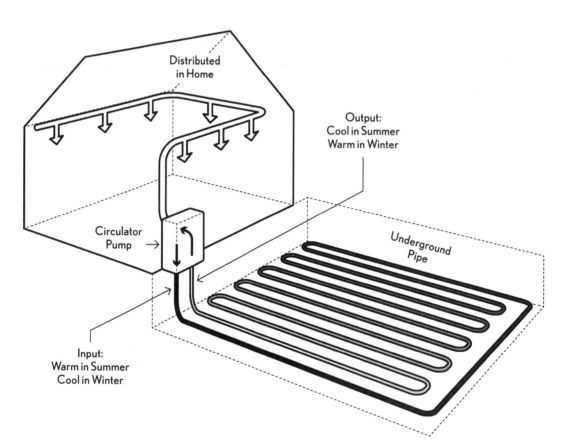

Distributed in Home

Output:
Cool in Summer
Warm in Winter

Circulator Pump →

Underground Pipe

Input:
Warm in Summer
Cool in Winter

HOT TIP Rocks make incredible thermal batteries, especially in mountainous environments. If you can incorporate rocks into your structure and place them on the southern wall, they will retain heat from the sun, sealing in warmth. They'll also help keep out predators, so they're great not only for your house but for your barns, chicken coops, goat sheds—you name it.

The reverse of all this works, too. In the summer, you'll be pushing hot air down, letting it cool off, and having it come back up to lower the temperatures indoors. It's an all-natural DIY air conditioner, and once it's installed, it requires zero maintenance and can last just about forever.

WHERE TO LIVE WHILE YOU BUILD

The problem with building on your land is that you have to live somewhere while that's happening. If you can afford it, you can stay in your current location while you're getting your homestead set up, or you can rent something nearby, but depending on your budget, that may not be an option. Tent living is tempting, but that may not work for you because of your climate, the size of your household, or simply because sleeping in a tent isn't particularly restful. If the climate is mild enough, you can build a cheap greenhouse and live in that surprisingly comfortably. Or you could consider an inexpensive mobile home like a Park Model—it's more sustainable than an RV and can likely be used as a guesthouse once your long-term home is built. Alternatively, an inexpensive "tiny home" can work well, though again, there can't be too many of you and you have to like each other a lot. At worst, you can throw up a shack with reclaimed or "unusable" wood from a nearby lumber mill, but you'd better plan to have your long-term home ready before winter.

Another idea is to get a CONEX box or shipping container—one of those big metal things you see on the back of semi trucks. They come in all different sizes and they are the perfect makeshift shelter, barn, or shed. You get one of those, cut a door in it, cut some windows (you can even frame them out and put glass in), and bam! You've got a place to live. Once your house is built, you can then use it for storage, or you could bury it in the ground as a shelter in case of emergency. You could buy several of them (or find them at a junkyard) and string them together into whatever configuration you like—bedrooms, kitchen, and living room.

If you want something a little more snazzy, there are companies that will take a container and outfit the inside to make it into a tiny home, wired with solar and everything. They send it to you, and all you have to do is switch it on.

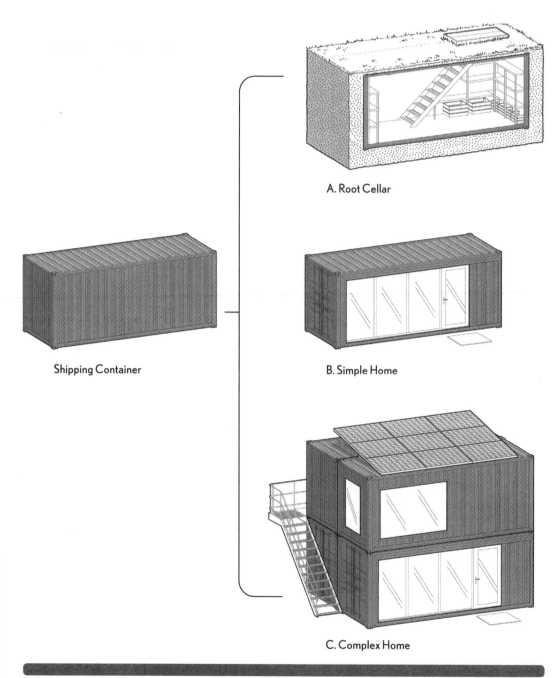

A. Root Cellar

Shipping Container

B. Simple Home

C. Complex Home

TOOLSHED ESSENTIALS

This list is divided into three sections—stuff you'll need immediately, stuff you'll need really soon, and stuff you'll need eventually but maybe want to save up for.

Right Now

- ☐ Chainsaw
- ☐ Axe
- ☐ Screwdriver/drill and screws
- ☐ Hammer and nails
- ☐ Table saw
- ☐ Tape measure
- ☐ Shovels (snow shovel, trench shovel, postholer)
- ☐ Pickaxe
- ☐ Wheelbarrow
- ☐ Machete
- ☐ Tiller
- ☐ Air compressor (whether for pneumatic tools or keeping tires squared away during winter months or dusting off anything or everything)
- ☐ Ladders (a step stool and an adjustable full-length one)
- ☐ Soldering iron
- ☐ Multimeter

Soon Enough

- ☐ Angle grinder
- ☐ Tractor
- ☐ Bow saw
- ☐ Sander
- ☐ Maul
- ☐ Pruners

Someday

- ☐ Chainsaw mill
- ☐ Splitter
- ☐ Backhoe
- ☐ ATV or utility vehicle

TOOLBOX ESSENTIALS

A well-equipped toolbox is a portable, convenient, and invaluable resource for doing basic maintenance. These are the tools you will rely on almost daily.

- ☐ Hammers (ball peen, club, mallet)
- ☐ Screwdrivers (slotted, Phillips, hex/Allen)
- ☐ Wrenches, with sockets
- ☐ Tape measure
- ☐ Pliers
- ☐ Utility knife
- ☐ Wire strippers
- ☐ Levels
- ☐ Clamps
- ☐ Flashlights (flood, spot, adjustable)
- ☐ Gloves
- ☐ Eye protection
- ☐ Ear protection

"The civilized man has built a coach, but has lost the use of his feet. He is supported on crutches, but lacks so much support of muscle. He has a fine Geneva watch, but he fails of the skill to tell the hour by the sun."

—**Ralph Waldo Emerson**

It is absolutely possible to live completely off-grid. If you've got enough solar panels and enough batteries to store the energy they gather, then you'll have all you need. Of course, rainy days happen, and when they do, you're going to have a lot less to work with. Most off-the-gridders do rely on a propane-fueled generator. Even if winter for you isn't cold, it does mean less sunlight. And a 1,000-gallon propane tank allows you to add in some of the power-sapping on-the-grid staples you may not want to give up, like constant water pressure. In years past, homesteaders were very dependent on propane and kerosene for their power needs. That said, if you're looking to go green, fossil fuels aren't helping the planet any. In fact, some states are considering doing away with selling propane altogether, so while you could power your own exclusively on a propane generator, it's best to build a system that uses it as a backup/supplement rather than your sole source of power. Also, propane generators are not maintenance free. You will need to either get really good at small engine repair or be prepared for calls to a repairman.

First things first, let's get a basic understanding of electricity and how it works, starting with electrons. Electrons are small particles that have an inherent negative charge—the movement of that charge is electricity. Things can get *a lot* more complicated than this, but these are the nuts and volts, if you will. There are four terms you need to know: voltage, current, resistance, and circuit. These four things allow us to manipulate and use electricity.

Voltage: the difference in charge between two points.

Current: the rate at which the charge is flowing.

Resistance: a material's tendency to resist current.

Circuit: a closed loop that allows charge to move from one place to another.

You can think of the circuit as a water tank. The amount of water is the charge, the water pressure is the voltage, and the flow of water is the current. The more water there is in the tank, the higher the charge, and the more pressure is measured at the end of the hose. You can think of the tank as a battery, a place where you can store electricity and release it. If you drain the tank by a certain amount, the pressure (voltage) decreases, and so does the current, like when a flashlight gets dimmer when the batteries run down.

With water, we measure the volume of water moving through the hose; with electricity, we measure the current moving through the circuit. Current is measured in amperes, or amps. Let's expand our circuit to two water tanks. Say each tank has the exact same amount of water, but the spigot on one tank is narrower than the other, so it has some resistance.

We have the same amount of pressure, or voltage, but the flow or current is less in the tank with the smaller spigot. If we want to make the flow equal again (i.e., compensate for resistance in one material), we have to increase the amount of water, or charge, in the tank with the smaller spigot, which will increase the voltage and therefore increase the current.

If voltage is called volts and current is measured by amps, resistance is measured by ohms, so that the application of one volt will push one amp, with one ohm representing the resistance between point a and point b. So, V (volts) = I (amps) × Ω (ohms). V=I × Ω is referred to as Ohm's Law. Diving into our basic algebra from high school, we can use this equation to determine how we need to adjust our current to account for resistance. Say you have

one volt on one side of the circuit, but a resistance of two on the other side. How much should the current be on that side to balance the equation? $1V = ?A \times 2\Omega$. Solving for A, we get .5.

Sometimes, you need to put in a resistor, because the amount of current coming in is more than your output can take—so if you have a 9-volt battery and a fragile LED that needs much less than that, you need a resistor to lower the current. If your LED can handle only .018 of that 9 volts, you can solve for your resistor like so: $\Omega = 9V / .018A$, which equals 500Ω. So that's the value of the resistor you need to buy. (As it happens, 500Ω is not a common resistor, but you can go up to 560Ω, which is, and know you'll be covered. When it comes to resistance, you need to meet the minimum.)

> **Basic electrical work (see page 240)**

WHY DO YOU NEED TO KNOW ALL THIS?

If your brain is shutting down—or, like mine, yelling at you that there's a reason you didn't do much math after high school—I promise, there is a reason you want to know this stuff. If you're going to be living off-grid, in the middle of nowhere, on your own piece of land handling your own shit, you want to be able to do the basics yourself. You want to know what you need to buy and what will work best with the system you have. You want to be able to do basic maintenance and repair. Sure, we all need to bring in the professionals sometimes, but the more you can handle on your own, the better.

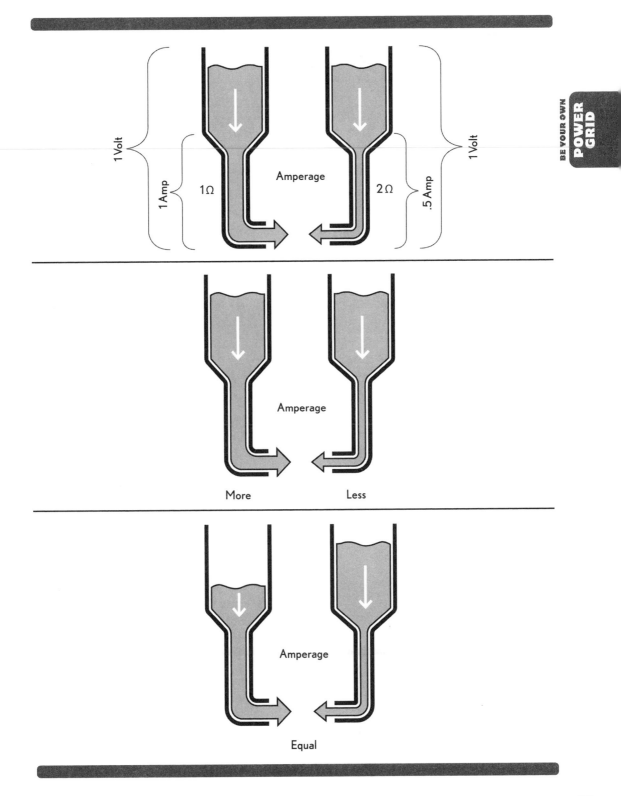

1 Volt

1 Amp

1Ω

Amperage

2Ω

.5 Amp

1 Volt

Amperage

More

Less

Amperage

Equal

Determining Your Power Needs

So how do you figure out how big a system you need? The Trayers live on around 22 watts, while the Rapiers, who also live in Idaho, use more like 350 (there are more of them, after all). Where do you land, and how do you know?

Most people in their ordinary, on-grid lives use a whopping 900 watts per day. That's a big, expensive system, and honestly more than you should be using while living the Rugged Life. You can figure out how to cut back by looking at what you are using. Check your power bills month to month, and then check the amps on your appliances and electronics. The following are the big energy vampires of the home:

→ Lighting   → Clothes dryer

→ Air conditioner   → Stove/oven

→ Electric furnace   → Dishwasher

→ Refrigerator   → Chest freezer

→ Water heater   → Water pump

The good news is that you can ditch or revamp any or all of these. You can use a solar water heater; heat your home with a woodstove; skip the air conditioner, the dryer, and the dishwasher; and switch over to LEDs. Throw out the television and the surround sound speakers. You can run your refrigerator, your water heater, your dryer, and stove on propane, though you're better off hanging your clothes on the line or building a root cellar or a spring cellar (where you store your items that need to be kept cold in a water-chilled container, kind of like keeping a six-pack in the stream while you fish).

You might look into an induction cooktop, which is incredibly energy-efficient. It uses electric current to heat, rather than thermal conduction, and can boil water up to 50 percent faster than an electric or gas stove. Or if you want to go old school, you can get a new or antique wood-burning cooktop, which will heat your house while you're at it (though you'll want to eat a salad or grill outside in the summer).

That'll knock out the big stuff, but to get down as low as you can, you'll want to get into the nitty-gritty. Look at your electrical draw like you look at calories in food. An iron draws a whopping 1,200 watts—and if you put the mister on, it goes up to 1,800. And what the hell do you even need an iron for? You're homesteading! Swap out your coffee maker for a French press, and find an antique coffee grinder like the Trayers have. Throw out the microwave while you are at it. Spend some

BREAKDOWN OF AVERAGE HOMESTEADING COSTS

Land

→ ½ acre, suburban: ~$100,000

→ 3 acres, rural: ~$30,000

House

→ Regular-sized: ~$300,000

→ Tiny: ~$20,000

Outbuildings

→ Shed: ~$3,000

→ Barn: ~$50,000

Power

→ Solar: ~$20,000

→ Wind: ~$30,000

→ Water: ~$10,000

Equipment

→ Tractor (Compact): ~$10,000

→ Pickup Truck: ~$56,000

→ Manure Spreader: ~$4,000

→ ATV: ~$3,500

→ Tools: ~$1,000

Livestock

→ Chickens: ~$30 per hen

→ Goats: ~$150 per goat

→ Sheep: ~$80 per lamb

→ Rabbits: ~$70 per rabbit

→ Pigs: ~$75 per hog

→ Cows: ~$1,000 per yearling

---

time lightening your electrical load before you take the plunge, to see how low you're willing to go. If you want, you can purchase a Kill A Watt, a handy-dandy meter that you can plug into anything and determine exactly how much it draws. It might be worth it to have an energy-efficient clothes washer, especially if you have a big family and don't live near a laundromat.

HOT TIP

"Choose laundry day based on the weather. If it's a sunny day, then, if you're on solar, you'll know you have plenty of charge to wash, and you'll know you can hang your clothes to dry."
—*The Rapiers*

The purpose of living a rugged life is not to be miserable. So design your power supply and appliances around your realistic needs and skills. If this means it's best for you to be tied into the grid, that is OK. Many modern homesteaders choose to be on the grid with solar panels and backup batteries.

Maybe back in the day we all survived just fine without electricity, but that's just not the way life is anymore. If the idea of going back to washboards and wood-burning ovens doesn't appeal to you, that doesn't make you an inauthentic homesteader, I promise. You get to choose how to make this lifestyle work for you.

Options for Power

Solar is the first and foremost power option, as it's the greenest, has no moving parts, and requires very little maintenance. Solar energy is harnessed via photovoltaic panels, which convert sunlight to energy. Unfortunately, it's still pretty damn expensive. You need photovoltaic solar panels, an inverter to convert the energy to usable electricity, and enough batteries to store all that you need—and let me tell you, those batteries cost a lot more than the ones you can get at the drugstore.

So if you're going off-grid (or if you want to stay on-grid but draw less), what you'll really be looking at is panels, an inverter, batteries, and a generator. The total cost to install a solar panel system to power a 1,500-square-foot house with electric items such as lights, a fridge, heat, a chest freezer, and a water pump is between $20,000 and $30,000. If you are looking to power a smaller portion of your home or a separate space for a business setup—an area that uses just LED lights, a computer, and Wi-Fi, you can get away with spending only between $5,000 and $10,000.

The truth is, if you're looking to save money, you're better off staying on-grid. Installation of enough solar to run your house won't pay for itself for decades. Factor in cloudy days, and you come to the depressing realization that for most people, solar alone can't cut it. You need to have some form of backup/supplement, whether it's the grid or a generator. Just so you have the info to help factor in, a 1,000-gallon propane tank costs between $1,500 and $3,500 to fill. Depending how you use it, that could be a year's worth of fuel or just a couple months. But again, cost is just one factor here; you should also balance it with the idea that these modern solar panels allow you a degree of independence and function that was unknown even in the early 2000s.

If you are building a new home, you should design it so that the solar panels can be placed on the roof where they will get the most sunlight. But if you've got land, you're not limited to roof square footage for your solar panels. In fact, keeping them on the ground will make them easier to clean and maintain. Point your solar panels south so they get the most sunlight, but you'll want to vary the angle at which they're pointing throughout the year. In the winter, angle them at 50°, but in the summer you'll have to move them to 15° as you follow the movement of the sun and the tilt of the planet. You can make this a little easier on yourself by hanging on to those big wooden spools you get when you purchase chicken wire, fencing, or cables. They look like something that would hold thread for Paul Bunyan's sewing machine. Lay them on their sides so they're like wheels, put bars across them, and attach your solar panels to the bars. You can roll the wheels back and forth to adjust the angle, and secure them in place with some rocks.

The limits of solar power are currently less about the sun and more about the

OFF-GRID POWER SETUP

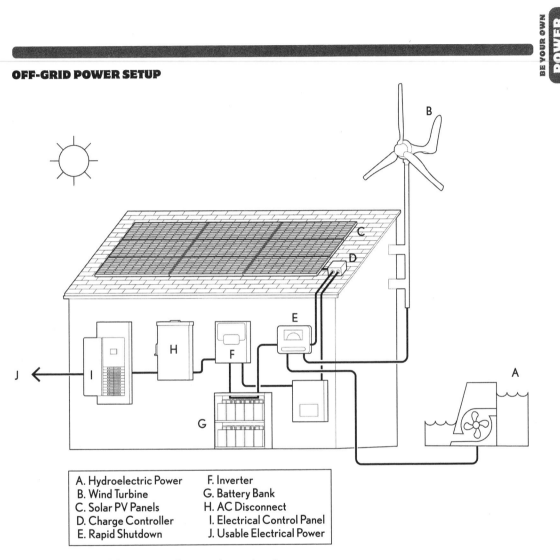

A. Hydroelectric Power
B. Wind Turbine
C. Solar PV Panels
D. Charge Controller
E. Rapid Shutdown
F. Inverter
G. Battery Bank
H. AC Disconnect
I. Electrical Control Panel
J. Usable Electrical Power

This model assumes you've got solar, wind, *and* water powering your home, which is ideal but probably unlikely—but if you can get two out of three, you'll be just fine.

SPINDLE-MOUNTED SOLAR PANELS

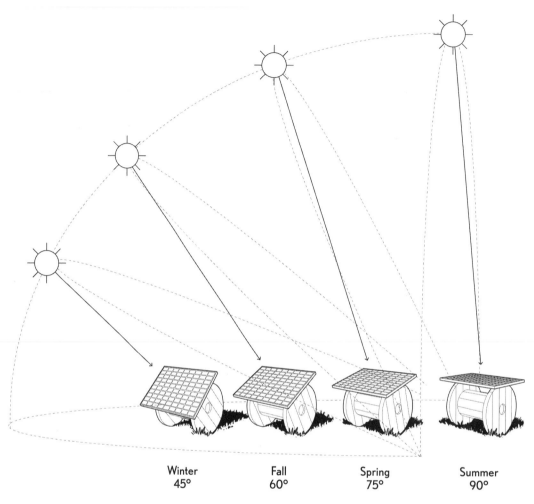

Roll your wheels every few months so that your solar panels follow the angle of the sun across the sky.

limits of battery storage. If you want to do a lot of activities at night in your home, you'll need a lot of storage and if there are days of no sunlight, you can't store anything. Also, batteries are made from rare earth metals such as lithium that are not in any way eco-friendly to mine from the earth. One innovation that seems to be around the corner is being able to take advantage of electric cars' big batteries. Hopefully, soon Tesla and other electric cars will allow you to link their batteries into your system as additional storage.

For safety reasons, make sure you store your batteries outside or in a shed. They're safe-ish . . . but not something you'd want indoors or around the kids. They create an off-gas, so it's important to install a fan that will blow it away.

Wind is another possibility. Depending on the average wind speed in your area (and various building and residential codes), you might want to purchase a residential-sized wind turbine. According to the U.S. Department of Energy's *Small Wind Guidebook*, a typical home requires a wind turbine that can generate between 5 and 15 kilowatts. The rotor size for a 10kW turbine is 23 feet in diameter, mounted on a tower more than 100 feet tall. Most towns won't let you plop something like that down in your front yard, but if you've got the real estate, it's workable. And despite their size, wind turbines are actually slightly cheaper to install than solar, though that will likely begin to change as the cost of solar goes down with its rise in popularity. On the other hand, like sunlight, wind speeds vary, and if there's no breeze, you've got no electricity. Wind turbines also have moving parts, which means more maintenance and more frequent repair than solar panels typically require. The fact is, most places in the country don't have enough wind—or more accurately, don't have the right kind of wind. Turbulence, or "dirty wind," when the air swirls around back and forth, doesn't work. You need a stiff, consistent wind flowing in one direction, which means large areas of open space. Of course, if you have that, you likely have lots of sunlight, too, so you might want to consider a solar-wind combo.

Microhydro electricity is not nearly as well known, but it's as old a form of power generation as there is. Think about water mills, where the river turns the wheel that spins the millstone to grind the flour. That's basically what we're talking about here. If you live on a river that is fast flowing and consistent, you can get anywhere from ten to a hundred times as much power as with solar and wind—and because you've got such a consistent source of energy, you don't need as many batteries to store it up.

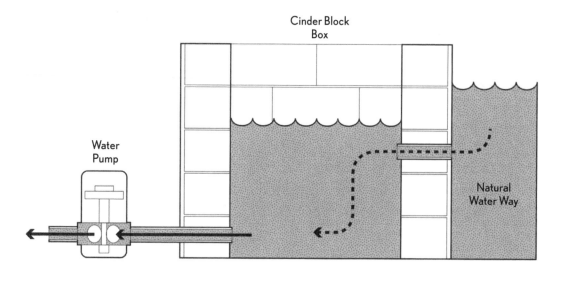

Cinder Block
Box

Water
Pump

Natural
Water Way

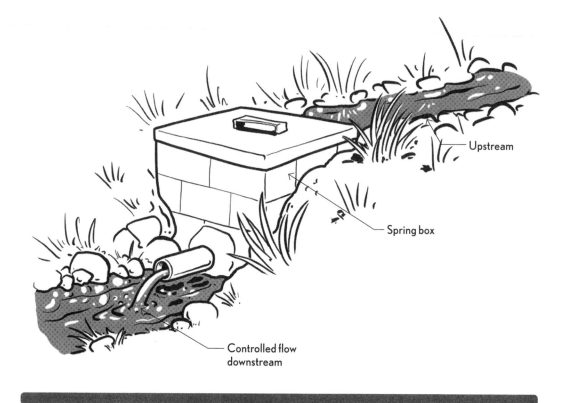

Upstream

Spring box

Controlled flow
downstream

Which sounds pretty great, but a consistently fast-flowing steep river (because you need a significant drop in order for the wheels to turn) is not commonly found on most properties. You can make this a bit easier on yourself by building a spring box. If you've got a stream uphill of your house, you can dam it off with some cinder blocks, creating a box that you can then smear with concrete to seal it. Hook up a PVC pipe down to your turbine, and you're in business—the spring box will regulate your flow as it fills up with water, and, bonus, it can serve as a refrigeration unit, like when you stick beers in the stream to keep them cold.

If your stream is *downhill* from your house, you can still make this work with some basic water physics, forcing that water uphill with a DIY ram pump. Create your dam and spring box, then attach a PVC pipe, forcing all the water coming out of the dam into that pipe. Using an elbow joint, attach a large PVC so that it stands vertical (yep, up in the air), with the remainder of your PVC guiding the water uphill toward your house. Close off the vertical pipe. When the water flows in from your dam, it will fill that vertical pipe, and then the pressure formed will pump your water uphill, so that it comes spurting in little bursts. Hook that up to your turbine (or to a water barrel if you just want water storage).

This technology is changing fast, and if you do have running water on your land, you've got some pretty good, if expensive, options out there. HOMER Energy (Hybrid Optimization of Multiple Energy Resources) is offering mini hydro turbines that make it so even a small stream can power a house. If you create a dam at your water source, you can hook it up to their turbine, which hooks up to the fuse box, and that water pressure is all yours. Though again, these things are not cheap, even in the already-expensive world of off-grid power.

HOT TIP

"No matter what kind of technology you use, know that like all technology, it will keep changing and being updated, and so it will almost immediately be out of date. Once you decide what kind of system you want, you need to buy it all at once, or it may well end up being incompatible with what's on the market in the future. Also, be sure to buy extra batteries."
—The Trayers

Shelter, potable water, and power are three of your biggest initial concerns. And they all come with major investment possibilities. Start with what you can reasonably spend right away and what you and your family can cut back on/live with. As we'll get in to with farming and raising animals, there is plenty of work to be done from morning to night so you won't have to worry about whether or not you have enough power stored up to watch Netflix, you'll be asleep. But also before you pull the plug, think about how much electricity you take for granted—computers, tablets, cell phones, air conditioners, giant fridges, HDTVs—and how much of this you are really ready to give up. This is where building a part-time cabin is ideal. It allows you to take breaks from the grid, to test what your power needs truly are, and to have a place to bug out to if the needs arise.

Water

Water is the lifeline of a homestead, but it's something most of us don't even think about. We just turn on the tap and let it run, not considering where all that water comes from. But being off-grid also means being off the water main, and you're going to go through *a lot* of water. Your garden, your animals, you—everything needs water, and honestly you'll want to have more than enough on hand at all times, because what if you need to mix concrete or give the dog a bath, or hell, just take a long goddamn shower sometimes? Water is not something you can take for granted.

Start by figuring out exactly how much water you absolutely need, and then round way up from there. Modern low-flush toilets take about 1.3 gallons to flush, though anyone conserving water should follow the golden rule: if it's yellow, let it mellow. Your standard energy-efficient washing machine uses around 19 gallons per load of laundry. This all adds up, so that usually, for a fully functioning one-acre homestead with two adults and 2.5 kids, you're going to need 50 gallons per day—not counting showers.

Okay, so where are you going to get all that water? There are a number of options, and if you can, you should try to take advantage of every single one. There is no such thing as enough redundancy when it comes to water.

Catchment means taking all the water that falls onto your roof and funneling it from the gutters into a water tank. Depending on the size of your household, it's recommended that you get a water tank of at least 10,000 gallons to make sure you have more than enough should you encounter a drought, and you'll need more than that if you're taking care of livestock.

If you have 1,000 square feet of roof surface, you can harness a lot of rainwater. Catchment area in square feet × rainfall inches × .623 = available water in gallons. So that 1,000 square feet of roof can capture approximately 600 gallons with just 1 inch of rainfall.

Depending on where you live, that could mean enough and more. If you're in a very rainy climate like the Pacific Northwest, you will likely be able to get all you need from the sky. But if you live in a place like New Mexico, Arizona, or another arid region, you'll have to be really smart about it—but that doesn't mean it's not worth doing. Say you get only 14 inches per year. Doing the math over that 1,000 square feet of roof, that still means you get 8,750 or so gallons of water annually.

Honestly, you should have catchments wherever possible—put them on your barn, your sheds, your chicken coop. Every single structure should have a gutter system. It doesn't all have to feed into the main tank; smaller structures can feed into rain barrels, ideally food-grade plastic barrels, but a new garbage can could work in a pinch. You could even just use 5-gallon plastic buckets to catch drips. Start simple and get creative as you figure out what you need and how to capture it.

Rain is free. Take advantage of it.

Well. If there's groundwater, you can also dig a well, though depending on where you live, this can be quite expensive. If you're drilling for an artesian well, you need to tap into the aquifer, which can be up to 500 feet down, which can cost you up to $15,000—*and* it will require an electric water pump, so you have to factor that into your energy usage costs.

On the other hand, if you live in a wet area, you can dig a surface well and set it up to gravity feed into your home. Obviously that's way less expensive, but you'll be at the mercy of climate change and drought season. If you go this route, make sure you're constantly testing the water, and always check any kind of well regularly for dead animals or other contaminants.

River. If there's a river on your property, or even a spring, you can use that—again, build a spring box.

No matter how you collect your water, put your tank up on a tower, creating your own water tower for gravity feed, adding in some old-school hand pumps that can completely take out the need for electricity to get water. Yes, it's a pain in the neck to build and haul up there, but you will be saving yourself so much in energy usage, it will be worth it.

FILTRATION

However you get your water, you're going to need to filter it. Don't use water directly from the tank even just to feed your livestock or water your garden. Bad water leads to bad vegetables, which leads to unhealthy humans.

If your water is toxic, it'll either kill your vegetables or they will absorb those toxins and pass them on to you when you sit down to dinner. Rainwater, pond water, even groundwater—all of it needs some sort of filtering system.

The easiest thing to do is create a biofilter. Say you've got a rain barrel alongside your pigpen, and that's what you're using to hydrate your pigs, because you're smart and you don't want to haul water around.

You can put a filter right in that barrel. Fill the bottom of it with rock, then layer charcoal over that, and then put a final layer of sand on top. Punch a tap in at the bottom down by the rocks, and there you have it—a standard filtration system that has cleared out insects, bird poop, leaves, you name it.

It's fine now to use for watering the garden, and your pigs will probably be fine, too. You want to create the exact same system for any water moving anywhere—you can put it in your big water tank, over by your water pump, or anywhere else water moves.

You shouldn't drink the water yet, though. There is still all manner of bacteria and so forth in there. Ultraviolet water filters kill 99.9 percent of all harmful microorganisms, and they do it without adding chemicals like chlorine or bleach. You can attach a small UV filter to that barrel—they are cheap and readily available. You can also attach a filter to your indoor faucet, so you always have potable water on tap.

WASTE

Okay, so that's how you're getting water in. What about how to get it out? Household wastewater divides into two categories: Graywater is waste from washing machines, sinks, tubs, and showers. This needs only minimal treatment before it can be released back into the soil. Blackwater, on the other hand, comes from your toilet, and needs to be carefully treated. If you can build your wastewater

treatment system so that it divides the graywater from the blackwater, your system can be smaller and more effective. You can let the graywater run into a pond or run it through perforated pipes to leach into the soil and gravel, watering your crops—make sure you're using only natural detergents, though. You can also run a pipe so that you're using graywater to flush your toilet. However, you'll need to do some research on this, as certain counties have strict waste management regulations.

Blackwater, being full of bacteria and unpleasant odor, needs to be handled more carefully. You have a few options:

Composting Toilet. There are some terrific composting toilets on the market, and you'd be amazed at how effective they are. Basically, you do your business, then you add some wood shavings, pine needles, or coffee grounds, dumping a half cup or so directly into the toilet—which rests above a container, like a pit toilet that doesn't stink. Once the container is full, you add it to a composter (not the one you're using to break down your kitchen waste) and it breaks down further until you

Blackwater

Graywater

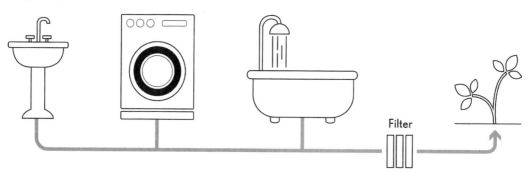

can absolutely use it as compost in your garden. This takes either pretty high heat or an extended period of time, up to two years or so. Some come with urine diverters, which sends the urine into a separate container (you can use it to add nitrogen to your garden). Feces will break down faster if it is kept separate from urine.

It's also simple enough to make your own composting toilet, and you may prefer to do so not just because of cost but because of ease. The Trayers, who obviously always have a lot of sawdust around, built their own because the container that comes with a commercial toilet is often too big and heavy to move easily. All you really need is a hole in the floor, a toilet seat, and a bucket underneath. Keep adding the sawdust and change that bucket out regularly, and smell will not be an issue. That said, you don't want your toilet to be right off your kitchen, for both aromatic and sanitary reasons. Creating a separate room or even structure will also allow you to put in multiple seats, which can be helpful if you've got a big household.

Nature's Head Composting Toilets.

These are quite similar to the kinds of toilets found in RVs and boats. They run on very little power, around 12 volts. They separate the urine and feces, and use fans to reduce smell. They use no water, and you can preload the feces bucket with compost to speed up the process of breaking it down. They're great, but they're also expensive, and they, too, need to be emptied regularly.

Septic System.
Used to be, you could just send your blackwater into a hole in the ground (also known as a cesspool), but that's illegal to build these days and not a great idea anyway, especially if you want your soil to thrive. A septic system works as your own personal sewage treatment center. Your blackwater enters a tank, and the oils and fats rise to the top while the solids sink to the bottom. The remaining liquid flows through into another tank, clears out further, and then enters a leach field via perforated pipes, allowing the water to be filtered in the soil. Your tank of solids and fats will need to be pumped out every five years or so. There are DIY options here, but to be up to code, you may need to hire a professional, which can get expensive.

Look, tempting as it may be, do not go out into the woods and squat. Build an outhouse, even when you're just getting started. A composting toilet really isn't a big deal to put together, and the sawdust does neutralize the smell. But it's not just about unpleasant odors; it's about basic hygiene. If you don't take care of yourself, you're not taking care of your homestead, and microscopic fecal matter can lead to typhoid, hepatitis, or many other manners of infection.

Cleanliness will prevent most of your medical issues. Make sure that however you set up your toilet, you've got a place to wash your hands immediately.

As far as the rest of your water needs, you can get a basic shower, the same kind of thing used in an RV. You can heat water on your woodstove for a sponge bath. Or you can run a Jacuzzi—as always, your energy and expense versus your needs and wants are entirely up to you.

3 | BE YOUR OWN FARMER

"Though I do not believe that a plant will spring up where no seed has been, I have great faith in a seed. Convince me that you have a seed there, and I am prepared to expect wonders."

—**Henry David Thoreau**

There is a difference between growing crops (traditional farming) and having a vegetable garden (food that sustains you). If you are considering having a farm big enough to grow feed for your animals and maybe even some commercial crops like corn, it will save you a great deal of headache and backache to purchase existing farmland. If you've ever been in New England, you've probably seen those picturesque old stone walls around fields. They weren't built because farmers liked how they looked or even to keep animals in or out (think how short they are), but because their land was filled with field-stones that had to come out before they could grow anything. That's some back-breaking work right there.

There are plenty of farms around the country with good soil and already cleared fields owned by families who are just no longer working the land. Do your research on exactly why the fields are fallow (test the soil and ask in town what people know about the farm). You can still build your modern homestead on the land while you live for a time in the existing structures, but farmland will give you a significant leg up. And hopefully there will be some of the previous family members around who have knowledge of the land and can help you get set up and sort out problems.

This gets at one of the major tenets of modern homesteading—you need other people. For both basic human contact and also for sharing knowledge and skills. Always be on the lookout for old-timers. These veteran farmers, builders, and off-the-gridders may smell of manure, wood smoke, and sweat. They tend to hang out at feed stores and auctions and are easily spotted by their beat-up trucks filled with hay and random farming parts. Look for them and do whatever you have to in order to make friends. Their help will get you through the hard times. Most homesteaders go the next step and build either a formal or loose network of bartering—one person has maple syrup, one person has wool from their sheep, one person has hand-churned butter, and they trade. There is also the many-hands-make-short-work theory in practice—whether it's a barn raising or everyone getting together in the fall for a pickling and canning party to jar up all those extra cucumbers and tomatoes.

If you do insist on buying land that's never been worked, here are some basics on how to clear it, till it, and sow it.

CLEARING

First, make a plan. You don't want to just clear willy-nilly. Figure out what you're going to use each section of land for, whether it's growing crops or pasture. It's perfectly fine to leave a little grove of shade trees in your pasture, but you wouldn't want it in your cornfield. Test your soil before you do any clearing—if you need to do some amending, you can, but if it's way off, you'll probably want to come up with another crop. And if you've got a lot of trees to fell, consider selling them to offset your costs.

Next, get your equipment. If you're clearing half an acre, you may be able to do much of it by hand, but if you're going full farmland, you're going to need some machines. A track harvester will help you pick up felled trees, while a stump grinder will help you get rid of the leftover stumps—or you can just wait for them to die before pulling them out, though that can take some time. If you've got rough underbrush, you can buy or rent a brush mower, or you can make use of some goats and pigs—goats for the brush, and pigs for the roots underneath.

If you've got big rocks to deal with, you'll need a digging bar, essentially a big crowbar, to help you lever them up and out, though if you have a lot of them, you'll probably need a backhoe. For smaller rocks, you can attach a box blade for turning up the rocks that can be gathered into piles; these rocks can then either be hauled away or, better yet, used to build stone walls or to fill drainage areas.

How to use a backhoe (see page 257)

READYING THE SOIL

Figure out what amendments your soil will need for your intended crop, whether it's nitrogen, lime, vermiculite, etc. If you're just starting out, you'll probably need to till your field—this won't be necessary forever, as overtilling can cause more harm than good, but if you're prepping a field for the first time, it's a good idea. Make sure the conditions are right for tilling by squeezing a handful of soil into a small ball. If it crumbles, it's dry enough to till.

If you've got a small garden, you can just use a spading fork, but if you're working over a large acreage, you'll need a rototiller. Turn up the soil, making sure not to go farther than 12 inches, and loosen it up. This will also help you mix in your amendments, compost, and whatever other soil-improving additives you'll be using.

Growing a Victory Garden

Growing your own food is sustainable, healthy, and damn satisfying. Food tastes better when it's seasoned with your own labor and time. And while it is a lot of work, most of your efforts come in with prep and maintenance—the plants do the growing all on their own.

If you're subsistence farming (growing and raising everything you need to eat), then you've got some math to do. The average person requires 2,300 calories per day. You'll need fruits and vegetables aplenty. What does that mean in terms of land? You'll need .44 acres per person, and that's not even including land set aside for livestock.

But whether you're working with acres and acres of crops, with a backyard garden bed, or with a simple window pot, you can achieve that same tasty satisfaction.

HOT TIP

BE YOUR OWN FARMER

Buying Farm Equipment. If you're only going to need something once or just once in a while, you're better off renting—there's no need to own your own backhoe unless you're constantly clearing fields. But you probably will need a tractor. It can be tempting to buy something secondhand—farm auctions are a great place to scout out used equipment and are an opportunity to meet old-timers who really know what they're doing. You'll probably be able to find hay balers, threshers, milking setups, and so forth. If you've got your heart set on really doing it old-style, you can probably find old-fashioned, oxen-pulled plows and the like.

For a decent-sized farm, you'll want a tractor with a deck between 46 and 54 inches with at least an 18-horsepower engine. If you can find an analog tractor, that would be amazing, both in terms of price and ease of repair. Just like with your car, the more computerized something is, the harder it is to fix. The best secondhand tractors to look for are the Swaraj 735 FE, the Eicher 364 SUPERDI, and the Ford 3600—these are powerful, reliable, and relatively easy to keep in repair.

Check your purchase carefully, though, because farmers *hate* throwing anything away—so if they're getting rid of it, there's a good chance there's something really wrong with it. But maybe you can use it for parts? Think ahead.

All that said, if you're working a smaller farm, you can pretty much get away with a four-wheeler. You can attach a wagon for loading, a tiller, and just about anything else. Plus, you know, they're fun.

Prep

It is so tempting to just start digging and planting seeds. But unless you've got good soil, those seeds are going to struggle. And know this: just because your neighbor's got a bountiful garden next door, that doesn't mean *your* soil is going to be up to par. Chances are, your neighbor did his homework and prepped, just as you should.

Now, if you're container gardening on your porch or outside your kitchen window, you're best off purchasing good, organic soil. Even if you've got a backyard garden, depending on the size of your plot, it may be easiest to just buy a truckload of soil.

But if you're working with what's in your ground already, then you need to see what that ground is like. If you live in an urban area or adjacent to a commercial area, it is critical to test the soil. There can be many poisonous and possible cancer-causing things in the soil, such as naturally occurring arsenic or toxins from factories' runoff. If you have lead or other toxins in the soil, you'll need to garden in containers. Outside of those dangers, you want to also test to get a breakdown of the soil's pH and nutrient levels. The ideal pH should be at around 6 or 7, though some crops, like blueberries, prefer more acidic soil, and others, like asparagus, are happier with a higher pH.

→ **Too acidic:** add ashes or garden lime.

→ **Too alkaline:** add coffee grounds or elemental sulfur.

The following nutrients are often deficient:

→ **Nitrogen.** Peas and beans are natural nitrogen fixers, and you can also use chicken manure.

→ **Phosphorus.** Soft rock phosphate, bat guano, and bone meal are all good antidotes.

→ **Potassium.** Ashes from your fireplace, banana peels, and potash work great as supplements.

If you want to grow a truly organic garden, there's a little more to it than simply not spraying it with pesticides. You have to buy organic soil, because I promise you the stuff you've got in the ground is definitely going to be contaminated by something or other. Two of the best soil enhancers are compost and manure, and both are key to successful organic farming without chemicals. When you treat it with amendments, you can't use anything chemical based, though worm casings and compost work great. If you use manure, make sure the animals are raised organically (they're usually not).

Your most effective organic pesticide is actually just organic dish soap diluted with water. Put it in a spray bottle and spritz away—that'll get rid of aphid infestations, mealybugs, leafhoppers, earwigs, and more.

Composting

Composting takes your scraps and turns them into gold—or at least, a fertilizer as good as gold. Beneficial microorganisms including bacteria and fungi will do all the work for you, but you have to give them the right ingredients and environment—and time. They require four things:

1. Nitrogen. Including the scraps from your cooking, greens, overripe fruits and vegetables, lawn clippings, and even fresh manure.

2. Carbon. Including dry matter like torn newspaper, cornstalks, dried leaves, straw, sawdust, or rotted hay.

3. Water. If your compost gets too dry, it'll stop the process—but you also don't want it to get too wet, either. Depending on where you live, you may need to never water it at all, or water it occasionally. Ideally, it should be moist but never drenched, and keeping it covered with a tarp or using a container like a composting bin will help it stay that way.

4. Oxygen. That said, you don't want to smother your compost. Turning it occasionally will introduce some air into the system. Again, the easiest way to do this is with a rotating bin, but you can also just take a pitchfork and turn the whole thing. If you have a tumbler, you'll probably have usable compost within three months; no tumbler and it may take up to a year.

CONTAINERS

I've mentioned rotating bins a couple of times, as they are ideal for the suburban homesteader. For an apartment homesteader, however, that might be too much, and you're better off using a bucket. You can keep it under your sink—compost smells good and loamy, and not at all like rotting food.

But if you're living only off of what you grow, even a bin won't be big enough for the amount of compost you'll be generating (and requiring). Instead, build a raised platform, either out of branches laid across one another or just with leftover pallets, and put a couple of perforated plastic pipes in the center of the pile, to keep oxygen flowing. This should make it so you rarely if ever need to turn it—which is good, since compost weighs a *ton*.

COMPOST TEA

Most often, you'll use your compost when you're tilling your soil to ready it for planting. But your growing plants can also benefit from some compost, offered in the form of "tea"—you can think of it as a shot of energy drink. Compost tea contains those beneficial microorganisms, putting them directly in the dirt so they can do their good work right around your plants, as well as soluble nutrients pulled from your compost. It'll make your plants hardier, improve the soil so that it requires less watering, stimulate root growth, and help fight off disease or pests.

You'll need the following:

→ 1 large handful of compost

→ 1 large handful of good soil

→ 2 handfuls of straw

→ 3 to 5 leaves from a healthy plant

→ Cheesecloth

→ Twine

→ ½ cup molasses

→ 5-gallon bucket filled with water

→ Fish tank aerator

→ Aquarium thermometer

Place the compost, soil, straw, and leaves inside the cheesecloth and tie it up with twine. Stir the molasses into the water, drop in your "tea bag," and turn on the aerator. Let your tea brew for 24 to 48 hours, making sure the temperature stays around 70°F. When you're ready to use it, dilute it to 3 parts tea to 1 part water. You can use a backpack sprayer, but do so early in the morning or late in the evening to avoid burning the leaves. Otherwise, simply use your diluted tea to water the ground around your plants.

COMPOST TEA

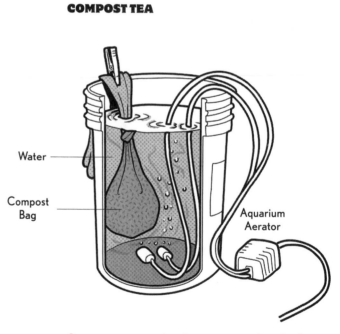

Water

Compost Bag

Aquarium Aerator

Compost tea is a quick and easy way to get beneficial microorganisms right into your soil.

Manure

Manure is *great* for your plants, but it's easy to use too much and end up harming them. The safest way to use manure is to add it to your compost, but you can also add it to your soil as you till it to ready it for planting—but be sure to do so well in advance, i.e., in the fall or winter, months before you plant in the spring. You want to give your manure plenty of time to break down. Alternatively, you can age your manure, which will also make it safer (store-bought manure is aged manure).

While chicken, horse, and cow manure are the most commonly used, just about any farm animal's droppings will be beneficial for your crops, including rabbit, goat, and even pig. Just stay away from cat, dog, and human feces, as they tend to contain parasites.

Pest Control

You'll be fighting with deer, crows, blue jays, cabbage moths, aphids, slugs, flea beetles, tomato hornworms, and probably a ton of other pests local to your area. Dogs can help with deer, but depending on the breed, they might also just want to make friends. There's a rumor that Ivory soap can keep animals away, but honestly, rain washes it off, so fencing or netting is necessary, though nothing works better than a shotgun.

Companion planting is a great way to keep smaller pests out without having to resort to pesticides or arms. Orange nasturtiums will fend off cabbage moths and help with pollination while they're at it. If you've got ants, plant some tansy; marigolds are another great natural pesticide. Certain plants will even attract predatory insects that will do the work for you. For example, planting dill can attract ladybugs, which feed on aphids and mealybugs.

HOT TIP

Rotate your crops regularly. This is great for your soil, and it will confuse the insects and other pests who expect to find a tasty snack and instead encounter something they dislike. And if you've got slugs, don't bother with a salt or copper barrier, as those don't really do much. Instead, fill a saucer with beer and let them drown their sorrows—and themselves.

What to Plant?

It's best to plant things that you know are likely to grow where you live. Trying to grow bananas in the Southwest is an exercise in frustration. You can do some research online or at the local garden center, but you might also want to ask your neighbors what they've had success with. Try your local County Extension office, in the Agricultural Department. This is an invaluable resource. And then, once you know what your options are, consider what you need. What is unavailable to you? If you live way out in the country, staples may be hard to get, so you'll want to grow vegetables such as carrots, potatoes, and broccoli.

HOT TIP Potatoes and beans are nutritious and stomach-filling foods. The potato especially has gotten a bad rap in the United States more from how it can be prepared (fried), not because of its lack of nutritious value. In fact, the simple potato, like beans, is a superfood that has lots of vitamins, carbs, and protein. Unlike what you may have read in diet books, carbs and protein together help make you feel full. Which means less of a need for meat-heavy meals. Also, potatoes and beans can be stored year round. And baked potatoes are incredibly easy to make. Just scrub your potatoes well and pick off the eyes (those white baby root things). Stab it several times with a fork. Rub a little olive oil on the skin, sprinkle with salt, and pop it in the oven at 400°F for an hour or so, until easily pierced with a fork.

If you're a suburban or city farmer, you're free to go a little more exotic, and try to grow things that you can't get as easily, or that you have to pay an arm and a leg for, like raspberries, jicama, watermelon radishes, or purple sweet potatoes.

You'll definitely want to try your hand at an herb garden. Herbs are basically weeds, so even the blackest of thumbs can get them to flourish. Plant some basil, mint, thyme, cilantro, parsley, etc. and save yourself (and the planet) from those expensive plastic containers of "fresh" herbs. They'll add a ton of flavor to your food, and you can grow them indoors, where they'll be on hand whenever you need them, all year long.

Raised beds. If you're somewhere between multiple acres and a windowsill, you might want to consider raised garden beds. Weeding is the bane of all farmers, and if you plant right in the ground, you're already operating at a disadvantage—the weeds are already there, just waiting to sprout up. Raised beds are simple to maintain, provide good drainage, and make it easy to harvest a variety of crops. And when one plant is done producing, it's no trouble to pull it out and put your next crop in.

Once your frame is built, you can either fill it with purchased soil if you never want to deal with weeds ever again or you can fill it with tested, fixed soil from the ground—you'll get weeds that first year, but they'll taper off if you stay on them.

This may seem obvious, but it's worth stating: make sure you're placing your garden bed in a place where it gets adequate sunlight and where it's close enough to the house so you can go grab a handful of basil when you want it, or do a casual weeding and watering on the regular.

DIY RAISED GARDEN BED

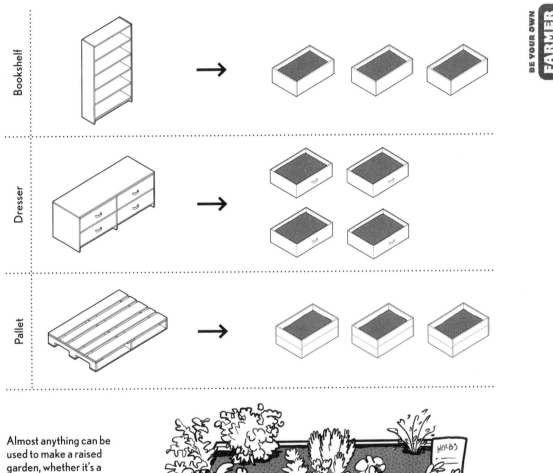

Bookshelf

Dresser

Pallet

Almost anything can be used to make a raised garden, whether it's a chest of drawers or a deconstructed bookshelf or a pallet. Just one drawer can be enough to get you started.

HERBS

Corn, beans, and squash are known as the Three Sisters, and have been a staple of Native American gardens for centuries. They work together synergistically, putting in all the effort of sustaining each other. Corn provides tall stalks for the beans to climb while the squash vines sprawl beneath. The beans then stabilize the tall corn during heavy winds. They're also natural nitrogen-fixers—the rhizobia in bean roots take in nitrogen from the air and convert it into forms that can be used by the corn and squash. The large squash leaves shade the ground, helping it retain moisture and keep out weeds.

They work together just as well nutritionally, too. Eating corn, beans, and squash at the same time forms a complete and balanced diet, with corn providing necessary carbohydrates, beans giving protein and amino acids, and squash supplying additional vitamins and minerals.

3 SISTERS

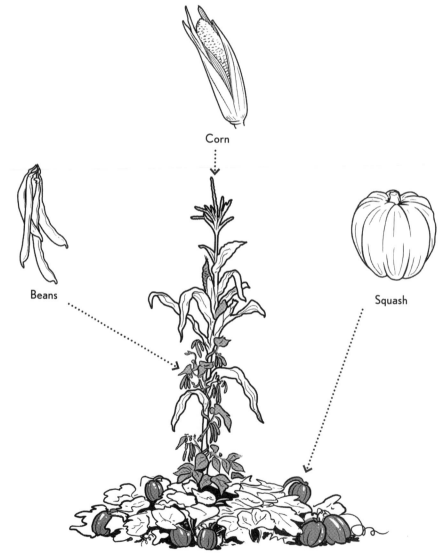

Corn

Beans

Squash

Small containers. Container gardening is the simplest of all. You can put a few barrels on your porch or in a smaller yard, and still produce plenty of food. Earthboxes are self-watering, which is extremely handy, but they can be pricey, and you don't actually have to use anything fancy. Building your own small garden box is very straightforward; you can even grow your crops atop a straw bale, which gives them excellent drainage.

You can also use old truck tires, bathtubs with holes drilled in, barrels, whatever—if it contains things and has drainage, it'll work.

HOT TIP

Growing Your Tomatoes Upside Down. To save space and allow for ease of picking, try growing your tomatoes upside down. This method works for any variety, from cherry tomatoes to heirlooms, and is a great option for the urban homesteader who might have limited space for a garden.

Waffle gardens. So-called waffle gardens were developed by the Zuni, a Pueblo people who live in what is now New Mexico. They designed this method of gardening to help manage arid, windy regions and in areas where the soil has a high clay content. It allows your crops to receive sunlight while still being somewhat protected from the wind.

UPSIDE-DOWN TOMATOES

HOW TO
WAFFLE GARDEN

Basically, you clear an area for your garden just as you would for any other. Till the soil, clear out weeds, etc. Then you dig a series of holes within that garden, say four by four two-foot-square holes, for a total of sixteen. Yep, it looks like a waffle.

Using the dirt from each of those holes, create a wall around each one, raising the earth up around it to serve as your barrier and windbreak.

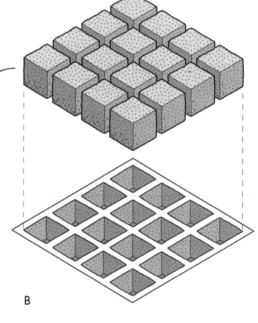

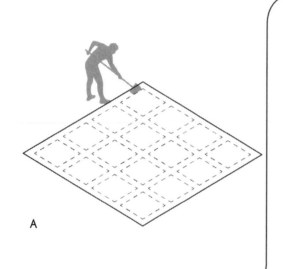

A

B

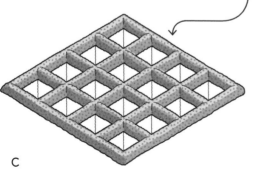

C

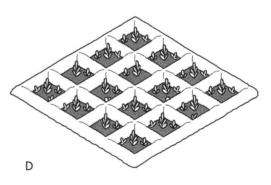

D

HOW TO
WATER YOUR GARDEN

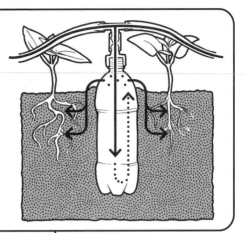

Get sixteen or so one-liter plastic water bottles (yep, those same ones we throw away every day) and punch some holes in the top of each. Stuff an old sock in there to keep them from getting clogged with soil.

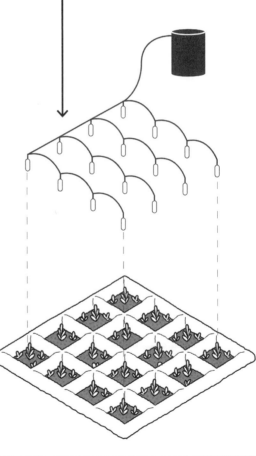

Plant a water bottle in the middle of each square, mouth up, then attach an irrigator pipette to each bottle.

Turn on your system, let gravity run water into the bottles, and let the bottles slowly release water into your soil.

When and What to Grow

Now that you have decided on what type of garden you'd like to plant, it's time to move on to some guidelines of where and when to plant and what to plant. It's helpful to follow the USDA Plant Hardiness Zone map to determine which plants are most likely to thrive where you live. You can zero in on your exact location using the USDA website (planthardiness.ars.usda.gov), but here are some basic parameters.

HOT TIP

Annuals versus Perennials.
An annual plant usually lasts just one season, while a perennial will come back year after year. So yeah, it's definitely easier to grow perennials . . . but some annuals are easy enough to grow and reseed that they're worth planting again and again.

Depending on where you live, certain crops will do better than others. Learning about your zone can give you a lot more information than this, but here's a basic overview—the foods listed are all easy to grow and good ones to start with:

ZONES 1, 2, AND 3

These northern zones have the shortest growing season in the United States—but that doesn't mean you can't grow plenty of food. You can protect your crops from over-night frosts with tarps to extend the season.

→ Leafy greens, including kale, chard, butter lettuce, and spinach

→ Herbs, especially parsley, cilantro, and basil

→ Summer squash

→ Cucumbers

→ Celery

→ Peas

→ Garlic

→ Root vegetables, including beets, radishes, carrots, and turnips

→ Rhubarb

→ Asparagus

→ Apples

→ Blackberries

→ Blueberries

HOT TIP

Crab apples are not great for eating, but they are a great source of pectin, so you don't have to buy pectin, just put a crab apple in with your other fruits for your jams. Since they bloom twice, they will also pollinate almost all of your other apple varieties. Or you can get a Frankentree, a fruit tree with other varieties grafted on—this tree will pollinate itself.

ZONE 4

As with the northern zones, you may want to invest in some tarps to extend your growing season. You should be able to grow all of the above, and the following fruits and vegetables as well.

→ Swiss chard

→ Leeks

→ Broccoli

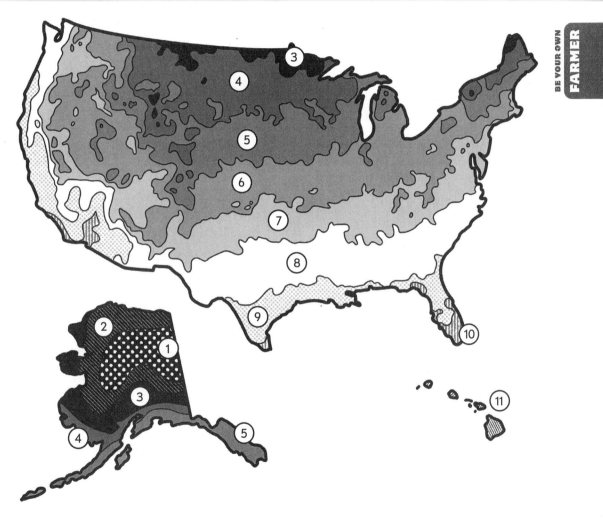

BE YOUR OWN FARMER

Zone 1: Last Frost: May 30. First Frost: August 30

Zone 2: Last Frost: May 15. First Frost: September 1

Zone 3: Last Frost: June 15. First Frost: September 15

Zone 4: Last Frost: June 1. First Frost: September 1

Zone 5: Last Frost: May 15. First Frost: October 15

Zone 6: Last Frost: May 1. First Frost: November 1

Zone 7: Last Frost: April 15. First Frost: November 15

Zone 8: Last Frost: April 1. First Frost: December 1

Zone 9: Last Frost: March 1. First Frost: December 1

Zones 10–11: No Freeze

- → Cabbage
- → Meyer lemon
- → Dwarf cherry
- → Grape
- → Raspberry
- → Mulberry
- → Strawberry
- → Cranberry

HOT TIP

Autumn-bearing raspberries planted in the spring will give you fruit later that same year. For strawberries and blueberries, though, you have to give them a little while to establish themselves, so only let them produce two fruits in their first year or two, so they can develop their root systems. After that, let them go crazy.

ZONE 5

Your options certainly expand as you get into Zone 5. You likely won't have to worry about overnight frosts for much of your growing season, and most of the above plants are still viable farther south. Your other choices include:

- → Brussels sprouts
- → Cauliflower
- → Chicory
- → Cress
- → Okra
- → Onions
- → Parsnips
- → Winter squash
- → Corn
- → Melon

- → Eggplant
- → Tomato
- → Pepper
- → Pears
- → Peaches
- → Plums
- → Persimmons
- → Apricots
- → Walnuts
- → Chestnuts

ZONE 6

This zone is about as temperate as it gets. It's wet enough that you aren't limited in what you can grow, but it's also not so cold that plants won't thrive. Nor is the season so short that your plants don't have time to reach full growth. You can grow most of the above, with the addition of these:

- → Rutabaga
- → Sweet potatoes
- → Any kind of beans, really
- → Fennel
- → Pears

ZONE 7

Things get a little hotter and drier as you venture farther south. You can still grow most of the above fruits and vegetables, but you'll have to put a little more effort into watering them. And with a longer, warmer growing season, you can try the following as well:

→ Figs

→ Nectarines

→ Bananas

ZONE 8

You've got even longer, hotter summers in Zone 8, which means you have to be careful of droughts, but it does offer an even greater variety of fruit options:

→ Oranges

→ Grapefruits

→ Tangerines

→ Kumquats

→ Avocado

ZONES 9, 10, AND 11

Living in any of these zones basically means you can grow and harvest cyclically all year round. There's a reason so much of our produce is grown in California. But again, the issue you run into is water. Your plants will grow only if you can keep them hydrated. If you're under a water restriction, relying only on the town water main may make that difficult, and if you're off the water main entirely, you need to make sure you have plenty of water in reserve to see you through those dry times.

YIELD PER ¼ ACRE

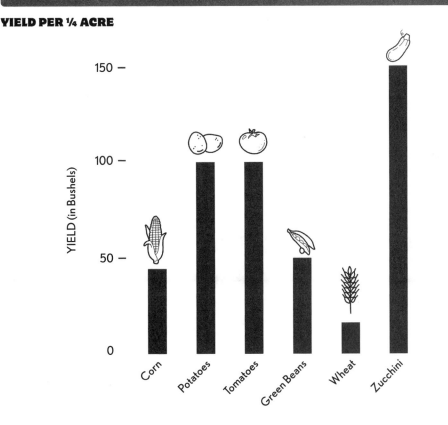

Planting Your Crops

Seeding. Your seeds will stand a much better chance of success if you sow them in smaller containers indoors in the early spring, rather than simply putting them in the ground. You want to give them all the help they can get. Egg cartons, small plastic pots, and peat pots work great. Fill them with a 1:1 mixture of peat or sphagnum moss and vermiculite (expanded mica) and/or perlite (volcanic ash), which will hold a lot of water and nurture your seeds as they sprout.

Sow your seeds, giving them adequate space (yes, even when they're so tiny you can barely see them) and scatter a thin layer of growing mixture over them. Put them in a place where they'll stay warm-ish, around 70° to 75°F, and where they'll receive plenty of sunlight. Keep their germinating mixture moist but never soaking, checking on it every day. Once your

HOT TIP

Make a map of your garden. When those seedlings start coming up, it can be really difficult to tell what they are at first, and if something isn't growing according to plan, you want to know what it is so you either (a) figure out what to do to help, or (b) try something else next time.

GARDEN MAP

seeds sprout, their first leaves will not be the "true" leaves, but a few days later their mature leaves will appear, at which point it's time to start fertilizing. A soluble plant food like Miracle-Gro or compost tea is ideal, but you'll want to water it down at the beginning, increasing in strength as your seedling matures.

While you're waiting, prep your garden. Dig a trench for your seedling and press the tines of a pitchfork deep into the dirt at the bottom of your trench, aerating the soil. Scatter a little compost, then refill your trench with the soil you removed, turning it and loosening it.

Transplanting. Your seeds are ready to transplant when they've matured enough to develop four true leaves. Soak the

growing medium, and then carefully lift out the plant with its rootball, thinning and removing any plants that are too crowded together. If you're using a peat pot, you can simply plant the entire pot, unpeeling it a little before placing it in the ground. Plant them carefully in your prepared garden, watering both the soil and the seedlings. They'll wilt, but they will spring back. Keep an eye on them, watering them just enough to wet the soil every day for a week, and try to keep your chickens or anyone else from snacking on them. If need be, cover your garden bed with netting.

Maintenance. Keep a regular stream of watering, sunlight, and weeding—or as much as possible, anyway. If your garden bed is out in your yard, you won't have much control over the weather. But if it's been dry for a while, water your plants and weed either during a drought or after a heavy rain.

Harvesting. For subsistence farmers, the system is the same for garden beds and container plants: harvest your plants when they're ready and when you're ready to eat them. If your salad greens are ready, it's time to eat a salad. If your beans are ready, then it's time to eat some beans. Go out and pick them right before you're ready to eat, and keep it up—harvesting is how you get your plants to continue producing. If they go to seed, they're done. If you can't

TRANSPLANT

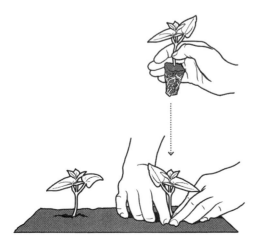

keep up with the supply, there are always friends and neighbors who are hungry.

As impressive as those giant vegetables are, they don't actually taste that good. Younger carrots are tastier than those giant horse carrots, and big beets are woody and hard when compared with tender baby beets.

Seed Saving. Since plants have a variety of methods of seed dispersal, there are a variety of methods for collecting their seeds. If you're working with a seed head, cut off most of the stem and place the seed head in a brown paper bag, tying it shut around the stem, and hang it upside down until the seeds have released. When you can hear them rattling around in there, open up the bag and clear out any remaining seeds, shaking them in a sieve to remove any debris. Pick out any smaller or discolored seeds, as they are likely unviable. Store your seeds in the refrigerator, which will keep them both cool and dry.

SEED SAVING

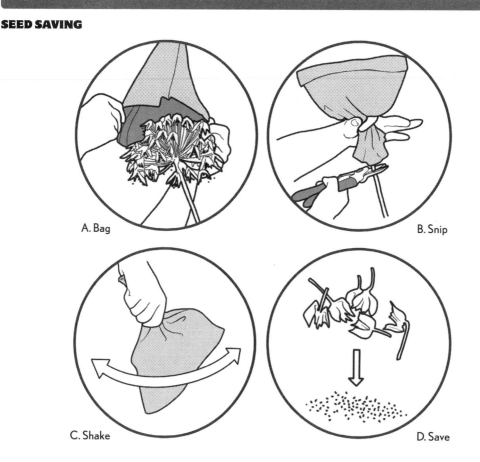

A. Bag

B. Snip

C. Shake

D. Save

Storing Your Food Year Round

ROOT CELLAR

The reality is, you're probably going to need a freezer for many things. For example, you can freeze fruits and vegetables to great success (just spread them out on a baking tray and pop them in a freezer; once they're fully frozen, you can transfer them to freezer bags). But if we're talking about storing a year's worth of food, and if you want to be eating what you grow year round, then you're going to need some storage space. Root cellars have been humanity's solution to this problem for hundreds of years, well before electricity was a part of daily life.

Remember how we talked about geothermal sanctuaries? If you dig down 6 to 8 feet into the earth, it will be around 50°F there. That is the case everywhere on Earth and throughout the year, summer and winter. Why do you think we put our dead bodies 6 feet under?

You can build your own root cellar by digging a 12-foot-deep hole, squaring it off with cinder blocks, lining it with concrete, building a roof and reinforcing it with rebar, and then cementing the whole thing. Make a hatch door and some stairs, and you've got a room with temperatures consistently around 50°F.

Root vegetables such as beets, carrots, potatoes, parsnips, rutabagas, and turnips all store well in a root cellar. You can also keep the bulbs or rhizomes from perennials here.

CANNING

For other, non-root vegetables, as well as fruits and meats, canning is a low-energy, inexpensive way to keep food around long after the growing season ends. You'll want to use recipes until you know what you're doing, but the USDA has a list of recommended processing times for different foods. There's a bit of a learning curve, and you want to make sure you do it right to prevent botulism. Botulism is a deadly neurotoxin that is technically all over the place, but in nonacidic anaerobic environments, it can grow to lethal levels. Check in with the National Center for Home Food Preservation for updated safety procedures, but for now, here are the basics.

Lingo

→ **Raw or cold pack:** uncooked fruits or vegetables that are packed in jars and processed with a hot liquid.

→ **Hot pack:** foods that are cooked slightly beforehand. Particularly useful for things like spinach, so you can break them down and get more in the jar.

→ **Headspace:** Refers to the space between the top of the food and the top of the jar. Most of the time you're going for half an inch, but some recipes will call for one inch.

HOW TO
BUILD A ROOT CELLAR

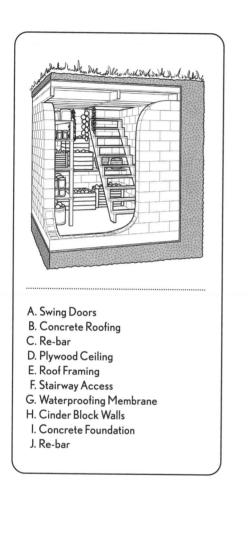

A. Swing Doors
B. Concrete Roofing
C. Re-bar
D. Plywood Ceiling
E. Roof Framing
F. Stairway Access
G. Waterproofing Membrane
H. Cinder Block Walls
I. Concrete Foundation
J. Re-bar

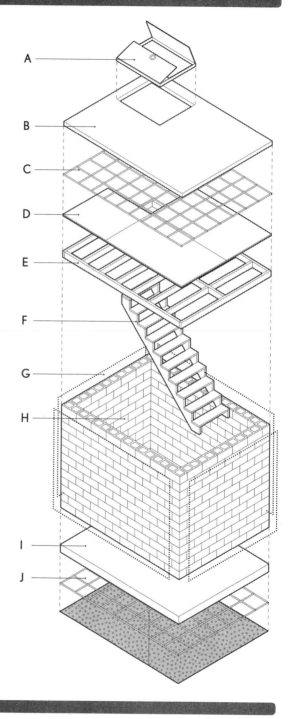

→ **Water bath:** Filled cans are boiled in a large stockpot filled with water to seal. Works well with high-acid and high-sugar foods like jam, tomatoes, or pickles.

→ **Pressure canning:** For low-acid foods, you need a pressure cooker to get the required temperature for safe preservation.

Supplies

→ **Mason jars**

→ **Pressure cooker** (FYI, Instant Pot has not been tested for this. You need a specialized pressure canner, which will run you about a hundred bucks.)

→ **Large sauce pot with lid and rack**

Quick and Easy Jam

4 cups fresh fruit (can be berries, apricots, peaches, etc.)
½ cup sugar
1 to 2 tablespoons lemon juice, or to taste

Cut up the fruit as needed until it's in half-inch chunks. Place it, the sugar, and the lemon juice in a saucepan and bring to a low boil. Let it simmer, stirring often, for 20 to 30 minutes, mashing up the fruit using a wooden spoon and helping it to break down into a mush. Pour into clean jars and seal with a water bath.

Pickling. An offshoot of canning, pickling allows you to preserve your foods using an acid (usually vinegar), boosting their flavor and helping them last longer. Pickling isn't reserved for cucumbers, as just about any vegetable can be pickled. Green vegetables should be blanched to preserve their color; you'll want to chop everything up into bite-sized or snack-sized pieces.

A basic brine is 1 part vinegar to 1 part water. You'll want to use a simple vinegar such as white or apple cider, reserving your aged balsamics for a salad dressing. From there, you can add spices and herbs, including dill, garlic, ginger, mustard seed, peppercorns, and turmeric. Experiment and see what works for you.

HOW TO
CAN

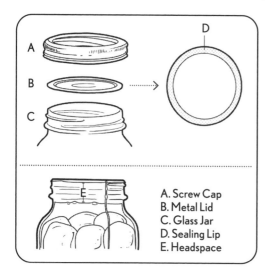

A. Screw Cap
B. Metal Lid
C. Glass Jar
D. Sealing Lip
E. Headspace

STEP 1: Prepare Food

Blanch it, chop it, wash it, whatever is needed according to the specific recipe.

STEP 2: Prepare Jars

Boil them first to sanitize them, and then pop them in a 200°F oven to keep them warm. Keep the lids out on the counter. Prepare your canning method. For a water bath, set the rack in the pot and fill the pot about halfway up with water. Bring it to a simmer and cover it.

*For a pressure cooker, place the rack inside and add 2–3 inches of water. Bring it to a simmer.

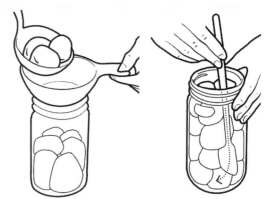

STEP 3: Fill Jars

Fill the jars with the prepared food, using oven mitts or a jar lifter. Don't burn yourself. Leave the correct amount of headspace in the jar. Use a rubber spatula to remove any air pockets in the jar.

STEP 4: Water Bath

Seal the jars. Wipe the rims clean and seal the lids. Place them into the water bath or pressure cooker. For a water bath, bring the water to a rolling boil and let your jars set for the time specified in the recipe.

*If using a pressure cooker, allow the cooker to come to the recommended pressure and start the processing time, then turn off the heat and let the pressure return to zero naturally.

STEP 5: Test + Store

Remove jars and test. Use oven mitts or a jar lifter to remove the jars. Let them sit for 12–24 hours. After that, check the seal. There's a little button on the top of a mason jar. It should be fully depressed. Store in a cool, dark place for up to 18 months.

SPOTLIGHT

The Norrises • Melissa grew up on the 15-acre farm in Washington State she works now, so this is the only lifestyle she's ever known or wanted. She was in high school before she first ate an Oreo, since her mom always baked cookies, and that's the same kind of life she wanted to provide for her kids. They live in the foothills of the Cascades, and raise 100 percent of their own meat, including beef, chickens, and pork. They believe in growing and harvesting their own food, and still seed and grow the same strain of heirloom Tarheel green pole beans Melissa's family has been cultivating for over a hundred years. Melissa teaches homesteading at melissaknorris.com.

Quick Pickle

1 pound fresh vegetable, whatever you
have on hand

1 cup white vinegar

1 cup water

1 tablespoon sugar

1 tablespoon salt

2 garlic cloves, crushed

1 teaspoon mustard seeds

1 teaspoon peppercorns

Sprig of fresh thyme

Cut up your vegetable into slices or sticks. Pack
them into your jars, leaving a half inch of headspace at the top. In a saucepan, bring the vinegar,
water, sugar, and salt to a simmer, then add your
garlic, mustard seeds, peppercorns, and herb.
Remove from the heat and pour into your jars,
leaving that half inch headspace. Seal with a
water bath.

Fermenting. The difference between
pickling and fermenting is that you don't
add an acid—the bacteria and sugars within
the food do it all on their own. It can seem
a little intimidating, but it's really not that
complicated. Standard vegetable fermentation uses salt to seal out mold and seal in
beneficial bacteria.

FREEZE-DRYING

Foods that contain high amounts of water
are ideal for freeze-drying, including
apples, berries, pears, potatoes, peppers,
carrots, and sweet potatoes. Once you get
good at it, you can try your hand at freeze-
drying chicken breasts, pork loins, etc. You
want to use the freshest food possible, the
ripest fruits and vegetables, and meats that
have just been cooked and cooled. Slice
your food into smallish chunks, then place
them in a sealed container. You'll need to
use a freezer set aside for just this purpose,
as opening and closing it will let in moisture and cause ice crystals to develop. Set
your freezer at its lowest possible setting,
then let your food sublimate, eliminating
all moisture. This will likely take around
three to five weeks.

To test whether it has been fully
freeze-dried, take out a chunk and let it
thaw on your counter. If it turns black,
it's not ready yet. But once it is ready, you
can store it in sealed plastic bags in your
pantry, your root cellar, a bug-out bag, or
wherever.

This process can also be done using
dry ice and a cooler. It will be much faster,
since it's so much colder—it'll probably
only take around 24 hours.

To reconstitute your freeze-dried food,
simply add boiling water slowly, just until
the food has absorbed enough moisture.

HOW TO FERMENT

STEP 1: Prepare Vegetables

Chop up your vegetables. The smaller they are, the faster they will ferment.

STEP 2: Prepare Brine

You'll want 1 tablespoon natural, noniodized salt per cup of water. As with pickling, you can add any other spices or flavorings you want.

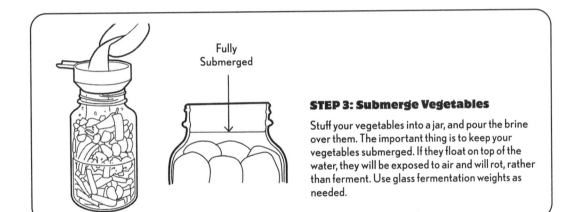

Fully Submerged

STEP 3: Submerge Vegetables

Stuff your vegetables into a jar, and pour the brine over them. The important thing is to keep your vegetables submerged. If they float on top of the water, they will be exposed to air and will rot, rather than ferment. Use glass fermentation weights as needed.

STEP 4: Seal

Tighten your lid, but don't seal it. Unlike with canning, you want to allow some air to move out, as the fermentation process will produce carbon dioxide. You don't want your jars to explode. Store them in a cool, dark place, and wait. Fermentation can take anywhere from three days to several months. Taste your vegetables every so often—they're ready when you say they are. They will keep for 1–2 years in the refrigerator.

Leave air gap

From Wheat to Bread

Part of growing your own food is thinking about how store-bought items are made. As you get more comfortable in the garden, you can be more adventuresome and even try your hand at growing wheat for your bread and pasta.

You'll need about a tenth of an acre set aside to grow enough wheat to feed a family of four for a year—that'll give you around 3.5 bushels of wheat, which is enough to make 31 loaves of bread. It takes around eight months for wheat to reach maturity and produce wheat berries, which is what you'll need to make flour. (They're also a delicious whole grain.) When it's ready, cut down your wheat with a scythe and thresh the wheat to remove the berries by whacking it against the inside of a bucket. You'll get some plant material in there you don't want, so set up an electric fan on low and drop handfuls of your wheat berries in the wind, down into a clean bucket. The plant material will blow away and the heavier berries will fall into the bucket.

You can mill your berries into flour using a coffee grinder, a blender, or a food processor. Although they won't make as consistent or fine a flour as commercial varieties, they will do the trick. But you can also purchase a dedicated grain-milling machine. Store your flour in the freezer, where it will last for up to six months.

This is unbleached, whole-grain wheat flour, so your favorite bread recipe will need some adjustment. Freshly milled flour requires more water, will ferment faster (meaning, the yeast won't need as much time to work), and you'll have a tighter crumb (meaning, a denser bread). You'll need to do some experimenting to see how your flour works.

Dealing with Winter

For those of you living in areas with true winter conditions, gardening can feel precarious and too short a growing season to invest too much time in. However, there are plenty of cool-weather crops that allow you to still grow bountiful vegetables. Onion, garlic, beets, radishes, carrots, cabbage, brussels sprouts, cauliflower, broccoli, and kale are all hardy down to the mid-twenty degrees (so can likely survive spring frosts). But even with the most winter-happy crops, there is always a little bit of work required to help them along.

At the end of fall, gather up your leaves *before* they start to go moldy. If they're dry, toss them in your compost, or let them dry in a wire bin first. Harvest anything still remaining, and pull up any annuals you have planted—if they're not going to come back, you might as well use them for compost! After your final harvest, top any raised beds with soil and sprinkle some manure or compost atop them, stirring it in and letting the soil improve during its resting season. You can scatter a layer of straw over the very top to seal it all in. Tidy up any trellises or other supports that might rot or get damaged over the winter.

Check all your machinery, making sure it's oiled, and fill your tanks so condensation doesn't form. Keep all your equipment in a protected shed.

Greenhouses are your best bet for maintaining a relatively consistent temperature for much of the year and extending your growing period. Sometimes, you'll need to cool down your temperatures, and you can install a fan. A greenhouse will also capture light and therefore heat, allowing you to start your crops earlier in the year and let them grow later as well. It will also help keep out predators and pests.

Greenhouses can be as fancy or as basic as you like. I tend to gravitate more toward the DIY and inexpensive, and you'd be surprised what you can create with some PVC and plastic sheeting. (I'm a big fan of PVC pipe. You'll be seeing a lot of it.)

HOT TIP

If you're trying to keep your greenhouse warmer for longer, you can put in a heat lamp . . . or you could save yourself some energy and money by using a thermal battery. Fill up a water barrel and paint it black. Put it on the south side of your greenhouse where the sun will hit it all day. It will heat up and retain that heat, keeping your greenhouse warm overnight. You can also take black garden hoses and fill them with water, then close them off and attach them to the south side wall, zigzagging them back and forth. The same principle applies—the sun heats them up, and they will heat your greenhouse.

Use winter as a time to plan out your next spring garden. Look back at your garden map and think about which crops worked and which didn't. Maybe it's time

HOW TO
FROM WHEAT TO BREAD

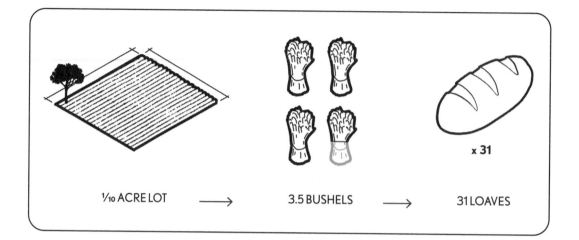

1/10 ACRE LOT → 3.5 BUSHELS → 31 LOAVES

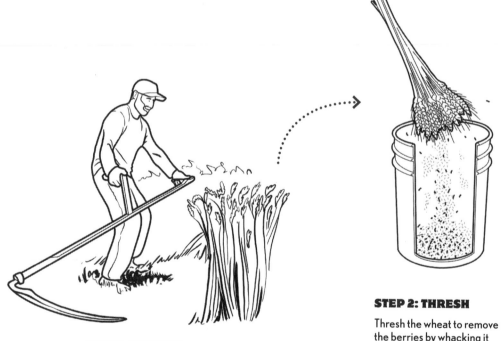

STEP 1: COLLECT

When it's ready, cut your wheat down with a scythe.

STEP 2: THRESH

Thresh the wheat to remove the berries by whacking it against the inside of a bucket. You'll get some plant material in there you don't want.

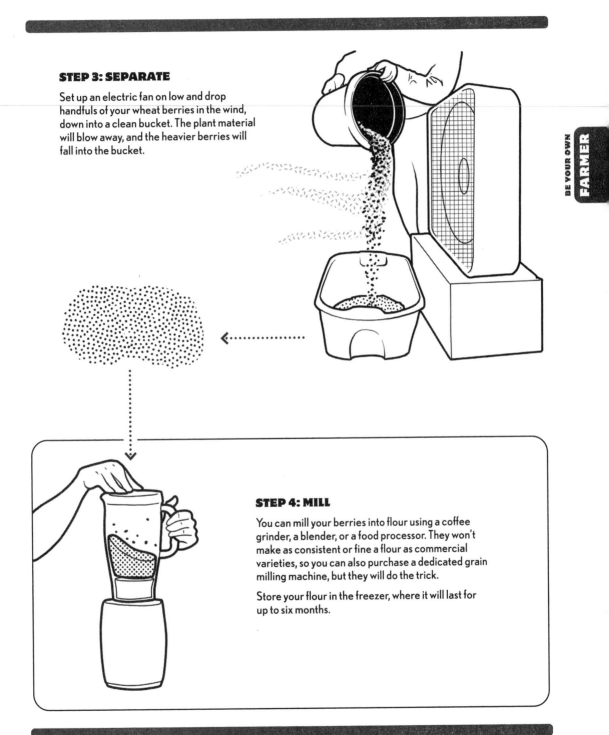

STEP 3: SEPARATE

Set up an electric fan on low and drop handfuls of your wheat berries in the wind, down into a clean bucket. The plant material will blow away, and the heavier berries will fall into the bucket.

STEP 4: MILL

You can mill your berries into flour using a coffee grinder, a blender, or a food processor. They won't make as consistent or fine a flour as commercial varieties, so you can also purchase a dedicated grain milling machine, but they will do the trick.

Store your flour in the freezer, where it will last for up to six months.

ANATOMY OF A GREENHOUSE

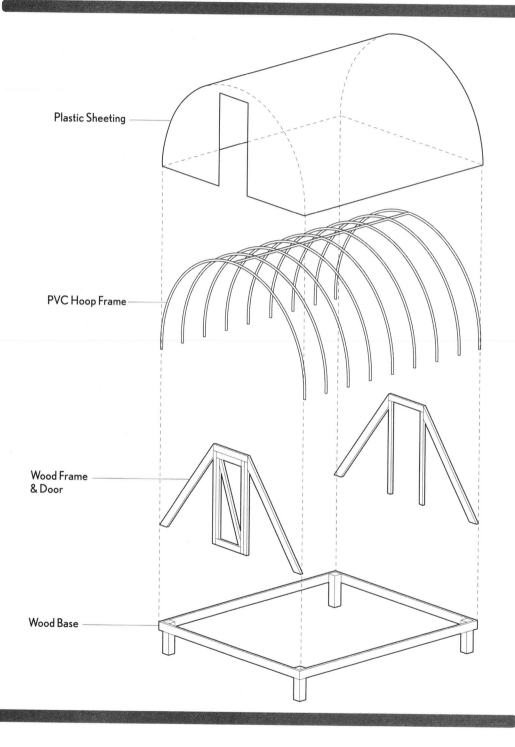

Plastic Sheeting

PVC Hoop Frame

Wood Frame
& Door

Wood Base

KEEPING IT WARM

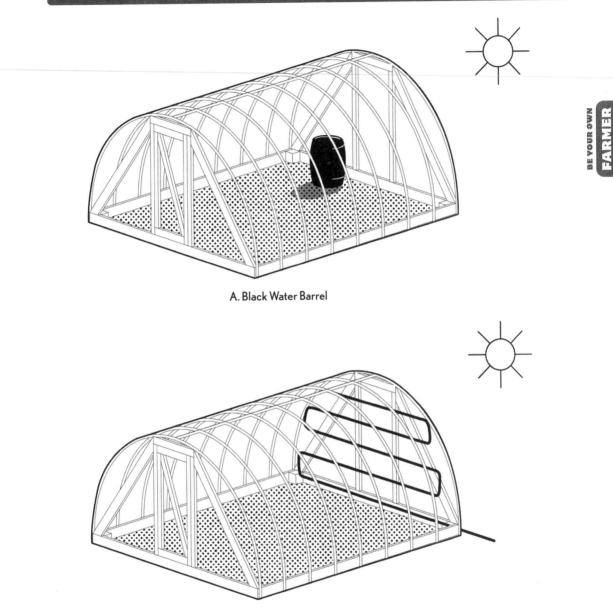

A. Black Water Barrel

B. Black Water Hose

to try a new plant or a new technique. You should also rotate your crops every four years to help your soil, so make sure you note on your map what you've planted and when. If you don't rotate, your crops will deplete your soil and you'll have to go through the whole amending process all over again.

FORAGING

You don't have to cultivate every single thing you want to eat. Unless you're planning on growing blackberries to sell, there's not really any reason to plant a big swath of plants you *know* will try to take over your whole farm—not when you can just go wander the woods and fields and pick them for free. No matter where you live, there is a host of wild foods available to you. You just have to know what to look for.

There are certain basic rules to observe:

→ Stay off of private property and don't overharvest.

→ Never take more than you need at any one time and don't strip a plant to the point where it'll die.

→ Don't dig up whole plants, and don't gather from anything rare or endangered. You want to be able to forage for years to come.

→ Eating right off the bush is a joy that cannot be dismissed, but after the first few tastes, it's better to take your food home and wash it before sampling any more. Nobody wants to eat animal urine or environmental waste.

→ *The last and most important rule is also the most obvious: Know what you're eating before you eat it. If you aren't sure what it is, don't eat it. Period.*

This is by no means an exhaustive list. There will be hundreds of varieties of edible wild plants that grow in the woods, fields, and parks close to where you live, no matter where you are. The following list is simply a collection of the most commonly found and most easily identified wild plants in the United States.

→ Amaranth (cook before eating)

→ Blackberries

→ Blueberries

→ Cattail (boil and eat the rootstock)

→ Chickweed

→ Chives

→ Clover

→ Dandelion

→ Kelp

→ Mulberries

→ Mustard greens

→ Nettles (cook before eating)

→ Plantains

→ Prickly pear cactus

→ Purslane

→ Raspberries

→ Seaweed (all green seaweed is edible)

→ Violets

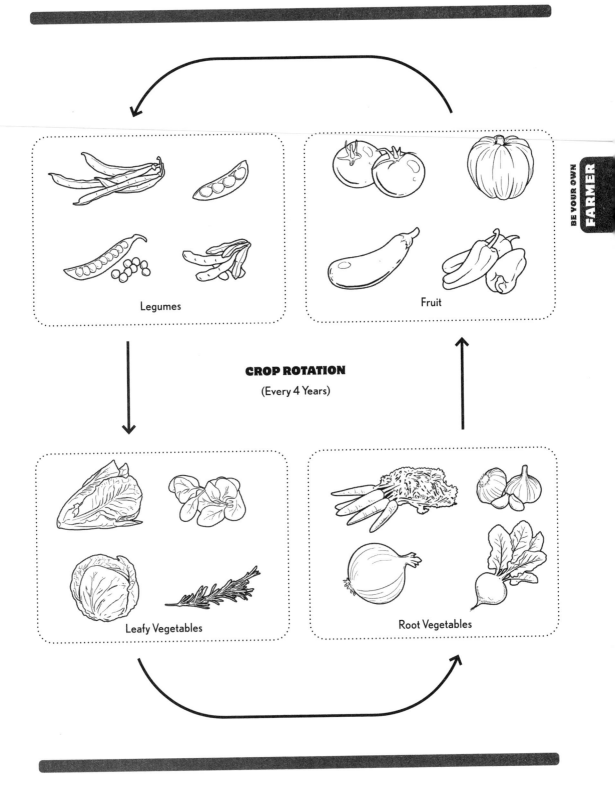

Legumes

Fruit

CROP ROTATION

(Every 4 Years)

Leafy Vegetables

Root Vegetables

POISON TEST

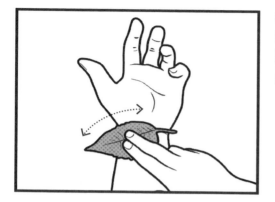

STEP 1: RUB

Rub the inside of your wrist with all parts of the plant, including the leaves, sap, and/or fruit. Wait 15 minutes to see if you have a reaction. If not, proceed to step two.

STEP 2: BITE

Take a small bite, hold it in your mouth for 15 minutes, then spit it out. Wait another 15 minutes to see if you have any swelling in the mouth or throat. If all goes well, proceed to step three.

STEP 3: SWALLOW

Take a small bite, this time swallowing it down. Make sure you haven't consumed anything in the past 8 hours, as it could interfere with the test. Wait for another 8 hours. If all goes well, you can eat this plant.

MUSHROOMS

Foraging for mushrooms is meditative, productive . . . and a little risky. There are mushroom identification apps, which can help, but they require power and cell service, which you may not necessarily have in the woods. Your best bet is to go out with your local mycologist society for a few trips—they can show you the good places to look and help you be sure about how to identify your mushrooms. This is yet again one of the countless examples of how making friends with someone with knowledge of the land is priceless; in this case, it could save your life.

Go mushroom hunting just after a heavy rain, which prompts the fruiting bodies to sprout. You'll have the best chance of success in the late summer or early fall. Cut off the top an inch from the base, allowing the mushroom to regrow.

→ **Giant puffballs.** Ranging in diameter from 4 to 12 inches, this big mushroom can form an entire meal, sliced, sautéed, and tossed into a stir-fry. It has a soft, marshmallow-like texture, is white or off-white, and has no visible stems or gills.

→ **Chanterelles.** These are the most popular foraged mushrooms, as they are fairly easy to identify and are quite delicious. They are a bright yellow, unlike their lookalike, jack-o'-lantern mushrooms, which are orange. They smell sweet and fresh, and grow in the ground on dead oak leaves (not in rotting logs).

→ **Oyster mushrooms.** These can be pale brown to light pink and they grow in stacks, like little stepping stones winding up trees or on fallen logs. They

TYPES OF EDIBLE MUSHROOMS

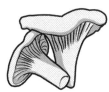

Giant Puffball

Chicken of the Woods

Oyster Mushroom

Chanterelle

Porcini

Lion's Mane

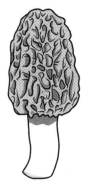

Morel

have pure white gills and a slightly off-center stem; they can be found in the spring or fall or even winter.

→ **Chicken of the woods.** This meaty-tasting mushroom is a bright orange-red and has no gills. It really does taste like chicken. They are commonly found growing around the base of dead or dying hardwood trees—usually oak, but often cherry or beech.

→ **Porcini.** Also known as King Boletes, these mushrooms have a distinctively rounded, dark cap and a fat stem. They have an earthy, rich flavor, and like to grow in semi-sunny places, usually beneath beeches or birches.

→ **Lion's mane.** This mushroom looks a bit like a cheerleader's white pom-pom. It may not look edible, but it is (and it's delicious), and there are no lookalikes, so if you see this, you're good to go. Lion's mane mushrooms grow higher up on the tree than most, up to 40 feet.

→ **Morel.** This variety of fungi with its honeycomb cap is prized by chefs as a delicacy. It can be found in forests in the springtime.

MAPLE SYRUP

If you live around sugar maples, absolutely tap them for your own maple syrup. It is one of nature's greatest gifts and it is so easy. Sugar maples (*Acer saccharum*) grow all over the Northeast and can also be found all the way down in Tennessee. Maple-tapping season occurs for four to six weeks beginning around March first, and your tapping rule of thumb is as follows: trunk diameter 12 to 20 inches = 1 tap, 21 to 27 inches = 2 taps, greater than 27 inches = 3 taps. If you don't follow these guidelines, you can end up harming the tree.

To tap the tree, drill a hole around 3 feet off the ground, making sure to leave at least 6 inches between your new hole and any previous ones. Most spiles (the thing that drains the sap) require a $5/16$ or $7/16$ drill bit. Drill your hole 2 to $2\frac{1}{2}$ inches deep, and work at a slight upward angle to allow gravity to pull on the sap. Check your shavings—if they're light-colored, great, but if they're dark, you may want to try a different spot.

How to operate a drill (see page 237).

Clear away any wood shavings, then insert the spile into the loop on the hook and insert it into the tap hole. Gently tap in the spile using a hammer. You should immediately see sap starting to drip—if not, it's not flowing yet. Hang a clean bucket by inserting the hook into a hole on the rim of your bucket, and then attach the lid to the spile, keeping anything from falling in while the sap is dripping.

Once you've collected all the sap you want, transfer it to a food-grade storage container—milk jugs or new, clean garbage cans work great, though make sure you disinfect them first. Use cheesecloth to filter out any contaminants. Like milk, sap must be kept cold and used quickly, so keep it in your refrigerator (outside works too, if there's snow on the ground) and boil it down within seven to ten days. You can technically drink the sap straight off, but it's better to boil it first to kill any bacteria—one minute at a rolling boil will do it.

To make maple syrup, keep it boiling to remove the excess water from the sap. This can take a while, as it takes ten gallons of sap to make one quart of syrup. That's a lot of steam, so most people like to boil their sap outdoors, either over a fire pit or using a grill. The boiling sap will eventually turn golden, though it'll still be quite fluid. At this point, it's fine to transfer it to a smaller pot and finish the boiling process indoors. Keep going until it reaches the syrupy consistency you're looking for, and keep an eye on it, as it tends to boil over. You can test whether it's ready by using a candy thermometer—the syrup is finished when it reaches 7°F above the boiling point of water. If you don't have a thermometer handy, dip a spoon into the boiling sap and watch it drip back into the pot. If it runs off the spoon smoothly in a sheet, it's probably ready. If it's still dripping in separate droplets, it needs more time. When it's ready, let your syrup cool.

There will still be some sediment, which you can filter out using a coffee filter or by letting it settle to the bottom of your container overnight. Sterilize your containers before bottling your syrup.

TAPPING A SUGAR MAPLE

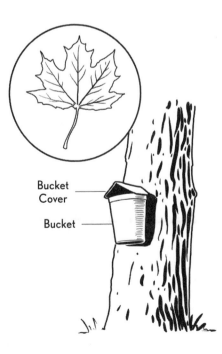

Bucket Cover

Bucket

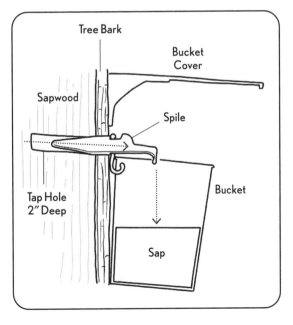

Tree Bark

Bucket Cover

Sapwood

Spile

Tap Hole 2" Deep

Bucket

Sap

"The cost of a thing is the amount of what I will call life which is required to be exchanged for it, immediately or in the long run."

—Henry David Thoreau

Growing and raising your own food is an essential part of the Rugged Life—perhaps the most essential. What could be more independent and self-sustaining than that? And you can do this no matter where you live or what your life is like, whether you commute to work from the suburbs or live way out in the country with acres and acres of land for your livestock to roam.

From one source or another you will need protein for your family to live on. Adult humans require a minimum of twelve ounces of protein per week, ideally more than that. While vegetable protein (soy, peanut butter, beans) is much cheaper, cleaner, and easier to source, it's not for everyone. If you enjoy meat, raising livestock is a great way to either supplement your grocery store trips or avoid Big Farm altogether. But for the off-gridders, hear this now: everything you do, all day, every day, will be in support of food. You'll be raising animals, caring for animals, butchering animals, and growing plants to feed you and your animals. Your whole life will revolve around their needs—so that they can meet your needs.

So start small. Get a couple of chickens, and see how you do. Is the work worth it? Are you able and willing to butcher them? Is it cost-effective? You can always get more animals.

SPOTLIGHT

The Rapiers • This incredible family welcomed me into their home in northern Idaho. They have seven kids, and each of them works the farm. (It's true—farmers didn't just have lots of kids back in the day because they were bored. Kids are workers.) I've never seen a more enthusiastic and handy crew, as they ran around in coonskin caps and herded sheep and chickens. It's their job to handle the carcass when a sheep drops dead, and they're the ones who have to go in and restart the water pump when it acts up. They didn't start out with a farming background but fell in love with the lifestyle, challenging as it is. All the kids are homeschooled, and there's space for dirt bikes and horses.

Staying Vegetarian. If you've got a nice field of soybeans, you can make soy milk and tofu with ease. Soy milk is just a precursor to tofu (just like milk is a precursor to cheese), and all that's needed is water, soybeans, and a coagulant—usually nigari (magnesium chloride) or gypsum (calcium sulfate). There isn't much difference between the two, though nigari produces a more distinct flavor.

Soak 3 cups dried soybeans overnight, covered with 2 inches of water. Once they're soft, drain them and place them in a blender with 8 cups water. Blend for a while, until they're creamy and smooth. Place the liquid in a large pot over medium heat and cook it down, stirring often and skimming off any foam—don't let it boil. Once it starts to get really foamy, remove it from the heat. Set a fine-mesh strainer over a mixing bowl, and line the strainer with cheesecloth. Pour the liquid over the cheesecloth and let it drip for an hour or two.

Gather the cheesecloth up into a sack and gently press on it to release any additional liquid—you'll have about 8 cups of very loose soy milk solids, also known as okara. Cook it a second time, letting it just steam over low heat for 5 minutes. Stir it up and remove any skin that has formed, then prep your coagulant by stirring 1 tablespoon coagulant into ½ cup water.

Stir your soy milk vigorously, then add a quarter of your coagulant. Mix it in, add another quarter, and then cover your pot and let it sit for 5 minutes or so. Add another quarter, let it sit again, and then add the final quarter. At this point you should see yellowish whey and white curds. Line a tofu mold with another swath of cheesecloth, then scoop out the curds with a slotted spoon, placing them in the mold. Cover them with some cheesecloth, place the top of the mold over them, and weigh it down. Let it sit for 15 to 30 minutes. After that, it's ready to chill and serve as you normally would! It will keep in the refrigerator for 3 to 5 days.

TOP TEN THINGS TO CONSIDER BEFORE RAISING ANIMALS FOR FOOD

If you're considering raising animals, it's easy to get overwhelmed and not know where to start. Here are the most important things to know before you dive in:

1. Find a good meat processor.

2. Put the telephone number of a good vet on speed dial.

3. If you're likely to have excess meat, have a plan for how you're going to sell it. Research local farmer's markets.

4. If you're going to sell milk, figure out what licenses and processing materials you need.

5. Make sure you're buying good stock from a reputable seller.

6. Build a sturdy fence.

7. Have a plan for what to do with all that manure.

8. Spend time with your animals to keep them docile and manageable—but don't get too attached.

9. Be realistic about what you have the time, money, and energy for.

10. Ask questions! Local farmers will always know something you don't.

Chickens

Chickens are the gateway animal for the modern homesteader. They require relatively little space and care, and they are a reliable source of food. You can keep up to a dozen chickens on a quarter acre lot (though that may not be allowed in your county), which will give you as many as a dozen eggs per day. So unless you *really like eggs*, you might want to keep only three or four.

Your best bets for egg-laying breeds include these:

→ **Golden Comet.** Actually a hybrid, this chicken will lay tons of eggs and eat relatively little food. They're low-maintenance and hardy.

→ **Rhode Island Red.** This hardy chicken is a great option because it lays eggs *and* makes for a tasty dinner. They're tough and self-reliant.

→ **Sussex.** Similarly, the Sussex can be used for either meat or eggs, and is quite tame and friendly—and unlike most chickens, these won't eat up your garden if you let them roam about.

→ **Buff Orpington.** Definitely don't get this chicken if you plan on eating it someday. It's very friendly and cuddly, and makes a great tame backyard chicken.

→ **Barnevelder.** This is a great option if you have a small fenced area and are concerned about your chicken getting out of it. Barnevelders are poor flyers and, unlike the others on this list, they don't require clipped wings.

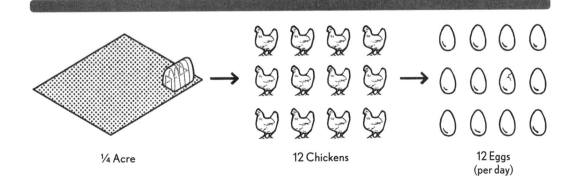

¼ Acre   12 Chickens   12 Eggs (per day)

A hen will lay best during her first year, and be less and less productive as she gets older. Eventually you'll want to turn her into a stew and replace her with a new chick; the turnover time is approximately two years.

That said, egg-laying chickens often don't make for particularly good eats. They tend to be small and stringy as they put all their energy into their eggs rather than fattening up. And, older chickens are much tougher than young chickens, so you'll want to look for soup or slow-cooking recipes. If you want chickens just for their meat and not eggs, you might consider an Australorp or a Cornish game hen.

You can also get a dual-breed chicken, which will have a good breast size *and* be a good layer. For that, you want a Cornish Cross, which will take around eight to ten weeks from hatching before they're ready to butcher. Don't go beyond that, though, in trying to stretch out their laying time, or they'll have organ failure.

HOT TIP

"Don't get a rooster. Roosters are loud and annoying, and your hens will lay eggs with or without them. If you want to grow your flock, you can get one—but you can also simply purchase chicks, which is both easier and quieter. That said, roosters can protect your flock from predators such as hawks, owls, and coons. But you're better off purchasing electric netting, which has the added benefit of being mobile."
—*The Rapiers*

COOPS

Chickens do require a coop to protect them from harsh weather and potential predators, but we're not talking about a chicken hotel here. Their needs are really very simple, and you can use scrap lumber and roofing to make one.

Basic Coop. It needs a roof, a ramp for the chickens to get up into it, a small doorway, and a larger door with a hatch for you to reach in and get your eggs—and clean out the coop. You'll need one nest box for every four chickens.

Mobile Coop. If you have the space for it, consider building a coop that you can pick up and move around the yard. There are a couple of advantages to this: (a) you won't have to clean out the coop as often; (b) the ground will be fertilized from all that chicken poop, making it an ideal place to plant crops.

HOT TIP

Make a Hoop Coop. A hoop coop looks a lot like the greenhouse on page 84—it's basically the same principle, just with chicken wire instead of plastic. It's fantastic because it will keep out predators, and it's just as straightforward and easy to build. If you put the chicken house on wheels, you can easily wheel the whole thing around to wherever you need it to go.

Some folks say that *free range* means letting your chickens go wherever the hell they want, and if that works for you, great. But the reality is that you will still need some form of perimeter for them, or you're basically just putting out feathery snacks for predators to come munch on. *Free range* doesn't mean "no fence." You have to have

HOW TO
BUILD A CHICKEN COOP

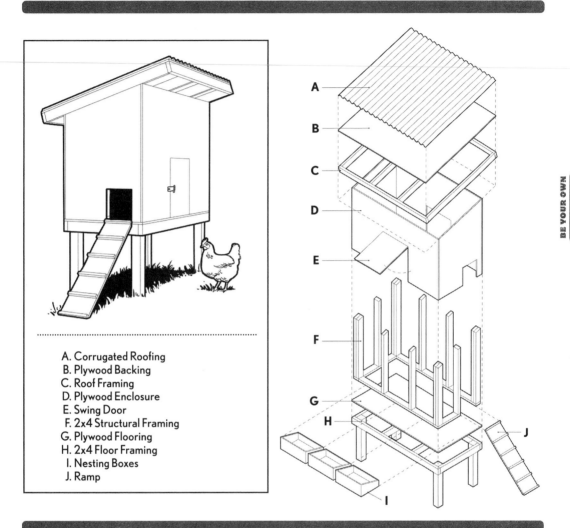

A. Corrugated Roofing
B. Plywood Backing
C. Roof Framing
D. Plywood Enclosure
E. Swing Door
F. 2x4 Structural Framing
G. Plywood Flooring
H. 2x4 Floor Framing
I. Nesting Boxes
J. Ramp

HOW TO
BUILD A HOOP COOP

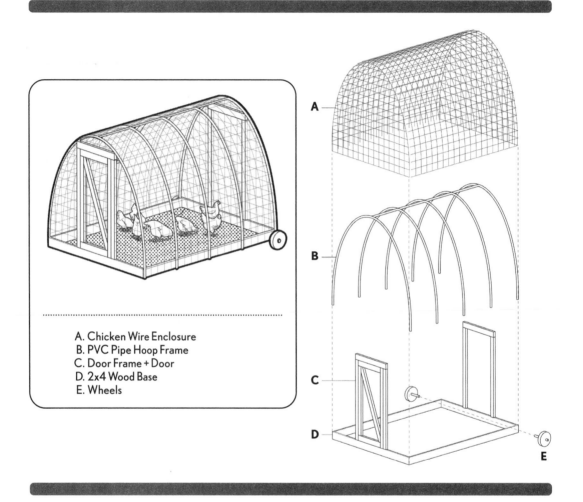

A. Chicken Wire Enclosure
B. PVC Pipe Hoop Frame
C. Door Frame + Door
D. 2x4 Wood Base
E. Wheels

Opposite: Birds will make a mess of anything, so
this kind of water feeder will need to be cleaned out
regularly, but the set-up will cut down on spills.

some kind of structure that will allow you to protect your birds.

Whatever you decide to build, build it to cover your worst-case scenarios. If you're building a chicken coop, it won't cost you much more to build one that's covered, protecting your flock from birds of prey, and it'll be worth it. If you live in snake country, you've got to put a skirt around everything, and the walls of the coop have to be tall enough so they can't slither over them.

FEEDING YOUR CHICKENS

In order to make sure your chickens are getting all the nutrients they need, you're probably best off purchasing chicken feed pellets from the farm supply store, but check to make sure its soy content isn't too high. It costs around $30 a month to keep five chickens, and you can support that diet (and save some money) by giving them a variety of other foodstuffs, including leftover table scraps and garden produce—chickens will eat just about anything (but don't give them raw potato peels, which they can't digest, or onions, garlic, or fish, which may end up flavoring the eggs). Letting your chickens roam about the yard will allow them to eat plants, seeds, and insects. If your chickens are foraging or eating scraps, they will need some grit to help them grind up the plant matter. You can scatter calcium grit for them as needed, which will have the added benefit of keeping the eggshells strong. Make sure your chickens have plenty of access to fresh water.

You can rig up a water feeder for your birds by taking a basic five-gallon bucket, putting a lid on it, and drilling some holes around the top of the bucket, just under the lid. Fill up with water and then place it upside down atop a flat garbage can lid. The water will spill out of the holes until the surface water level equalizes, refilling

DIY WATER FEEDER

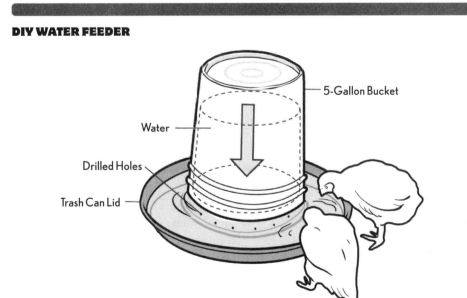

5-Gallon Bucket

Water

Drilled Holes

Trash Can Lid

itself as your birds drink their water. This trick won't work for goats and pigs, as they'll just knock it over or step in it, but it's great for birds.

If the neighbors are complaining, or if your town doesn't allow livestock, try registering your chickens as emotional support animals.

BASIC CARE

On a daily basis you'll need to do the following: check water, feed your chickens, collect their eggs, and hang out with them a little. Making sure they stay socialized will make it much easier to manage any issues that may come up. Once a month, you'll need to do a deep-clean, including changing their bedding and nesting boxes, cleaning out their water and food containers, and giving each chicken a full check over, making sure there aren't any injuries or issues that need to be handled. Wings will need to be clipped annually—all you need to do there is snip off the tips of their flight wings, cutting five to six feathers about a third of the way down.

If at any point they need a vet visit, you're looking at an average fee of around $75.

COLLECTING EGGS

You'll want to collect the eggs as soon after they are laid as possible. They'll be fresh and less likely to be broken or soiled. If you can, collect them at noon and in the evening just before putting your chickens to bed. If your chickens are free range, you're really going to have to hunt, like it's Easter every day.

How many eggs you get will depend on the length of the day—so you'll probably get more eggs in the summer, though you can purchase lights to extend their laying time. Also, every chicken goes through a period when they're molting (shedding old feathers to make way for new ones), and therefore not laying, so stagger the ages of your chickens so you have a steady supply.

Know this: the egg comes out the same hole as the poop, so you'll want to wipe it off a little. But *do not wash it*. Eggs come with a natural seal against bacteria called the cuticle or bloom, and with your own, fresh eggs, that means you don't have to refrigerate them. That's right, you can just leave 'em out on the counter, where they'll stay good for about two weeks.

Hens will lay eggs whether there's a rooster around or not, but if you do have a rooster, you need to keep an eye on him and make sure he's not fertilizing your eggs—no one likes cracking an egg and finding a chicken fetus inside. If you're not sure and don't want to check by cracking it, try holding the egg up to a lamp or other light source and see if there's a shadow inside.

BUTCHERING

You may not be ready at first to harvest your chickens. You may feel it will be tough to butcher your chickens yourself, and you can always hire a farmer or custom slaughterer if you're handling a whole flock, but if you're tackling just one chicken, it's probably something you're going to have to do on your own. The good news is fowl are one of the easiest animals to process (once you get over chopping the head off).

The Norrises do their chickens in batches, and they can get through twenty-five chickens start to finish in less than three hours. If you're doing several chickens at once, you're best off purchasing or renting a scalding tank—it'll just be something like ten bucks for two days, and it's totally worth it. You might also want an automatic plucker—you hook a hose up, spin it, and you've got your plucked chicken in less than thirty seconds.

You might ask yourself, Why would I want to do all of them at once? What am I going to do with all that meat? It's really just about efficiency, and if it works better for you to kill your chickens as needed and not have to worry about the freezer space, then do that.

HOT TIP **Get a Chest Freezer.** Sure, it's a power draw, but it's probably the most important appliance you can have. This freezer will act as your grocery store. Label and date everything and do your best to keep it organized, and you can store enough food to last you all winter. Another thing to check out is investing in vacuum sealing. It helps preserve frozen food even longer.

Either way, make sure you exhaust this resource to the nth degree. Using all the parts is basic homesteading philosophy. On night 1, you roast your chicken, then make stock with the carcass. Take the feet, scald them and skin them, and make stock with them, too, adding in your carrot peels, onion skins, celery ends, whatever you're not using. Chicken feet are an excellent source of collagen and gelatin.

HOT TIP **Get Some Turkeys.** Turkeys are basically big chickens, so the same principles apply. You could probably get away with a turkey or two living with your flock of chickens, though more than that and flock dynamics will get dicey. You could raise those turkeys for meat, and your chickens for their eggs. Turkeys are incredibly easy to raise and care for.

BE YOUR OWN **BUTCHER**

101

HOW TO
BUTCHER A CHICKEN

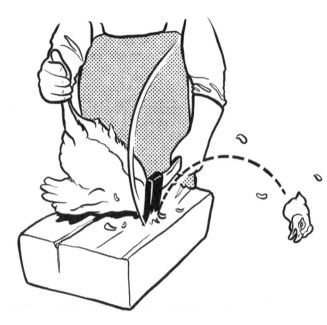

STEP 1: AXE

Catch your chicken and hold her by her feet. This will make her instinctively stick her neck out. Using a sharp, clean axe, place her on a chopping block (a stump will do) and with one firm swing, take her head off. Yes, her body will twitch, but she is in fact dead. You can also hang her upside down and slit her throat, allowing her to drain out, but this is less humane.

STEP 2: DE-FEATHER

Boil some water in a large pot and dunk the chicken in it three or four times—no more than that or it will begin to cook. This scalding process will help the feathers come out more easily. When you've finished plucking, run a blowtorch over the skin to char any remaining bits of feathers.

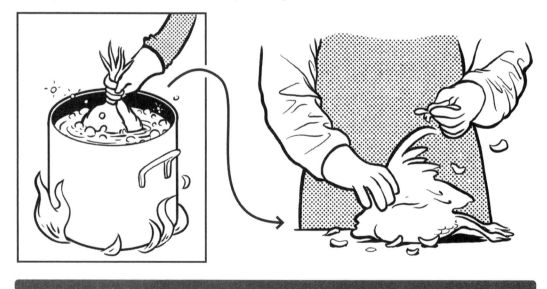

STEP 3: GUT

Remove the chicken's head if it hasn't been removed already. Hang the body upside down. Using a sharp knife, slit downward from the groin, being careful not to pierce the organs or intestines. The organs will begin to fall out, though you'll need to cut them free. If you keep pigs, they'll be happy to eat the refuse.

STEP 4: RINSE

Rinse the chicken thoroughly inside and out, making sure you got all the organ bits.

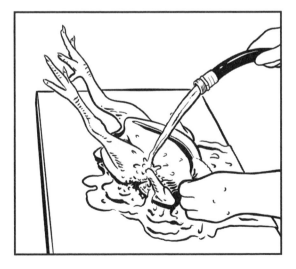

CUTS OF CHICKEN

A. Neck
B. Breast
C. Wing
D. Back
E. Thigh
F. Leg
G. Feet

Goats

Goats are some of the most useful animals to have around. You can make cheese and soap from their milk, and they are what you call "opportunistic eaters"—which means they'll eat just about anything. That can be annoying if you've left a shirt or a pair of shoes outside and the goats got them, but it's also extremely helpful if, say, you need to clear out a patch of brush for a new field. You also won't need to purchase as much feed, though on average you'll spend around $240 per goat every year.

A dairy goat will give you about 90 quarts of milk every month for most of the year. You can make cheese, yogurt, and ice cream, and give any leftover milk to your chickens or pigs. As with chickens, any goat will give you meat, but if you want a goat that is better for slaughtering than milking, consider getting a Boer or Spanish goat.

The best goats for milking include these:

→ **Alpine.** This dairy goat thrives in cooler climates.

→ **LaMancha.** This dairy goat will do better in warmer environments.

→ **African Pygmy.** This tiny goat requires less space, less food, and produces sweeter milk, as it contains more fat.

HOT TIP

"Goats are herd animals, and one lonely goat will be very unhappy. Get more than one, or have your goats share their living space with other animals—they get along well with cows, sheep, and donkeys, as well as cats and dogs. An intact male goat is a buck, and you don't really want him around unless you're breeding. On the other hand, wethers, or castrated males, are great pack animals, and can haul up to 40 percent of their body weight." –*The Rapiers*

SHELTER

Goats don't really need much in the way of shelter. An unused shed will do, or even a simple lean-to or four-sided structure. You just want to make sure they can get out of the rain and cold, and that you can clean it out easily. Packed dirt or cement is fine for a floor; cover it with straw or noncedar wood shavings. Whatever hay your goats don't eat should go right on that floor. You can replace the bedding seasonally, but spread a fresh layer on top more often.

Your goats will be happiest with some space to run around and things to climb on, so you can stack pallets or put some old tires out—but make sure those are tough tractor tires, because a goat will try to chew on anything. Similarly, a goat will try to get out of anything, and making a fence goat-proof is one of homesteading's great trials. You need a strong fence with small enough gaps that the goat can't wiggle through. Frankly, electric fences are probably your best bet, but you could also use chain link or wooden rails.

GOAT SHELTERS

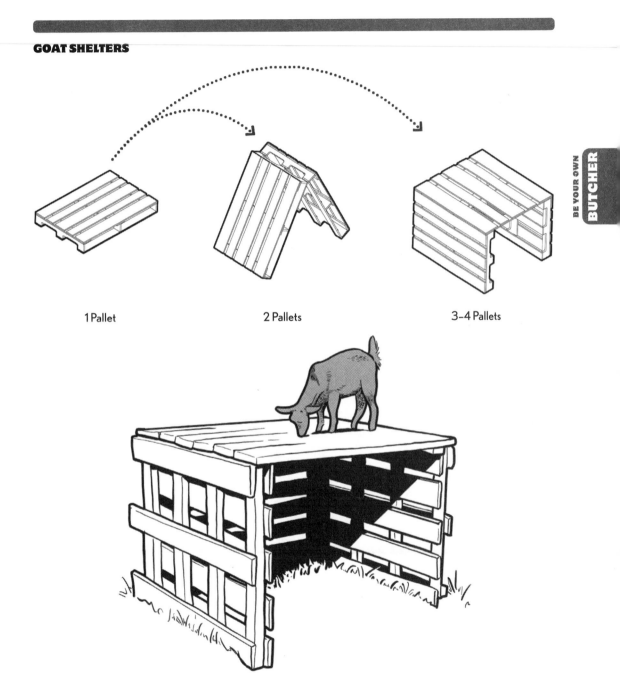

1 Pallet

2 Pallets

3–4 Pallets

BE YOUR OWN
BUTCHER

105

FEEDING YOUR GOATS

Letting your goats graze around is good for them and saves you money on feed. But if you want their milk to taste good, you probably don't want to let them munch on brambles. Instead, set them free in a maintained pasture (i.e., one that you're keeping clear of wild onion, garlic, or anything else that will affect the flavor of the milk). Rotate their grazing area weekly so it doesn't get overgrazed or muddied.

Your goats will still need plenty of hay—about four pounds of hay per goat per day. But goats won't eat more than they need, so just make sure there's plenty of clean, fresh hay available. Try for a hay that is half grass and half legume, which should support nutrition and be a little less expensive than full legume. When you have a high-producing dairy goat, she will likely need some concentrate to provide additional nutrients. You'll also want some baking soda to keep your goats' rumen acidity at an optimal level and some salt to help with digestion.

The more water a goat drinks, the more milk she will provide. Fill a 5-gallon bucket with clean water and place it outside the goat shed, ideally through a hole in the fence so they can drink without knocking it over. Refill it often, giving them cool water in the summer and warm water in the winter.

BASIC CARE

As long as goats have plenty of good pasture, sunshine, and food and water, they're relatively easy to care for. They need their hooves trimmed every four to six weeks, but you should spend time with them every day. Be very gentle in your approach, as goats are naturally nervous. Use a rope halter and don't restrain them more than is absolutely necessary. Check them regularly for loss of appetite, limping, listlessness, labored breathing, diarrhea, discharge from the eyes or nose, and abnormal body temperature.

Common issues can include upper respiratory infections, parasites including lungworm, bloat, and abscesses. Keep their vaccinations up to date and give them regular checkups. Care from your veterinarian will probably cost between $50 and $250 per year, per goat.

MILKING A GOAT

Give your goat some hay or concentrate to munch on and she'll be happy and relaxed as you milk her. Talk to her or sing to her, and be gentle. If you tug her teat, scratch her, or pull on her hair, she'll kick over the milking pail. Keep her hairs trimmed and your nails short. Wipe down the udder with a baby wipe to remove any dirt.

Squeeze the teat rather than pulling on it. This takes some practice. Use your thumb and forefinger to apply a steady pressure—this will keep the milk from going back up into the udder—and then use your remaining fingers to draw the milk down and out. The teat will become soft and flat when the udder is empty. When you're done, spray the teats with a teat dip to keep out bacteria—and rub them with some Bag Balm if the teats are getting dry or chapped.

For the modern homesteader, a few jars of milk from a couple of goats can be placed in a refrigerator to cool immediately after milking. If you've got lots of goats and therefore lots of milk, immerse your

HOW TO
MILK A GOAT

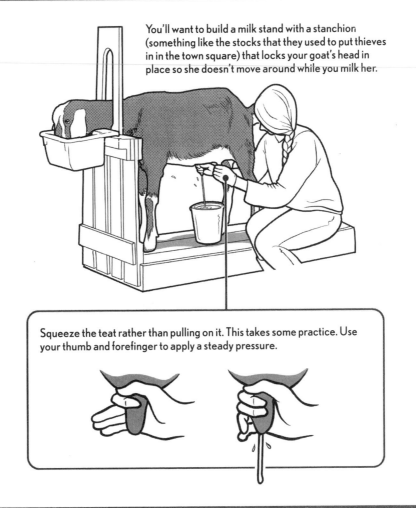

You'll want to build a milk stand with a stanchion (something like the stocks that they used to put thieves in in the town square) that locks your goat's head in place so she doesn't move around while you milk her.

Squeeze the teat rather than pulling on it. This takes some practice. Use your thumb and forefinger to apply a steady pressure.

containers in an ice bath to cool them rapidly before moving them to a refrigerator. You can pasteurize your milk using an Instant Pot or on the stove—all it takes is heating it to 165°F for fifteen seconds.

HOT TIP

"Spend time with your goats, scratching them and calling them by name. A socialized goat will be a lot easier to milk and maintain. And hook them up to a goat cart! They'll haul stuff for you, and even give the kids rides."—*The Rapiers*

HOW TO
MAKE GOAT CHEESE

STEP 1: BOIL

Heat a quart of goat milk to 180°F or until the surface is foamy and bubbling gently.

STEP 2: MIX

Turn off the heat and stir in a cup of lemon juice or vinegar. Stir it well, and let it sit for 10 minutes while it curdles.

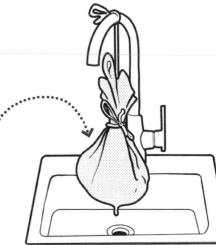

90:00

STEP 3: STRAIN

Take two layers of damp cheesecloth and place them in a colander in the sink. Gently pour the mixture into the cheesecloth and tie it into a bundle. Hang the bundle from your faucet and let it drip for at least 90 minutes.

STEP 4: ADD FLAVOR

Stir in salt to taste, and add herbs of your choice. Store in the refrigerator and use within 3–4 days.

Sheep

Sheep and goats get along well, and require basically the same care and feeding. The Rapiers raise sheep and sell the lambs for meat—a lamb is a bit more manageable, volume-wise. Oftentimes, they eat them, too, or even the older sheep (mutton) once they've stopped dropping lambs. (Of course, with mutton, you've got a gamey flavor, so you'll want to use it in a stew with plenty of spices.) Also, if one of your lambs dies, it's not the huge loss that a cow death would be, with so much money and time gone down the drain. Lambs are ready to butcher at six to eight months.

Sheep have other benefits, too. They are natural lawnmowers, for starters, and who wants to add mowing the lawn to the already way-too-long list of things to do? They also grow wool, which can be useful for you and can make you some extra money. The most popular sheep breeds are those that can be raised for both their meat *and* their wool, though their wool won't earn as much as other breeds' raised solely for their wool.

→ **Merino.** Merino makes an incredibly soft wool, and is relatively easy to spin. The meat is decent.

→ **Turcana.** This coarser wool is more often used to make carpets, and both the meat and dairy products are tasty.

→ **Dorper.** This breed can handle drier, warmer areas than others. Its wool is used in commercial clothing manufacturing.

SHEEP TO WOOL

If you're planning on selling your sheep's wool, know that it's a bit of a pain. Commercial producers will probably get you only 50¢ per pound, which hardly seems worth it. However, if you're raising a Merino or, better yet, a rarer wool sheep, such as Bluefaced Leicester, Cormo, Polwarth, or Targhee, you can get some decent money selling their wool to hand spinners at sheep and wool festivals. For good, clean fleece you can get up to $20 per pound. That's a much better profit margin . . . but you've got to put in the work. Like all animals, sheep poop, and believe me, there's nothing grosser than trying to get it out of their wool; most hand spinners prefer to purchase clean wool. So you'll need to cut away (or skirt) any unusable wool. You can cut down on that waste by putting your sheep in jackets, keeping their wool free of fecal matter, burrs, and bugs.

You can hire a shearer to come trim your sheep, and it's not that expensive. A flock of fifteen sheep will cost you about $15 per sheep, and a shearer may trim the hooves for you while they're at it.

How to spin wool (see page 182).

Rabbits

Now, here is a good source of meat. As the saying goes, rabbits breed like rabbits, ensuring you have an ever-renewing food supply. It's a low amount of feed for a decent amount of meat, they don't require much space, and it's a pretty fast turnaround—they only need to be six to eight weeks old before they're big enough to eat.

They're also delicious, and their fur is useful and profitable, too. There is a downside—that kind of turnaround means you're always butchering rabbits, and you get tired of it pretty quickly. But if you're in hard times and you want to be as self-sufficient as possible, you could store up hundreds of pounds of pellets and raise your protein in your garage, living off of them for months and months.

Rabbit droppings make great fertilizer and, unlike chicken poop, the pellets aren't so high in nitrate that you have to process them first—you can just scatter them right into your garden.

Here's the thing, though: rabbits are really cute. They're sweet and snuggly, and so before investing in rabbits with the intention of slaughtering them, consider whether you (and your family) are really up for it.

The best meat rabbit breeds include the following:

→ **Californian.** This rabbit has a great meat-to-bone ratio.

→ **New Zealand.** This is the most popular meat rabbit breed because of its full, well-muscled body.

→ **Florida White.** This slightly smaller rabbit is ideal for a smaller family that won't be able to go through quite as much meat.

SHELTER

Rabbits live in hutches, which is basically an elevated box. You want it to be up off the ground so the poop can fall out, and it will keep them safe from predators. Predators (including foxes, badgers, coyotes, and snakes) love rabbits. Rabbits are most comfortable at temperatures between 50 and 70°F, so if it's hot out, make sure you've got your rabbits in the shade with plenty of air circulation. You can move your hutch into a barn if it's too cold out, but as long as they stay dry, they can actually handle pretty cold weather. An outdoor cage can be kept dry simply by stapling on plastic sheeting, but you want to make sure there's still some air circulation. Let the cage warm up in the winter sun and keep it out of the wind.

For all these reasons, a portable hutch is a good idea. You can move your rabbits' nitrogen- and phosphorus-rich fertilizer to areas you'll want to plant crops, and you can place them in the sun or shade as needed. If you're only planning on keeping a couple of rabbits, it's actually more cost-effective to buy a ready-made hutch, or at least a kit you can put together yourself. You have to buy a lot of supplies to build a hutch, so if you're going to have several rabbits, it does make sense to build from scratch.

If you want to keep your rabbit numbers down, make sure they're of the same sex. Rabbits are sociable animals and you'll want to keep them in pairs, or up to three in a single hutch. They will also need space to move around and some protected grass to nibble at, so it's a good idea to have a small fenced area for them to roam about in. Rabbits are naturally afraid of being picked up—the ground is awfully far away—but if you get them used to it from when they're young, they won't mind so much. That said, if you're planning on butchering them, maybe don't let your kids snuggle them all the time—that can make it pretty hard when it comes time to eat.

FEEDING YOUR RABBITS

Commercial rabbit feed is the way to go. It provides balanced nutrition, and you won't need to supplement with things like salt licks. Your rabbits will enjoy some nice fresh hay, but be careful what fruits and vegetables you give them, because despite what stories of Peter Rabbit have told us, rabbits can't actually eat anything they find in a garden. That said, they do like alfalfa, apples, beets, carrots, lettuce, and turnips. As with all animals, rabbits require a steady source of fresh water. Drop feeders are great, but be careful they don't freeze in the winter.

RABBIT HUTCH

BASIC CARE

One thing to note—if you're allergic to cats, you're probably also allergic to rabbits. And like cats, rabbits will scratch you, and they can carry bacteria in their claws. Wash all scratches immediately so they don't get infected.

Rabbits need to spend several hours a day outside their cage. Their bodies are designed for running and jumping. Set up a fenced area and watch them closely—they're also designed to dig. Clean out the cage at least once a week and brush them regularly. Check for discharge from the eyes or nose, dark red urine, fur loss, and for diarrhea. An average vet bill will run you between $25 and $50.

BREEDING YOUR RABBITS

When your doe starts marking with her scent by rubbing her chin against the feeder or other surfaces, check her genitals—if they are red, she's probably ready to breed. That said, she may not be in the mood. As the joke goes, men always are, and women need some coaxing, and the same is true for rabbits. Take the doe to the buck's cage rather than vice versa so she doesn't feel the need to defend her territory. If he has to chase her, give them ten minutes or so, and if they still haven't worked it out, try again another time. But if she raises her hindquarters, it's on. You'll know when they're finished when the buck gives a squeal and falls down to rest. Rabbits: not that different from humans.

You can expect the litter to arrive in about a month, and your pregnant doe will not need much extra food. She will need a wooden nest box filled with hay or straw. Once she's kindled (given birth), she will be quite nervous and overprotective, as mothers tend to be. Distract her with a snack and check on her babies, removing any that have died. After about three weeks, the kits will come out of the nest box, and you can start handling them and giving them some love, getting them used to human contact.

BUTCHERING

If you are processing a bunch of rabbits at once, it's completely fine to send them out for harvesting. It's time consuming to break this small animal down. But if you would like to do it at home, the illustration shows you how.

Opposite: Having a portable hutch will allow you to take advantage of all that good manure.

HOW TO
BUTCHER A RABBIT

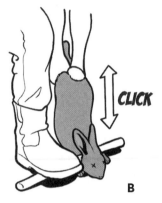

A

B

STEP 1: CULLING

Basically, you bop them over the head really hard with a bat. Do it hard and fast so they don't suffer. There are also things called "Hopper Poppers" available if you can't bring yourself to do this.

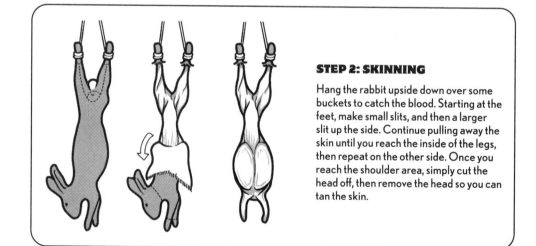

STEP 2: SKINNING

Hang the rabbit upside down over some buckets to catch the blood. Starting at the feet, make small slits, and then a larger slit up the side. Continue pulling away the skin until you reach the inside of the legs, then repeat on the other side. Once you reach the shoulder area, simply cut the head off, then remove the head so you can tan the skin.

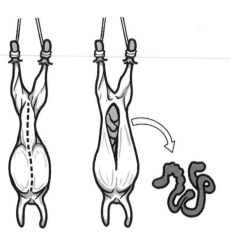

STEP 3: GUTTING

Starting at the anus, cut straight down the rabbit's chest, being careful not to pierce any organs. They will begin to fall out as you go, so try to get them to fall into the bucket. Cut out the anus and then hose down the body.

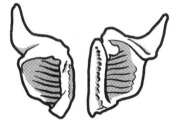

STEP 4: SECTIONING

Cut off the belly fat for bacon. Snip off the front and hind legs, and soak the pieces in cool water for a day to get the blood out.

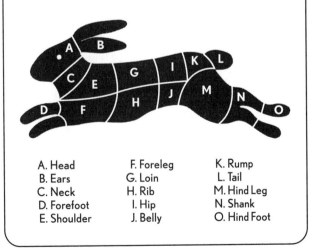

A. Head
B. Ears
C. Neck
D. Forefoot
E. Shoulder

F. Foreleg
G. Loin
H. Rib
I. Hip
J. Belly

K. Rump
L. Tail
M. Hind Leg
N. Shank
O. Hind Foot

Pigs

Hogs take up more space than rabbits, but they provide way more food. If you're looking to sell your meat or if you've got a lot of mouths to feed, pigs are the way to go. Their rooting can also dig up a garden bed for you faster than anything. A goat will strip a blackberry plant for you, but a pig will dig up the roots.

That said, they are more expensive, and it takes a while before they're ready to eat, around six or seven months. And they are messy, hard work. The Rapier kids hate dealing with the pigs, and take turns for who has to do the job. It gets really muddy in a sty, and you have to haul buckets of water to clean it out. Pigs are smart and they're also big and strong, which can make them hard to deal with.

You're best off buying a pig from a local farm. That way, you can check out the setup and see how big your piglet is likely to get. Buying a pig at auction means they are likely stressed out and may have been exposed to disease or toxins. Look for a barrow (castrated male) or a gilt (a young female) to avoid a boar taint in the meat.

The easiest starter pig breeds include:

→ **Berkshire.** Very common, and durable. Good, lean meat.

→ **Poland China.** Also common and durable. Good, lean meat.

→ **Spotted.** Fast-growing and durable. Commonly available.

SHELTER

Trust me, you don't want hogs roaming around the place. Free-range pigs are not a good idea. Goats and sheep can hang out together, but pigs are aggressive and they dig up everything. Build a separate hog pen. You can put it near your garden, where you can easily toss in waste for your pigs to snack on. Their shelter needn't be fancy—just a three-sided plywood roofed structure will work, though you'll want planks for the floor so it doesn't get slippery. Depending on where you live, you can simply fence off the rest of the pen and let them live on the ground, but if it's rainy and likely to get too muddy, you'll want to build a planked "porch" as well, which will allow waste to fall through. If you've got piglets, you'll want to put some chicken wire over the shelter to protect them from birds of prey. No matter what your shelter ends up being, make sure you've got a strong fence around the pen.

FEEDING YOUR PIGS

A pig's digestive system is remarkably similar to a human's, and they can basically live off of corn and soybeans, probably running you around $100 to $200 per pig over the course of its life before slaughter—it takes around six months for them to grow to butchering size. You can just make sure the feeder is full of fresh food and let your pigs fatten themselves up. Supplement their feed with scraps from the garden and with some animal protein like eggs,

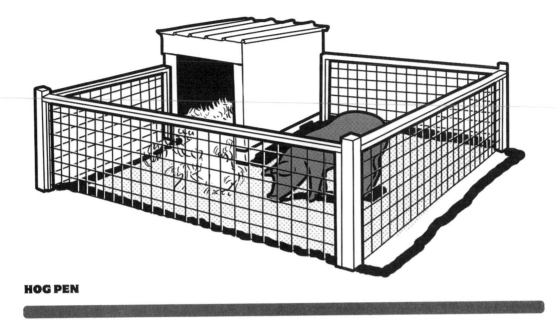

HOG PEN

fish, or dairy. Just, you know, don't give them pork.

DEALING WITH HOGS

These aren't wild boars; most hogs are gentle and chill. But they are big, and if they get upset, they can hurt you. Don't back them into a corner and make them panic, and remember that if you stay calm, so will they. However, getting them to go where you want to can be a challenge. Using a snare and gripping tongs will help restrain a market-ready pig, while a smaller, younger pig can be grabbed by the ears and hind legs. Avoid the tail, as it's attached to the spine.

If you're breeding pigs, you need to have the ability to keep your boar away from your sow. Once he's gotten her pregnant, get him out of there. Boars are, well, boorish. He will keep harassing that sow, push her back into heat, and if he bothers her enough, she'll abort her litter and you'll end up with a bunch of stillborn piglets. Put him someplace separate so everyone can just chill out.

BASIC CARE

Pigs are prone to health problems, including respiratory infection, but these can be reduced if you keep their housing sanitary and make sure they have plenty of fresh water and good feed. Clean out their bedding often. They prefer straw as it allows them to nest, but they'll make a mess of it.

Check them every day for physical or behavioral changes. Poor appetite, lethargy, and labored breathing are all signs that something could be wrong, and you should consult a vet right away.

Due to their weight, pigs often have hoof problems. Keep their hooves trimmed (the less active they are, the more frequent trimming they will need). Horse hoof

117

nippers work well on pigs. Watch out for infection, including swelling, abscesses, limping, or any cracks in the hoof. Male pigs will also need their bottom tusks trimmed every three to six months, or they will injure your other pigs. A noncheckup vet visit could cost around $400.

USING THE MEAT

Honestly, if you're keeping hogs, you're probably pretty comfortable with slaughtering and butchering and we don't need to go into that here. The same basic principles apply; this animal is just a lot bigger. A *lot* bigger, so you are going to need to shoot it to kill it, and unfortunately, pigs are among the most difficult of animals to shoot. The target is really small, and certain breeds have concave faces, making it even more difficult. Aim for the middle of the forehead, shooting toward the tail at one finger's width above eye level.

The size means you've got a lot of meat to work with.

I recommend finding out if there are any smokehouses in your area. They will often fully process your meat, smoke it, and package it all up for you. But if you want to handle it yourself, you can freeze it, grind some of the lesser cuts into sausages, or preserve it. Mix in some fat with your lean meat when you're grinding to preserve the flavor, probably about 25 percent, and grind twice; you want to use the coarsest setting first, then mix in any spices (traditional Italian sausage uses parsley, oregano, fennel seed, paprika, red pepper flakes, onion flakes, garlic powder, and salt and pepper). Push it through the finer setting and then shape it. Use it or freeze it.

To cure your pork, you'll need sugar and noniodized salt. The salt will inhibit bacterial growth as well as dry it out.

CUTS OF PORK

A. Hock
B. Ham
C. Bacon
D. Spare Ribs
E. Loin
F. Back Fat
G. Shoulder
H. Picnic Ham
I. Neck
J. Jowl
K. Head
L. Ears
M. Snout

The sugar will bring out the flavor in the meat that may have been overwhelmed by the salt. You can also add saltpeter, or nitrate, which has some health risks with overconsumption, but will help prevent botulism.

LONZINO

→ Ground pork loin

→ Noniodized salt

→ Sugar

→ Curing salt (available for purchase online)

→ Spices (see above)

To figure out how much of each ingredient you need, weigh your pork loin, and use 2.5 percent of the overall weight in salt, 2.5 percent in sugar, and .25 percent in curing salt. Use your spices to taste, as every curer has their own secret recipe. Mix all your dry ingredients, and then rub them well into the meat. Cover it in plastic wrap and refrigerate for a week. Remove it and test it for firmness. If it's clear the salt has penetrated, unwrap it, rinse it off, and let it sit on a rack for a couple of hours. Tie it up with twine and hang it in a cool, dry place for at least two weeks and up to six months. If you see white mold growing, that's fine— it's doing its work. If you see black or green mold, wipe your meat down with white vinegar to clean it off. It'll be ready when it's very firm and a nice dark red. It'll get harder and drier the longer it hangs, so take it down when it's still soft enough to slice. Enjoy as you would prosciutto.

Cattle

If you've got the land for it, these are easy to raise and provide a ton of meat and dairy. The Norrises raise cows, and they say that these are probably about the easiest meat animals there are—they require little to no care or attention, and in the summer they can pretty much live off your land without needing any additional feed, and can usually live off of rainwater as long as your environment isn't too dry. Cows will happily consume 2 percent of their body weight every day. In the colder months, you'll have to feed them, but you can give them a bit less since they aren't moving around so much. You're looking at spending anywhere from $700 to $900 in hay per cow, which is a lot, but if you're growing corn, you can offset that by giving them corn husks.

You can avoid bloat by moving gradually from hay to grass and vice versa with the changing seasons, and you only need to increase their feed a little when the weather gets cold. The amount of meat you get in exchange for your daily effort is staggering. You'll have good fencing, because if your cow gets out and causes a car accident, in most states you'll be liable—but that's true of all livestock. A two-year-old cow is ready to butcher—any longer than that and the money you're spending on feed makes it less cost-effective.

That said, in order for it to be worth it, you need a *lot* of land, one to two acres per cow. Less than that, and you're buying too much feed, so are better off getting your steaks at the store. The other issue is, when you butcher a cow, you've got a *lot* of meat on your hands. Maybe that's a good thing, depending on how much freezer space you have, or if you're able to sell it.

Suggested breeds:

→ **Angus.** This is the most popular breed of beef cattle. They're very hardy and can handle cold winters. They're big and muscular, and are known to calve easily.

→ **Holstein Friesian.** This dairy cow will keep pumping out milk, giving an average of 25 liters per day.

→ **Simmental.** Most cattle are bred for either dairy or milk, but Simmentals are good choices for either. They produce plenty of milk, mature quickly, and are quite large.

→ **Brahman.** If you live in a hotter climate, this is the meat cow for you. They can tolerate heat and are also less prone to parasites and disease than most breeds.

BASIC CARE

Cows may not require much care, but they do require some, and the thing is, the bigger the animal, the more expensive it is when something goes wrong.

Check on them every day, including their feed, bedding, salt and mineral licks, and water supply. Cattle can feel anxious when trapped, and they're big animals. Watch your feet, and run your hands over them often to help them feel comfortable with you—this will also allow you to check them for sores, and for issues with their hooves, which need to be trimmed once or twice a year.

Cattle are prone to bloat (overeating grain) and mastitis (infection of the mammary glands), both of which can be minimized by being careful with their feed and cleanliness. If they do show signs of either, or of foot rot or respiratory issues, you should contact your vet immediately—this animal is too expensive to risk. You should have a bovine veterinarian check your heifers every three months. You're looking at an average of $100 per cow per visit.

AMOUNTS TO FEED A FAMILY OF FOUR

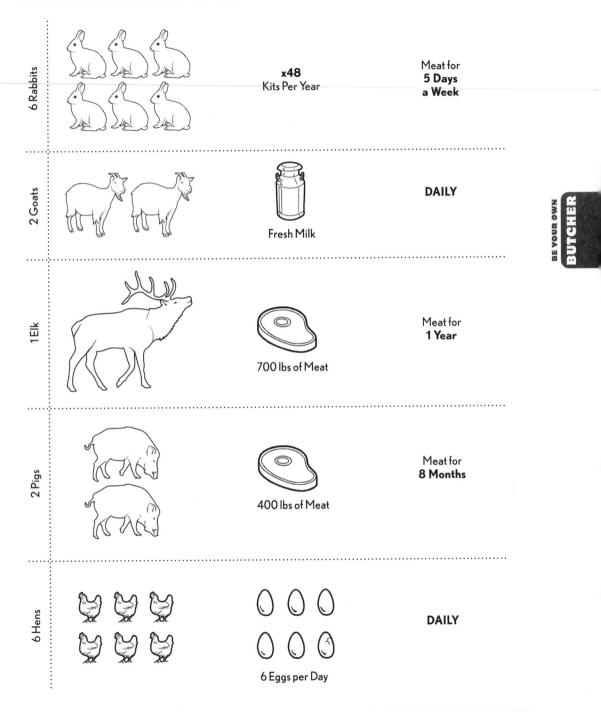

6 Rabbits

x48
Kits Per Year

Meat for
**5 Days
a Week**

2 Goats

Fresh Milk

DAILY

1 Elk

700 lbs of Meat

Meat for
1 Year

2 Pigs

400 lbs of Meat

Meat for
8 Months

6 Hens

6 Eggs per Day

DAILY

BE YOUR OWN
BUTCHER

Smoking Meat

It's a good idea to always have a year's supply of food preserved and ready. You just never know what might happen. Chest freezers are ideal, but you can also smoke the meat. This technique likely dates back to the Paleolithic era, and smoked meat is *delicious.* The methods for smoking meat for preservation, versus for flavor, are only slightly different. You can certainly use an electric smoker, in which case all you have to do is turn it on and set a timer, but honestly that's way less cool and provides less flexibility. You can make your own smoker out of a 55-gallon drum—no welding required.

You can also make one out of an old refrigerator, which is handy since it's already got doors on it. If you haven't got one you want to get rid of, you can probably find one at a junkyard. Cut a chimney at the top with a hacksaw, then cut a hole in the side near the bottom of the fridge. Make your firebox out of cinder blocks, then force the smoke and heat through the hole into the fridge.

The best smoke to use comes from wood chips, a lot of them. You can use whatever you have on hand, as long as it's not from chemically treated wood, or from conifers, which can be toxic.

Start by salting your meat. This works for anything—fish, game, cow, goat, pig, whatever. Cut it down to manageable size, then rub natural, noniodized salt all over the exterior. Add some spices to your rub as desired—cumin, paprika, chili powder, whatever you like. Let it rest in the fridge, and then once the blood runs out, dump it and give it another rub. Alternatively, you can brine it by soaking it in salt water mixed with sugar and spices—you want enough salt so that a potato can float, and leave your meat in there for a couple of days.

Next, cure it by roasting it quickly over a hot bed of coals—a fire pit will work great. The idea here isn't to cook the meat, but to quickly get all the moisture out. This will extend its shelf life.

Now it's time to smoke it. The two key words are *low* and *slow*—don't rush this process. You want the heat from the smoke to do the work on your meat, not the heat source itself. Smoking something for 24 hours at 150°F will ensure that it's actually preserved and won't need any refrigeration. Obviously it's cooked well before that, so you can take some out earlier for dinner. You'll know your meat is ready when it cracks and breaks, rather than bends. Store it in a cool, dry place.

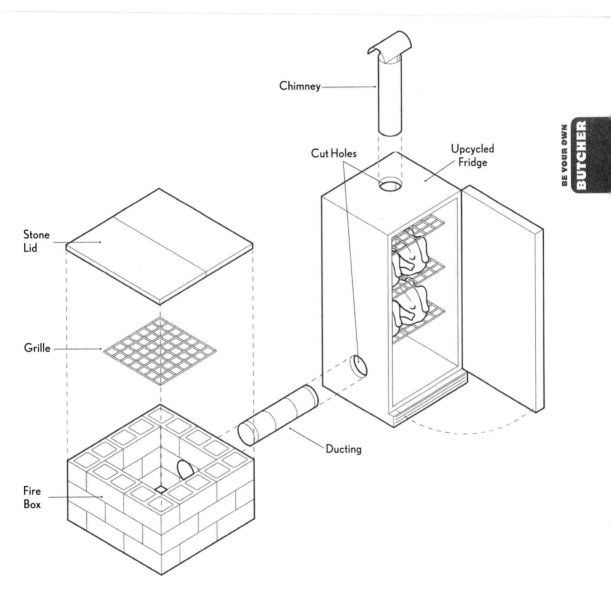

Chimney

Cut Holes

Upcycled
Fridge

Stone
Lid

Grille

Fire
Box

Ducting

BE YOUR OWN
BUTCHER

Bees

Yeah, bees sting, but they're great. They don't require much effort, they'll keep your garden and fruit trees healthy, and their honey will keep your immune system happy, not to mention your sweet tooth. If you've never tasted good, fresh honey before, you're in for a treat. It's so much better than the stuff that comes in the little plastic bear.

Speaking of bees, Winnie the Pooh isn't kidding: honey is a definite bear magnet. If you live in bear territory, you'll need to put in an electric fence. A line stretching from post to post will zap a bear's nose and convince him he's better off going elsewhere for his dessert.

You can get your bees from a fellow beekeeper or you can mail-order them. You'll want to begin with a small package of bees to help you gain confidence before building up to a full hive, though this will mean that you won't be able to harvest honey that first year. It's okay—you'll have plenty to do figuring out how to manage your bees and get used to each other.

You'll have three types of bees in your colony: your queen bee (we all know what she does), your drones (who live their lives tending to the queen), and your workers. The worker bees go out, forage, and make honey, and they're the ones helping your garden. They're also the ones most likely to sting you. Drones don't have stingers and the queen almost never leaves.

→ **Carniolan bees.** These bees are great if you live in a colder, wetter climate.

→ **Caucasian bees.** These bees are a little more difficult to establish and have a lower production rate than Carniolans, but they are quite gentle and also tend to winter well.

SHELTER

Those stacked boxes that you've seen beekeepers working with are for the more advanced honey harvesters. For getting started, you really only need a top bar hive, which is basically a wooden box on stilts.

HOT TIP
Rooftop hives are becoming increasingly common, and bees are great in cities or suburbs. That said, you may get some neighbors complaining. This may seem shortsighted as bees help everyone, but if your pal Jim has a daughter who will go into anaphylactic shock if she's stung by a bee, it's somewhat understandable. Barring that, gifts of honey help relations—and check your city ordinances.

FEEDING YOUR BEES

Your bees are not your pets and they will forage on their own. They consume nectar as an energy source and pollen for supplemental vitamins. Make sure they have access to fresh water at all times, and if you notice that their production is declining, you can give them a carbo boost with a sugar syrup; sugar syrups can also help stimulate larval growth.

LANGSTROTH HIVE

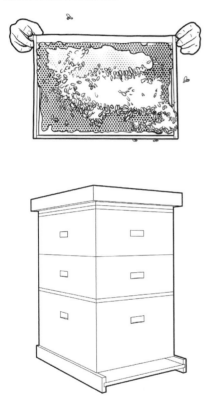

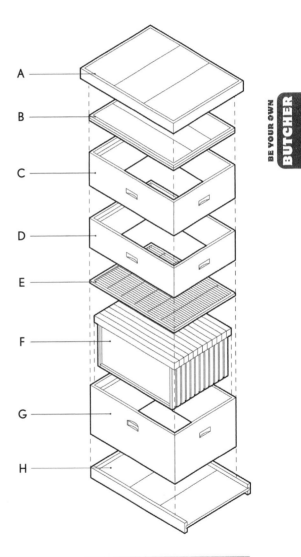

A. Outer Cover
B. Inner Cover
C. Medium-Depth Super
D. Shallow Extracting Super
E. Queen Extracting
F. Wood Frames
G. Full-Depth Hive Body
H. Bottom Board

TOP BAR HIVE

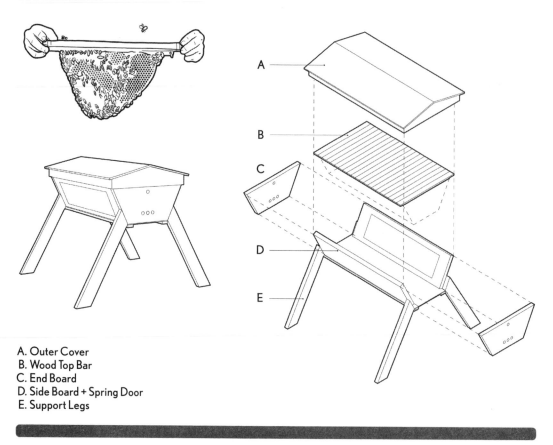

A. Outer Cover
B. Wood Top Bar
C. End Board
D. Side Board + Spring Door
E. Support Legs

EQUIPMENT

Nobody likes getting stung, but here's the hard truth: you will get stung, no matter how much protective gear you wear, so there's no real point in getting those hazmat suits. Instead, wear long cotton sleeves with rubber bands around the cuffs, and long cotton pants in light colors (red or black may trigger your bees, much like red triggers a bull). Tuck your pants into your socks. Wearing gloves will help you feel a little safer, but most beekeepers give up on them after the first year or two. Don't wear any perfume, cologne, or jewelry.

All of that said, the hat with veil is one piece of equipment you don't want to do without. Get one and wear it.

THE RUGGED LIFE

How to Minimize Bee Stings

Go out to the hive on a sunny day when the bees aren't at home. Using a smoker will definitely help keep them calm. When you do get stung, scrape the stinger out using your fingernail as soon as you can to stop the flow of venom.

PROPER BEEKEEPING ATTIRE

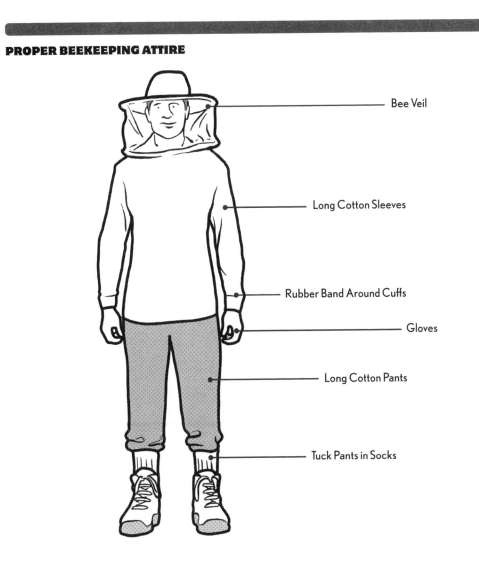

Bee Veil

Long Cotton Sleeves

Rubber Band Around Cuffs

Gloves

Long Cotton Pants

Tuck Pants in Socks

HOW TO
HARVEST HONEY

Monitoring your hive will help you know when it's ready to harvest. The nectar will finish flowing at the end of the season, and the frame will be capped with wax. Make sure there are other supers full of honey to feed your bees— you only want to take their excess.

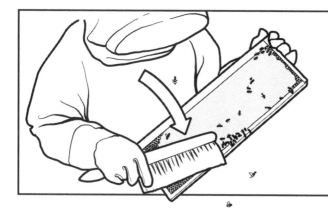

STEP 1

Hit the frame against the ground to knock off as many bees as you can, and use a brush to get the rest off. You won't get all of them, so don't worry about it.

STEP 2

Cut the comb from the frame and separate the wax into chunks to let the honey drain off into a clean plastic bucket.

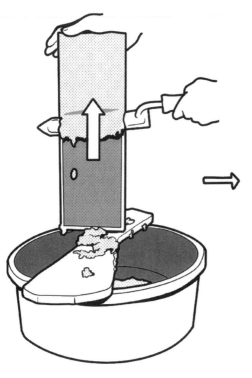

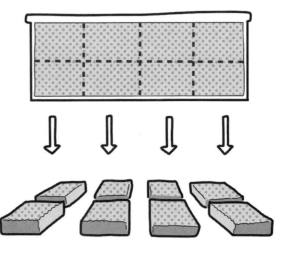

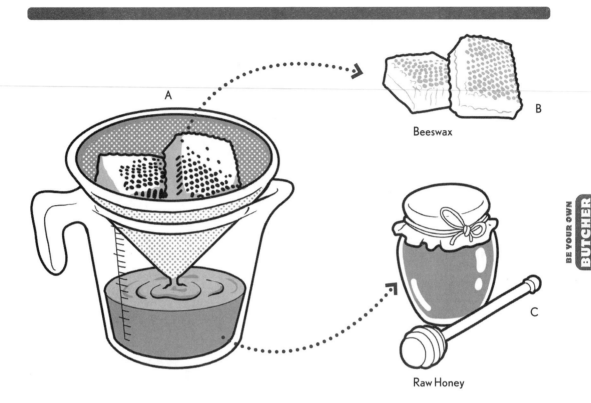

A

B

Beeswax

C

Raw Honey

STEP 3

A. Put the honey in a strainer and let it drip. It's helpful to let it sit in the sun, as it'll drip faster if it's warmer. That said, if it's really humid, the honey will absorb a lot of water from the air, so you may elect to drain your honey indoors with a dehumidifier running.

B. Raw honey is naturally antibacterial and filled with proteins and enzymes. It will eventually crystallize, but if you gently reheat it, it will become liquid again. Enjoy it, but don't give it to any babies.

C. The beeswax, too, is incredibly useful. You can use it in salves and balms (see Chapter 9), as a lubricant for carpentry, and to make your own candles.

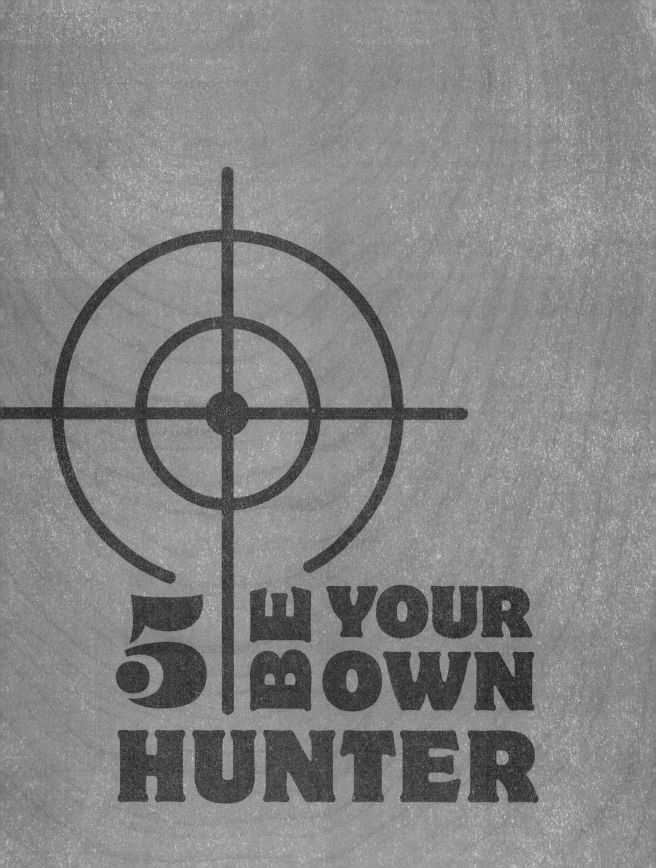

> *"It is not enough to be industrious; so are the ants. What are you industrious about?"*
>
> **—Henry David Thoreau**

If dealing with livestock doesn't sound like the way you want to spend your time (and, yeah, it is a lot of time), then you can always go get your food out in the wild. Hunting is extremely satisfying, and it can also be cost-effective, since you're not spending a ton of money on feed, care, and housing, not to mention veterinarian bills. A white-tailed deer can get you 60 pounds of meat.

Of course, what you're going to be able to eat depends on where you live and your access to game—and your skill. It's not as easy as just standing in the woods and waiting for your dinner to come to you. As with everything else, there's research and prep involved.

Hunting on even your own private land is regulated by the state you live in. Every state has its own rules, limits, zones, licenses, tags, seasons (for what you can hunt and by what method), and bag limits (how many of an animal you can harvest). A lot depends on the size of the herds in your state and the amount of regulation in your state. The best place to start is to look up hunting rules on your state's fish and game website. Almost all hunting happens in the fall, but if your state uses a lottery system, you may need to enter early. For some prized big game, you may even need to enter years in advance of when you hope to hunt.

Where to Go

After you've worked through all the regulations in your state, figuring out the best spots—and determining how to get access to them—is the next most important part of the hunting process. As you prepare, you're going to be studying maps, scouting locations, chatting with other hunters, and calling up government agencies and local landowners to gain permission to hunt in certain areas.

So what are those areas? Well, you've got your public lands and your private lands. Public land is government-owned and is designated available for hunting. Public land often has large herds but will also be more crowded with hunters. Private land is not open to the public, and you need to get special permission from the owner. Obviously, there's a lot to be said for the ease of hunting public lands, but they do tend to be more crowded, which can be a problem. Not everyone is going to be as well researched, skilled, and prepared as you are.

If you can hunt on your own land or get access to some form of private land, you'll be sharing the ground and the animals with fewer people, which makes hunting a lot easier and often much more productive. That said, a private landowner makes the rules, and you have to abide by them if you want to be invited back. And they may decide they just don't want you and your gunshots around anymore—it happens. When it does, don't despair. You should have more than one beloved hunting spot, anyway.

Of course, if you've got the land for it, *you* get to make the rules. You can hunt the deer that are eating your fruit trees.

FINDING GAME

Once you've got your location picked out, you've got to figure out where the game is. Do your research and do your recon. One of the best ways to do this is by setting up an infrared camera survey. This requires time, planning, and equipment, but it'll give you the most information. You'll be able to estimate deer density, sex ratio, buck ages, and more. Of course, the larger your sample, the more accurate it will be, so the more acreage you can include in your survey area the better.

Timing. Your survey should be conducted either in early fall or late winter, as that's when you're likely to get does and fawns as well as bucks. Basically, you want to start your survey within one week of buck velvet-shedding; if you're too late, you'll see only bucks, and miss out on counting does and fawns.

Baiting. Follow all the rules and regulations around feeding and baiting in your state, but if you are allowed, prebait the area for seven to ten days before beginning your survey.

Planning. Draw a grid on a map of the area and designate one camera for each grid. If your area is smaller than 1,000 acres, you'll need one camera for every hundred acres. More than that, and you can stretch to one camera for every 150 or so acres. Yeah, that's a lot of cameras, but if you can get together with some buddies, you can probably cobble together enough.

Setup. Clear ground-level debris at each camera site to allow for clearer images. Face the camera north if possible to avoid backlighting, and place it 15 to 20 feet away from the bait. Monitor your cameras for those first seven to ten days of prebaiting to make sure your equipment is working and the deer are showing up.

Survey. An ideal survey length is two weeks, which should allow you to capture the majority of the herd. Refresh memory cards, batteries, and bait as needed, but try to keep activity and scent to a minimum. At the end of the survey time, compile your images and count your individual deer. You'll want to put together a list of shoot/don't shoot bucks based on their age range; do your research so you know how to identify the age of a buck or fawn.

DO IT OLD SCHOOL

Yes, using cameras is a lot of effort, but it's worth it. However, if technology isn't your thing or you just don't have the money, you can always hunt like humans have done since we first decided meat was good: identify game trails.

Here's the thing about animals—they pretty much do the same thing every day. After all, like a homesteader, they're focused on just three things: food, water, shelter. And when they've got it worked out, they follow the same path from their bedding area to their sources of food and water, over and over again. With heavier game like boar, deer, elk, and so forth, that means they wear a pretty heavy path through the woods. Smaller animals such as rabbits, raccoons, and possums won't leave such distinct markers, but you can see paths through tall grasses or a disturbance in the leaves on the forest floor.

Of course, just because a path exists doesn't mean it's currently in use, but there are a few ways to determine if a game trail is active. If you see tracks or scat, then yeah, it's probably in use. You might also see scrapes or rubs on the ground or on trees where white-tailed deer have been

marking an area. Boar or wild hogs will root around in the dirt, noticeably disturbing the forest floor.

Finding a game trail is often a matter of just paying attention. It's good to know your hunting area, period, so spend some time hiking around and keeping your eyes open. Go foraging and collect some firewood while you're at it. If you find a source of fresh water, that's a good place to start poking around. If you find an area where the grass is flattened, that's a likely bedding area, and you may find game trails leading from there as well.

TREE STAND

A tree stand will help you to get a clearer shot, allowing for a clean kill.

Safety First

You're probably going to use guns to hunt. They're the most efficient type of arm. That said, if you've got the skills for it, you may want to take advantage of bow-hunting season, which will give you earlier access to game. If you're super old school, you can get into muzzleloader hunting, using guns that, like in Civil War times, are front-loading only (though they don't really look like they used to anymore). Muzzleloader season comes right after bow-hunting season.

I'm mostly going to be talking about rifle hunting, but whatever you use, know this: if it can kill an animal, it can also kill you or your loved ones, so practice basic safety precautions.

GUNS AND GAME

A basic single action rifle will do for just about anything. After all, you want to be a good enough shot that one shot is all it takes. You'll get great accuracy from a bolt action or single-shot rifle, and you'll be forced to make every shot count.

That said, dangerous game including wild boar or bear make having just one shot available to you a little risky, no matter your skill level, in which case you'll want a gun with more bullets to allow you to follow up your shot quickly.

There are three weight classes for game.

Small game includes tree squirrels, cottontails, rats, ground squirrels, and marmots. Foxes, coyotes, bobcats, and other small predators also fall under this category. You'll want expanding bullets to ensure quick kills, but avoid frangibles (bullets that disintegrate on impact) for meat hunting, though they'd be fine for shooting anything you don't plan on consuming.

Medium game includes deer, pronghorn antelope, goats, boar, and wild hogs—anything between 51 and 300 pounds. Since this is a pretty wide category, it makes sense to look at short-range versus long-range shooting. For short-range hunting in the woods, you can use anything that is marked "medium game at long range," and you'll also want to get ammunition with some expansion to ensure ethical kills.

Large game includes anything over 300 pounds, such as nondangerous game like elk and moose. You'll need a lot of force to have a single-shot kill here. This class also includes most North American dangerous game, such as boar, cougars, wolves, and bears. Never shoot a dangerous animal unless you are certain you can kill it in one shot. If an enraged bear is charging you, you're not going to have time for a second shot. You'll need one caliber for short range hunting of large game, and another for long range.

RULES FOR HANDLING FIREARMS

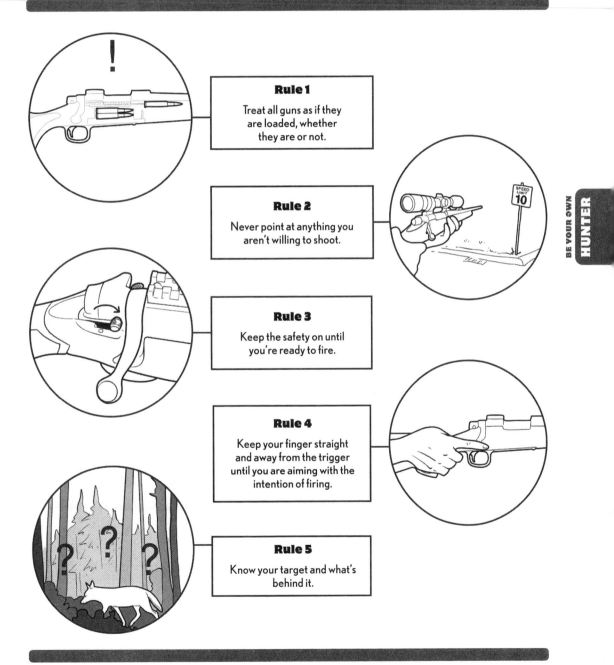

Rule 1
Treat all guns as if they are loaded, whether they are or not.

Rule 2
Never point at anything you aren't willing to shoot.

Rule 3
Keep the safety on until you're ready to fire.

Rule 4
Keep your finger straight and away from the trigger until you are aiming with the intention of firing.

Rule 5
Know your target and what's behind it.

BE YOUR OWN HUNTER

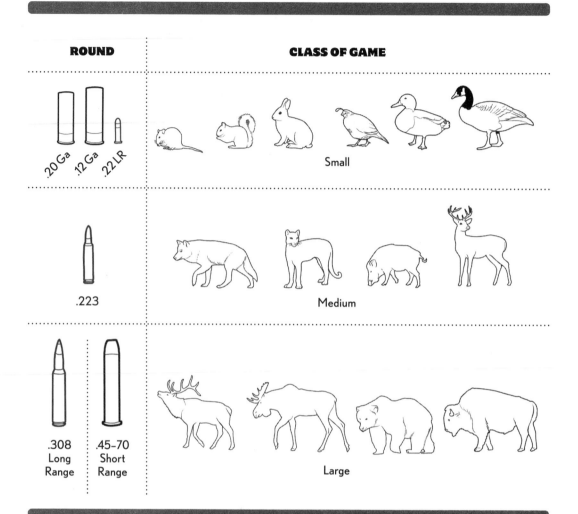

ROUND	CLASS OF GAME
.20 Ga .12 Ga .22 LR	Small
.223	Medium
.308 Long Range .45–70 Short Range	Large

COMMON HUNTING BULLET TYPES

→ **Ballistic.** Accurate with good expansion potential, so an appropriate choice for hunting.

→ **Boat tail.** The bottom of the bullet is curved, making it more accurate over long distances. Good for long-range hunting.

→ **Wad cutter.** Good for paper target practice.

Basic Gun Overview

There are a lot of guns out there, and you'll like some of them more than others. I'm going to give you a quick overview of the basics, but as always, do your research and practice to see what works best for you.

PARTS OF A HUNTING RIFLE

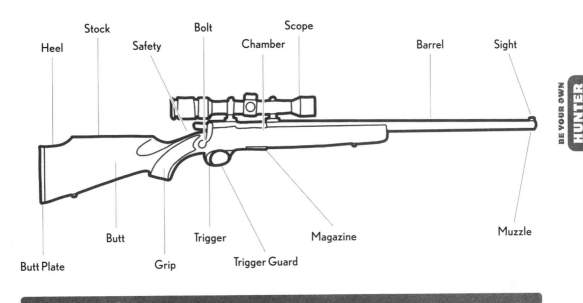

Heel · Stock · Safety · Bolt · Chamber · Scope · Barrel · Sight

Butt Plate · Butt · Grip · Trigger · Trigger Guard · Magazine · Muzzle

BULLETS

Heavier bullets are longer than lighter bullets in the same caliber (caliber means the diameter of the barrel of the gun). They are more aerodynamic and their added mass increases their momentum, so they can shoot farther and hit harder. But they have more recoil and are more expensive.

Cartridges (also known as "rounds") refer to a firearm ammunition that have a number of parts: the bullet or projectile itself, the propellant (usually gunpowder or cordite), the primer that ignites the propellant, the case that holds it all together, and the rim that allows you to grab the cartridge after the bullet has been fired.

DIFFERING ACTIONS

→ **Break action.** This is a manual, single-shot action. It's compact and lightweight, but reloading is slow, and you have to move the entire gun to do so, which means you need to aim all over again.

→ **Falling block action.** Also single shot, but more rigid and accurate. Allows you to reload while aiming, but tends to be expensive.

→ **Bolt action.** Can be single shot or hold a magazine, and are easy and fast to reload while aiming. Popular for hunting, with good reason, as they are very accurate and easy to use.

→ **Lever action.** Even faster to reload than bolt action, but you cannot use pointed bullets. Ideal for short-range hunting.

→ **Pump action.** Seen in movies a lot; with pump action you slide the fore-end backward and forward to reload. This is the fastest manual-action reload available.

TYPICAL CALIBERS

I prefer to stockpile common military rounds due to their availability, cost, and proven effectiveness. Gun geeks will dispute these choices, knowing very well that bullet placement is all that matters, but that is my two cents.

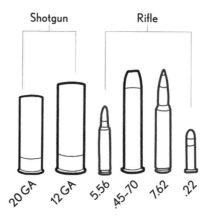

SIGHTING IN YOUR RIFLE

Ultimately, bullet placement matters much more than the type of round you're using. You can buy all the fancy bullets in the world, but if you don't put them in the right spot, they won't do a thing. If you put a .223 in the heart of an elk, that elk will go down. We only shoot with bigger rounds when we need more distance or a harder impact—but even then, bullet placement is what really matters. Ethical kills require accurate shooting, and unless you're sneaky enough to be able to walk up to your game and shoot it in the face, you're going to need a scope, and you're going to need to calibrate it properly before you even head out to the woods.

Start with some paper target shooting. Set yourself up so you're 25 yards away from the paper and aim at the bull's-eye. Fire, and check your shot. Odds are, you were nowhere close. Don't take this personally or take it to mean you can't do this—rifles aren't always super accurate and you need to adjust your sights accordingly. Where did your shot go?

Let's say it was low and to the left. That tells you that your horizontal crosshair (which manages the elevation of your shot) *and* your vertical crosshair (which is how you adjust the windage of your shot) need some work. Raising the horizontal crosshair on your scope will make your shot go higher; moving your vertical crosshair to the right will make your shot go farther right. Do this a little at a time and check your shot each time, until you've got it hitting the bull's-eye.

Step back to 100 yards. How accurate are you now? In all likelihood, the windage will still be accurate, but the increased distance will make your shot go low. Make some more adjustments until you feel confident in your sights and your aim. Once you've got your gun figured out on paper, *then* you can feel good about taking it to the woods or fields.

PROPER HUNTING ATTIRE

If you're out hunting in a crowded area that might be filled with hunters of unknown skill level, wear bright colors. Yeah, game will see you, too, but the last thing you want is to get shot by some idiot. Indeed, many states require deer hunters to wear bright orange—which is handy, since deer have trouble seeing the color orange. But if it's safe and legal, wearing camouflage to match your hunting terrain is recommended. Temperatures can shift, so layer up. If you're shooting long-range, a camo undershirt isn't really necessary, but if you're close range, it can really make a difference. Avoid shiny belt buckles and make sure your jacket has plenty of pockets.

HOT TIP

"Put cayenne pepper in your boots to keep your feet warm and help with circulation."
—The Trayers

SHOT PLACEMENT FOR AN ETHICAL KILL

When you're trying to kill an animal, aim for the heart and lungs. If you can, shoot the animal broadside, i.e., when it's perpendicular to you. Shooting at the crease in the shoulder should allow the bullet to go through both lungs, resulting in a fast kill that also hits only minor bones in the ribs, preserving most of the meat. Quartering shots, i.e., shots at an angle, also work, but you'll damage the meat in one of the shoulders.

In some instances, you'll need to anchor the animal, dropping it in its tracks. That can happen when you've got a charging predator, or when you're shooting on a slope and don't want to send your mountain goat tumbling off a cliff. To anchor, aim in the center of the animal's scapula. This will break the shoulder, making it difficult for the animal to move, and send a shock to the nervous system. You'll lose a good portion of shoulder meat, but you should have an instant kill.

HUNTING CHECKLIST

BEFORE THE HUNT

- ☐ Hunter Safety Course
- ☐ Hunting License
- ☐ Driver's License or other ID
- ☐ Deer Tag(s)
- ☐ Landowner Permission
- ☐ Setup Tree Stand / Blind
- ☐ Scent-Control Clothing

DURING THE HUNT: EQUIPMENT

- ☐ Ammo
- ☐ Ammo Case
- ☐ Binoculars
- ☐ Rifle or Bow
- ☐ Backpack
- ☐ Knife Sharpener
- ☐ Toilet Paper
- ☐ Headlamp
- ☐ Food / Water
- ☐ Scent Attractant
- ☐ Two-way Radios
- ☐ Dry Towel
- ☐ Batteries
- ☐ Hand Warmers
- ☐ Lighter / Matches
- ☐ Trail-marking Tape
- ☐ Game Calls
- ☐ GPS

DURING THE HUNT: CLOTHING

- ☐ Jacket
- ☐ Inner Layer (Long Layer)
- ☐ Outer Layer (Puncture Resistant)
- ☐ Orange Vest / Hat (Check Regulations)
- ☐ Boots
- ☐ Socks
- ☐ Gloves
- ☐ Rainwear

AFTER THE HUNT

- ☐ Gutter Gloves
- ☐ Permanent Marker
- ☐ Processing Knives
- ☐ Cooler
- ☐ Butt-Out Tool
- ☐ Deer Drag
- ☐ Pelvic Saw

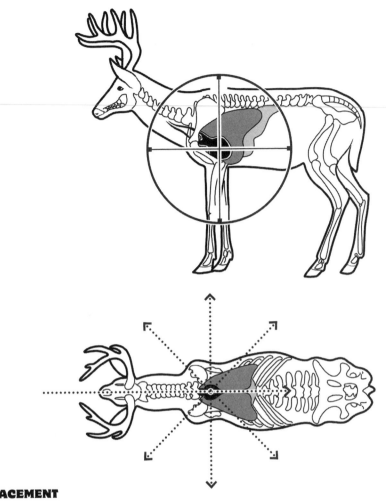

SHOT PLACEMENT

FIELD-DRESSING YOUR GAME

Don't haul that whole carcass back home. A grizzly is more than happy to walk 20 miles to get a free meal, and you don't want it coming around your house. Plus, why carry all that? Not to mention, the sooner you process your meat after death, the better it will be.

First things first, hang your game in the shade if it's small enough, and if not, prop it open to help it cool faster. Skinning the animal as soon as possible will also help it cool down. Dig out the entrails. You don't need to bury them if you're far enough from habitation, but make sure you're not someplace where dogs could come and drag them home. From there, you can take it home either on a game cart or in a backpack to process or deliver it to a meat processor.

HOW TO
FIELD-DRESS A DEER

1. First things first, hang your game in the shade if it's small enough, and if not, prop it open to help it cool faster.

2. Skin the animal as soon as possible to help it cool.

3. Dig out the entrails. You don't need to bury them if you're far enough from habitation, but be sure you're not someplace where dogs could come and drag them home.

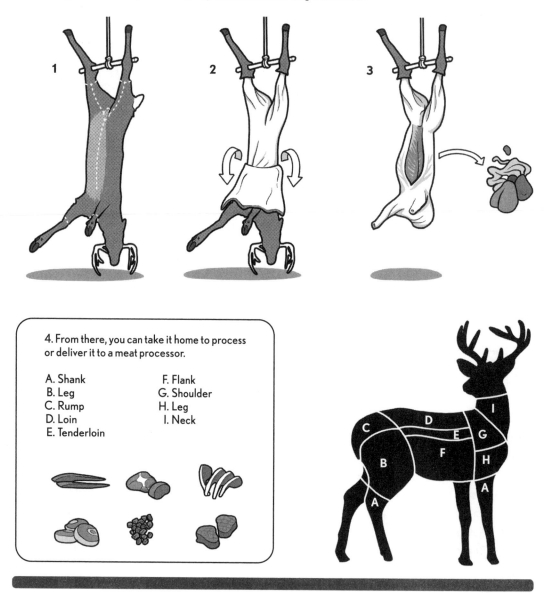

4. From there, you can take it home to process or deliver it to a meat processor.

A. Shank
B. Leg
C. Rump
D. Loin
E. Tenderloin
F. Flank
G. Shoulder
H. Leg
I. Neck

Snares

Another option is to set snares. A snare is basically a steel-cable loop placed in an animal's predicted path, capturing the animal by the neck or leg. They're surprisingly effective, but you do run the risk of snaring an animal you hadn't intended to, like a lost dog, for instance. That said, they are lightweight, compact, simple to use, and don't cost much at all. You'll need to do some research on the licensing and season requirements in your state, and most important of all, be careful where you set your snares. You'll want to keep your snares clean and free of human odor, so boil them in water and baking soda, and then wear gloves to keep your scent from getting all over them.

HOT TIP Snares can definitely be useful to set around your property targeting predators, but be careful not to accidentally capture any of your livestock or pets.

Snares are best for smaller game—definitely nothing bigger than a deer—so don't set them in elk wintering areas or within a pasture. Don't set them near carcasses or you'll end up capturing scavengers. If you do capture a dog, you should be able to get it free relatively uninjured, but it's best to avoid it, so keep your snares out of hunting-dog territory. Always mark the locations of your snares carefully on your map, for you'll need to check them regularly—in fact, most states require that you check them every day.

SIMPLE WIRE SNARE TRAP

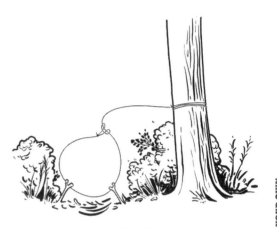

A. Fixed Trap

B. Sprung Trap

FIXED SNARE

This is a flexible snare, as you can make it out of pretty much anything you have on hand, whether it's wire or a braided-steel cable, and it'll catch most animals, including rabbits, ground birds, coyotes, foxes, raccoons, and beavers.

DEER TRAIL SNARE

This snare won't kill the deer, but it will hold it there until you arrive. Set your snare between two trees along the deer's path, at its eye level.

SNARE PLACEMENT

Just like with hunting, snare placement requires knowing the movements and routes of your game.

→ **Deer.** As with rifle hunting, you can use cameras and walking around to determine the paths between a deer's sleeping area and its water source.

→ **Beaver.** Look for dams or den entrances and place your snare nearby.

→ **Coyote.** Watch for trails in thickets or to and from carcasses.

How to Tan a Hide

In the spirit of using every part of the animal, here's a quick guide for how to tan a hide. This focuses on deerskin, but you could use similar methods for elk, rabbit, or even bear.

1. Skin the deer. Hang it up, then start at the bends of the legs, working toward the belly—you're trying to make it so you can lift the skin off in one whole piece. A sharp knife will help you as you tug the skin away from the muscle.

2. Fleshing. There will still be some fat and muscle attached to the skin, and this needs to come off. Place the skin over a fleshing beam (a wood plank that looks much like an ironing board) hair-side down, and work to pull away the fat, muscle, and

membrane. In this case, you *don't* want your fleshing knife to be all that sharp—a dull knife will allow you put pressure on the skin without piercing it.

3. For Hair-On Tanning Only: Salt the hide. Rub the interior all over, getting into all the edges. Let the salt draw out the moisture overnight, then scrape off any wet salt. Reapply dry salt, and continue to scrape and reapply until the salt is no longer drawing out moisture.

4. For Hair-Off Tanning Only: Float the skin in an alkaline solution to release the hair. Wearing eye protection and gloves, mix 8 ounces hydrated lime powder with 7.5 gallons of water. Gently agitate the skin in the mixture, then let it rest until evening. Agitate it at night, and again in the morning, checking to see if the hair has loosened. It should be ready after two or three days. Remove the skin from the bucking solution, and wring it out gently. Put the skin back on the fleshing beam, and use a dull fleshing knife to scrape off the hair. Scrape it once more to remove the grain, a thin layer of skin that sits under the hair—the grain should peel off in thin sheets, leaving a white skin underneath. Rinse the bucking solution in a mixture of 3 ounces deliming powder and 5 gallons of water, soaking it for 4 to 6 hours, then rinse in cool water.

5. Pickle the skin by soaking it in a mixture of 20 ounces pickling crystals, 7 gallons of water and 7 pounds of salt. Check your pH, as you want it to be between 1.0 and 2.0, so adjust the salt and pickling crystals as necessary. Stir twice a day for two to three days—it's ready when you can poke it gently without leaving a mark. Remove it from the solution and wring it gently.

6. Bring the skin back to a normal pH by neutralizing it in water and baking soda. Add 3 to 4 gallons of water and stir in enough baking soda until the pH is between 4.0 and 5.0. Let the skin soak for 30 minutes, adding more water as needed to keep the pH in range.

7. Let the skin dry on the fleshing beam until it is no longer dripping, then coat the inside of the skin with Curatan oil, repeating several times to make sure it is very well oiled. Let it dry overnight.

8. Now comes the work. Pull and stretch the skin in all directions, bending it over sawhorses, working at it at least an hour a day, pulling and stretching until it's completely dry. Keep it at for several days—the more it's worked, the softer it'll be. If any places become hard, add more Curatan oil.

9. When it's completely dry and softened, place the skin on a flat surface and hand-sand the interior using coarse sandpaper.

HOW TO
TAN A HIDE

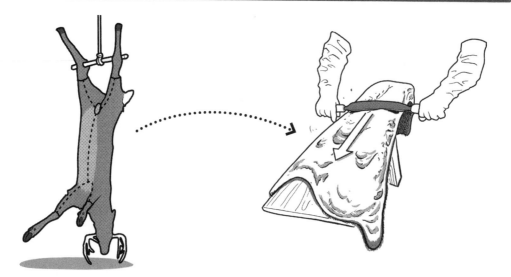

STEP 1

Skin the deer.

STEP 2

Flesh the inside hide.

Remove moisture

Alkaline Solution:
7.5 gallons of water
8 ounces hydrated lime powder

STEP 3

**For Hair-On Tanning
Only:** Salt the inside hide.

STEP 4

For Hair-Off Tanning Only:
Float skin in an alkaline solution
and scrape off remaining hair.

pH: 1.0–2.0 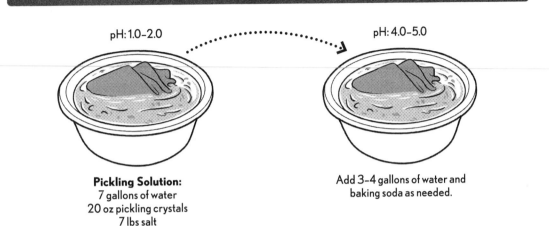 pH: 4.0–5.0

Pickling Solution:
7 gallons of water
20 oz pickling crystals
7 lbs salt

Add 3–4 gallons of water and
baking soda as needed.

STEP 5

Pickle the skin. Let sit for 2–3
days, stirring twice a day.

STEP 6

Bring skin to normal pH.

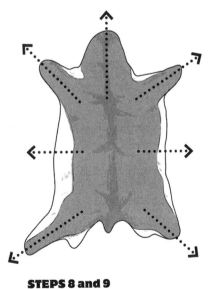

STEP 7

Coat the inside of the skin with
Curatan oil. Let sit overnight.

STEPS 8 and 9

Stretch skin in all directions.
Sand interior with coarse grit.

Fishing

If anything, fishing requires even more patience than hunting does, but it is a meditative, restorative, and peaceful way to spend your time—and you end up with something delicious to eat at the end of the day. Ideally, anyway. Fishing is an unpredictable activity, and fish can be sneaky little buggers. But here are some best practices that can help you have the highest chance of success.

RESEARCH

It always, always comes down to doing your homework. You can't just stick your rod in anywhere and assume you're going to land a big one. You've got to know where the good spots are, and you can start by going online and checking out forums, local fishing associations, and tourism guides. You'll also want to look up local regulations on licenses, permits, catch rates, etc. and definitely make sure you follow those guidelines. Your best bet is going to be the local bait shop. The workers there will be knowledgeable and friendly—and will likely be able to give you some good tips about where to go for what kind of fish. You can also check out a daily fishing forecast online at Farmer's Almanac, which will use data from your location and forecast tide and moon phases, helping you figure out ideal times to fish for the species you want to catch. There are, of course, plenty of apps available, too.

You can also invest in a fishfinder, a piece of technology that uses sonar to help, well, find fish. They can run the gamut in both cost and capabilities (anything from $10 to $2,000), and can be used from shore, from a kayak or small boat, or out at sea. You might also want a temperature gauge, to help you figure out whether fish are relaxing or out swimming around. On a day that's too hot or too cold—either extreme—cold-blooded fish will be more sluggish and less interested in checking out what you're dangling. While you can probably feel whether it's hot or cold, a temperature gauge will give you more precise and minute-by-minute information. Bright sunlight also affects fish activity, which is why dawn and dusk are such popular times, and cloudy days or light rain are ideal. And keep an eye on the weather. Wind disturbs water and pushes up surface food, and storms increase feeding immediately before a cold front, while warm fronts immediately put fish into a feeding frenzy.

CHOOSING A ROD

Your choice of rod is dependent on your choice of fish. What do you want to catch? You'll need a rod to suit.

Smaller freshwater fish. Ultra-light fishing rods for use with 4- to 8-pound lines are great for panfish or trout. They're made with lightweight graphite and allow plenty of sensitivity, so you can feel even the slightest nibble.

Larger freshwater fish. For something like bass fishing, you'll probably want a medium-heavy baitcasting rod, so you can use a heavy enough line with accuracy. That will work with spinnerbaits or swim jigs with single hooks. But if you prefer crankbaits, you'll want a medium-power rod with more flexibility.

Saltwater fish. The above principles apply for the size of the fish, but with saltwater you'll want some corrosion protection. Apart from that, it's once again about the fish you want to catch. Maybe you'll need a heavy-action fiberglass rod for something big or a medium-light action rod for something smaller.

CHOOSING A REEL AND LINE

Choosing your reel, like choosing your rod, depends on the kind of fish you want to catch and what sort of lures or bait you'll be using. After that, it's a matter of preference and what kind of fishing you feel most comfortable with. There are a lot of different reels on the market, but they boil down to four basic types.

For bigger fish, you'll need a bigger reel that can hold more, heavier line. Spool capacity is given by length and the pound-test fishing line that it applies to. Choose a reel that matches your fishing rod, so they can both handle fishing line of the same strength.

TYPES OF LINE

→ **Monofilament.** Mono is less expensive than other lines, stretches to absorb shocks, is abrasion resistant, and uniformly round in cross section, which helps keep it neat on the spool. Monofilament is easy to tie knots in, but can suffer from "memory" where it loops in the shape of the spool. It's great for fishing in saltwater. However, it's not as strong as braid for its diameter, taking on more space on the spool for its strength. It's also made of nylon, which breaks down over time.

→ **Braid.** Braid is very strong for a given diameter, often twice as strong as mono, so you can pack more line on a spool at a given pound test, and it sinks faster, casts farther, and trolls deeper than mono. It also has no memory so loops and twists aren't a problem, making braid one of the best fishing lines for spinning reels. Braid doesn't break down in sunlight, so you can keep it on the spool year after year. And it doesn't stretch at all, so you can feel every bump of the bottom and nudge from a fish—but that can also make it more difficult to catch the fish, requiring a bit more skill. It is also more expensive, and it's very slippery and difficult to cut. It's not see-through, which makes it easier for the fish to see, but you can use a leader line to hide it.

→ **Fluorocarbon.** Fluorocarbon makes for great leader material. It's completely invisible underwater and very abrasion resistant, making it the perfect complement to braid.

149

PARTS OF A FISHING ROD

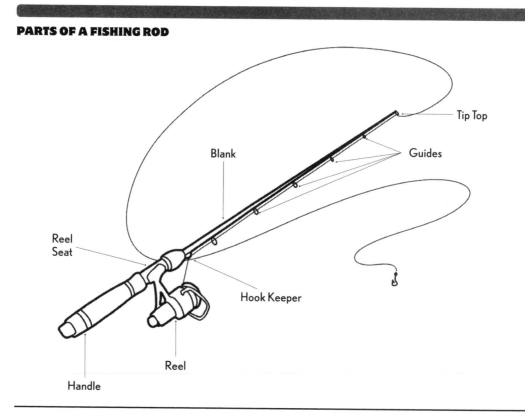

Tip Top

Guides

Blank

Reel
Seat

Hook Keeper

Reel

Handle

REEL TYPES

Spincast

Fly Reel

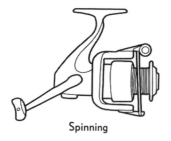

Spinning

Baitcaster

→ **Wire.** If you're dealing with a toothy fish like mackerel and tuna, you'll want wire for your leader line. It comes in both single strand and braided varieties.

A NOTE ON FLY-FISHING

Fly-fishing is a glorious way to spend a day. You reach a kind of meditative state, and you get to do it in some of the most beautiful places in the world.

That said, it's pretty complicated to master and there's a lot of gear involved. I love gear, but using it all is difficult to explain in book form. Suffice it to say—I highly recommend fly-fishing, and you should do some research on it, and consider taking a class or workshop.

CHOOSING A HOOK

Fishing hook sizes are generally referred to by a number from the smallest (size 32) to the largest (size 19/0). For hook sizes from 32 to 1, the larger the number, the smaller the hook. If your hook is too big, a smaller fish will strike but just take the bait and swim away. If it's too small, a larger fish might swallow it entirely, which isn't an ethical fishing practice. So depending on what you're looking to catch, you'll want to have a variety of hook sizes available, so you can fish what's there.

TERMINAL TACKLE

There's a lot of other stuff on your line besides a hook. You've got bobbers and floats, weights, snaps, and swivels.

Bobbers and floats keep your line on the surface, allowing you to watch to see if you've got a bite (a float is a more streamlined and sensitive bobber). A weight will pull your bait down, helping you find deeper, larger fish. You can set the distance between the bobber and the weight as desired.

Weights and sinkers can be as small as a BB or as heavy as a few ounces. The tiny BB-shaped ones are called split-shots, and have a groove in the middle that you can slide your line into, then pinch the weight shut. They're made of either lead or tungsten, and are soft enough that you can use your fingers or your fishing pliers to crimp it closed. That's often all you need to get your bait down to the bottom. Oftentimes, just a single split shot will provide all the weight you need to get a bait to the bottom.

When you're using bobbers and sinkers together, you'll want some snaps and swivels. Swivels join two parts of your line so that the far end spins freely, preventing tangles on the spool while allowing the lure to dance and spin freely and believably. Snaps are swivels that lock in place, allowing you to quickly attach a hook.

BAIT

Once you've got your equipment, found a good spot, and know what kinds of fish are swimming around in there, you need to know what they'll want to snack on. You can use live or artificial bait. In this instance, "live" refers to anything that was once living; you don't have to keep them wriggling or anything. That said, if your bait *is* alive, it does stand a better chance of attracting a fish, so do your best to keep it that way by baiting carefully and casting

ANATOMY OF A HOOK

A. The Eye: The eye is where you connect the hook to the line or lure.

B. The Shank: The shank is the connection between the bend and the eye.

C. The Barb: The barb is the projection extending backwards from the point that keeps the fish from unhooking.

D. The Point: The point of a fish hook is the sharp end that penetrates the mouth of a fish.

E. The Gap: The gap is the distance between the point of the hook and the shank.

F. The Bend: The bend is the curve in the hook.

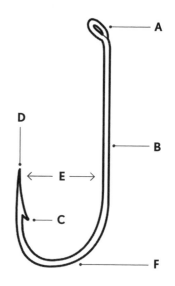

gently. You can purchase all kinds of bait or you can catch your own by either digging up worms or catching smaller fish (sometimes called rats) that you can then use to catch something you'd want to eat. Artificial bait can be more expensive, but it can also be a lot more fun and give you more control—you need to know how to use each type of lure, however. Again, do your research.

➜ **Live, freshwater.** Worms, leeches, minnows, crayfish, crickets, and grasshoppers.

➜ **Live, saltwater.** Strips of squid, eels, crabs, and cut-up pieces of fish.

➜ **Artificial.** Spinners, crankbaits, jigs, poppers, flies, and spoons in a variety of sizes, styles, and colors.

HOT TIP

Making Your Own Pole and Line. For best results, you're going to want something commercially made, but knowing how to make your own pole and line can still come in handy. Bamboo poles are a classic, and they absolutely catch fish. If you don't have bamboo, any flexible stick will work. You want something around four to five feet long and about an inch in diameter. Tie some fishing line to the thickest part of the stick (that'll be your handle) and then wind it up the pole until you reach the tip. Tie it off again, holding it in place, but don't cut the line. Extend the line three feet or so, then cut it and attach your fishing hook. You can put a bobber on there, too, if you like.

HOW TO FISH

At its core, fishing is pretty basic. You put the bait on a hook, you wait for the fish to come, the fish bites, you pull it in, the end. And there are many fishermen who do pretty much that, with varying levels of success. But if you want to have a little more control over your own success, there are some skills you can pick up:

Casting. This is your first and most important step. You want to know how to get your line way out there, and you definitely want to avoid catching your hook on some rocks or bystanders. Practice doing this at home before you go, just to get the feel of your rod.

The best kind of reel for beginning anglers is a spincaster. They don't cost much and are easy to maintain and use. The line comes enclosed in a plastic housing that will minimize tangles, which is definitely helpful. They are less powerful and less accurate than baitcasters, but they can still cast light and heavy lures without breaking your line.

Once you're a little more comfortable, you can look into baitcasting. This style of reel casting uses a revolving-spool and relies on the weight of the lure to pull the line even farther and with more accuracy. It's a little tricky to master, but once you get the hang of it, you'll be able to get your lure right where you want it.

Setting the hook. How do you even know if you've got a fish on there? With wave action or the current of the river, it can be hard to tell what's pulling on your line. Attaching a bobber or small float to your line can be a visual aid, but even that only gives you so much information. What's a nudge, what's a nibble, and what's a real *bite* that can hook your fish?

The short answer is, don't get too excited if you feel a gentle tug or your bobber disappears for a second. Wait until you *really* feel something, and your bobber goes all the way underwater. When that happens, reel in your slack, keeping the line tight, and give the rod a firm—but not too jerky—pull up. This will set the hook.

Reeling it in. Once you've set the hook, the fish is likely to take notice and start trying to escape. It might jump, dodge behind obstacles, swim away, or seek the bottom. A smaller fish will be easy enough to reel in as your strength combined with that of your rod will be enough to overpower it. But don't underestimate the strength of a larger fish—they're strong bastards, and they often can be a challenge for even the most experienced angler, and it's easy to end up with a broken line.

You can avoid this with drag fishing. Drag is friction created by a pair of plates inside the reel. If a fish pulls on the line hard enough, it will overcome this friction, and the reel will spin the other way, letting line out—this seems counterintuitive, but it's better than having the line break. Set your drag before your first cast, so that if you do catch a big one, you'll be ready.

HOW TO SET DRAG

1. Test your drag with your gloved hand, pulling on the line directly above the reel. Tighten it by turning the front drag adjustment a few clicks to the right. If need be, you can loosen it by turning it to the left— it's better to have it be too loose and have

HOW TO
CAST A SPINNING REEL

1. Hold the rod at about waist level, angling it so that the reel is below the rod, letting the bait or lure hang 10 to 18 inches below the end of the rod.

2. Hook the line with your forefinger, and open the bail, but don't let go of the line yet. Pull the rod tip back so the tip sweeps over your dominant shoulder.

3. Whip it forward swiftly, pointing the rod tip where you want the line to go. As the rod comes forward, release the line with your finger so the weight of the lure and the force of your cast pull the line off the reel. Close the bail.

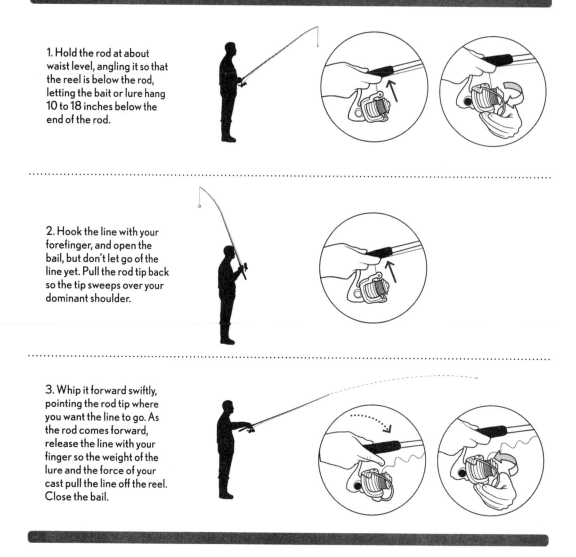

HOW TO
CAST A BAITCASTING REEL

1. Hold the rod about waist level, grasping it so that the reel is above the rod, with the bait or lure hanging 8 to 10 inches below the tip of the rod.

2. Push the button to put the reel in free spool while holding your thumb against the spool to prevent it from unwinding.

3. Pull the rod back so the tip sweeps over your dominant shoulder, and then bring it forward swiftly, pointing the rod tip at your target.

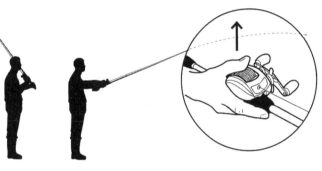

4. As the rod crosses your shoulder, remove some pressure from the spool while keeping your thumb gently on the line to prevent backlash.

5. Reel once or twice to engage the anti-reverse.

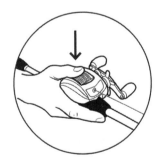
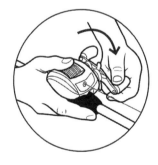

to fight the fish a little longer, instead of setting it too tight and breaking your line.

2. If you're not confident working by feel, you can get a small spring scale. Hold your rod at a 45° angle and hook the scale. Your drag setting should allow the line to hold a third to half of the weight before moving.

3. If you are using braided fishing line rather than monofilament, you'll want to test the line by wrapping it a few times around the handle of your fishing pliers. Don't use your hands, because braid can slice right into your fingers.

You'll know you've hooked a big one when the drag engages and your reel speeds into reverse, pulling line. This is not the time to try to reel it back in—if the fish is pulling that hard, you're just going to break the line. Chill. You've got time. Keep your rod at a 45° angle to the water, aiming it straight at the fish, and let that fish tire itself out swimming away. When the drag stops moving and buzzing, crank that line back in.

The pump and reel technique is a great method for big fish. Lift the tip of your rod like you're trying to point it skyward—this will bend your rod pretty hard, but don't worry about it, the rod can take it. As you lower the tip back to 45°, reel in your line, keeping even pressure on the fish. Repeat this process until you've got all the line pulled in—and a fish in your hands.

REMOVING A FISHING HOOK

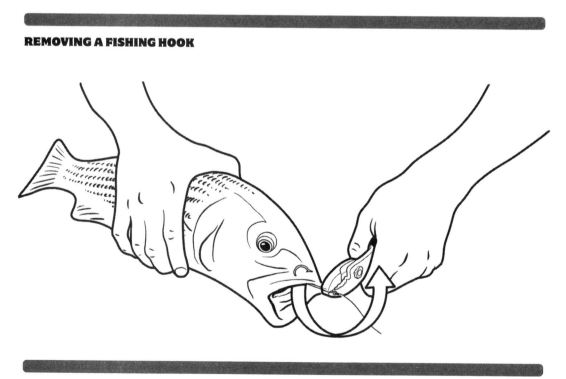

GILLNET

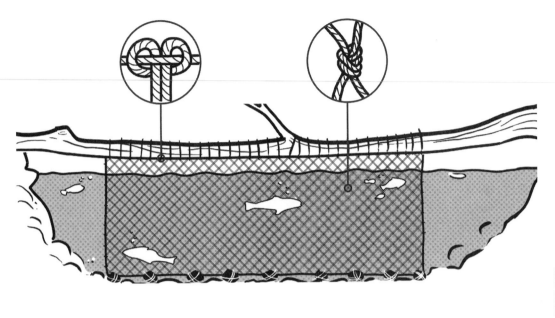

CAST NET

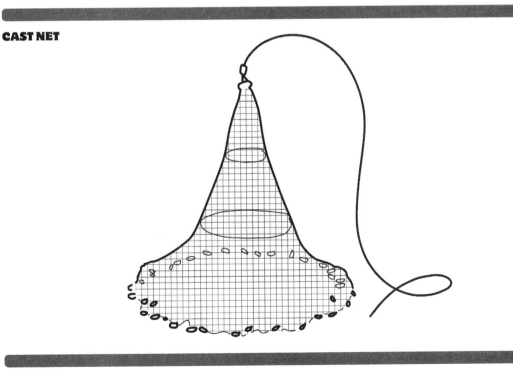

NET FISHING

There are two basic types of net fishing you would do from land—fixed net and cast net. Net fishing depends on being clear on the size of the fish you are aiming for. If the holes in your net are too big, the fish you want to catch will swim through it. But if the fish is too big, it might tear your net. It's important, as always, to do your research and know what fish will be near your net.

→ **Fixed net.** A fixed net is placed in a location you're reasonably sure a fish will swim into, and it is checked regularly—it's basically a snare for fish. You can place your net where it will block the passage of migrating fish (like salmon, for instance). Ideally you'll want a gillnet, set up so that it has a floatline along the top and a leadline along the bottom, with the netting hanging straight up and down in the water like a fence. It'll be secured in place with floats and weights (you can also let it float with the current, but keep an eye on it, for ghost nets are a real problem).

If it's set up properly, your fish won't be able to see the net, and when it swims up to it, it sticks its head through the mesh and catches its gills on the twine. This keeps the fish alive until you get there.

→ **Cast net.** A cast net is thrown out over a smaller area once you've seen a fish there, captures the fish, and is then hauled back in. It's typically relatively small, so you can control it, and it is circular in shape with small weights all around the edge. Cast nets work best for bait or forage fish in waters no deeper than their radius, and in areas free of reeds or branches. Typically you throw it out into the water using both hands, with an arcing circular motion. Just like with any kind of casting, this takes some practice, so do it in your yard a few times to make sure you're really getting the net to open up fully.

The net will start to close as soon as it begins to sink. As soon as it hits the bottom, pull it shut using the lead line and haul it in. If you work fast, you'll catch a ton of baitfish this way. But know that the net is pretty heavy to pull back in, so don't try to catch more than you can haul.

YOU'VE CAUGHT A FISH. NOW WHAT?

You'll want to either keep the fish alive or have a cooler on hand to keep it on ice immediately. Fish spoils fast, so keeping it chilled is key. You can put it directly on the ice, but make sure the meltwater can drain out, because the water will spoil the fish.

Once you get home, wash the fish in cold water and dry it with a clean cloth. Wrap it up—waxed paper is great—and put it in a freezer-safe plastic bag, getting out as much of the air as you can. It'll keep in a refrigerator for up to two days before it needs to either be eaten or frozen. It will last in a freezer for three to twelve months, depending on the type of fish.

Some fish are small enough to eat whole, and a baked whole fish is delicious, or you can fillet it into smaller pieces. But first, you've got to clean it.

Scaling. All this means is removing scales from the fish. You can get a specially designed scaler or just use the back of a knife. Place your scaler near the tail and rub it along the skin as you move toward the head. If the scales are sharp, you'll want to wear gloves; there are some chainmail fish-cleaning gloves that can provide extra protection.

Gutting. Insert your knife into the fish's anus, which will be near the tail. Cut forward toward the head on the underside of the fish—the knife will stop when you get there. Open up the cavity and use your hands to remove the organs. Rinse the cavity clean. If you don't intend to eat the head, just cut it off.

Filleting. Lay the fish on its side on a flat surface. If you know you're only going to be using the fillets, you don't need to scale or remove the fish's head. Turn your blade toward the tail and cut along the top of the ribs, using the backbone as a guide. Once you've freed the top, insert the knife close to the rib bones and slice away the entire section, pulling it from the ribs. Then, with the skin side down, insert the knife blade near the tail, about a half inch away. Holding the tail firmly, saw parallel to the skin in order to free the fillet from the skin. Turn the fish over and repeat on the other side.

HOW TO ROAST A WHOLE FISH

Set your oven temp to 450°F. Scale, gut, and rinse your fish, then pat it dry and place it in a roasting pan. Score the fish by cutting slits through the skin on the top, then brush it with olive oil, set some lemon slices atop and around it, and sprinkle it with salt and pepper, adding other spices as desired. Put some garlic slices in the cavity of the fish, and sprinkle it with whatever herbs you have on hand. Cook for 18 to 20 minutes, depending on the size of your fish, so check it often by slicing into it, as it's easy to overcook. Squeeze more lemon over the top and dig in.

HOW TO
CLEAN A FISH

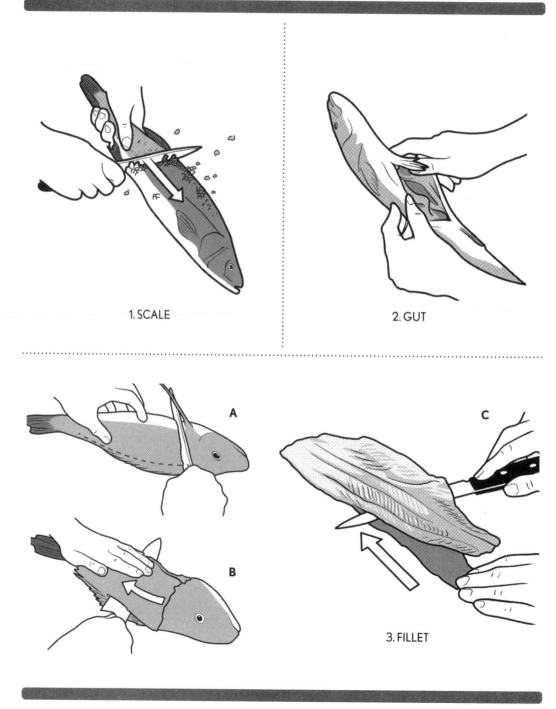

1. SCALE

2. GUT

A

B

C

3. FILLET

COMMON KNOTS

There are dozens of knots and it's an easy—and fun!—rabbit hole to fall down into. Once you get really into fishing, you'll get really into tying knots. But for now, these are the ones you'll want to know:

Fisherman's knot. This is the most popular knot for attaching hook to line.

1. Thread 2 or 3 inches of line through the eye of the hook, then pull it back parallel with the main line.

2. Holding the end together with the main line, spin the hook 5 or 6 times so the end twists around the line.

3. Thread the end into the loop created above the hook and below the twist, then back through the larger loop you've just created. Pull tight.

Palomar knot. This is one of the strongest knots and one of the easiest to learn. It's best for securing your hook with braided fishing line.

1. Take around 12 inches of line, double it and thread it through the eye of your fishing hook.

2. Tie an overhand knot in the doubled fishing line by forming a loop and passing the end through it. Let your hook hang loosely. Don't let the lines twist.

3. Pull the end of your loop down and pass it over your hook.

4. Moisten the line (spit works) and pull both ends to draw up your knot. Trim the excess line.

Rapala knot. Named for the company that invented it, this knot is best for attaching lures to fluorocarbon lines.

1. Tie an overhand knot 5 to 6 inches above the tag end of your fishing line.

2. Run the tag end through the eye of your lure or hook, then through the overhand knot.

3. Wrap it around your standing line three times, and then push your tag end through the back of your overhand knot.

4. Run the tag end through the loop you just formed in the previous step.

5. Pull on the main line, tag end, and hook or lure to tighten the knot down.

Hangman's knot (or noose). This style of knot is great for monofilament and terminal tackle, but it's so versatile it can be used in a range of fishing scenarios, particularly attaching your line to your reel.

1. Run your line through the eye and double it back. This should form a circle.

2. Wrap the tag end around the double line six times and then pull through the loop.

3. Next, moisten your line and pull your main line to tighten.

COMMON KNOTS

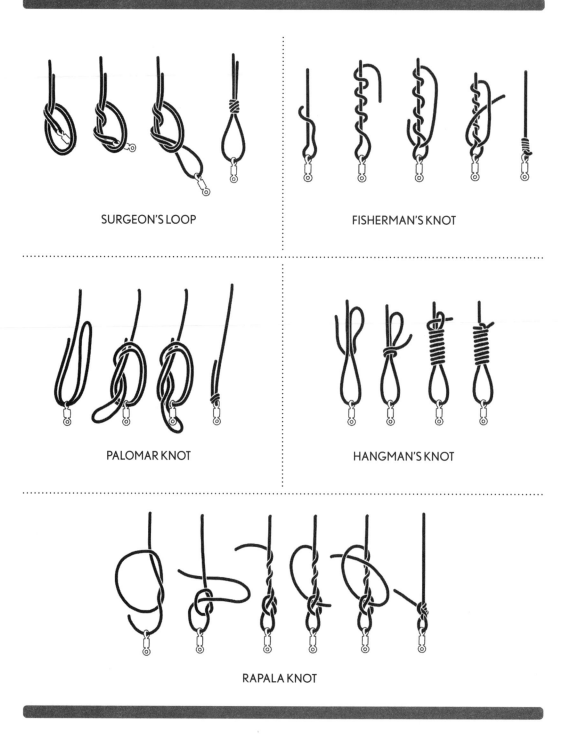

SURGEON'S LOOP

FISHERMAN'S KNOT

PALOMAR KNOT

HANGMAN'S KNOT

RAPALA KNOT

4. Finish by pulling the main line to slide your knot down to your eye of the hook or swivel.

Surgeon's loop knot. This knot is great for attaching a lead, joining lines of different weight.

1. Put your leader line next to your main line.

2. Create an overhand knot by pushing the long piece and leader of your main line through the loop.

3. Make a second overhand knot by moving the previous ends through your loop.

4. Wet the line and slowly tighten by pulling all of the ends.

5. Trim your tags.

FIRST AID

Fishing can be dangerous. It's easy to cut yourself, and it's even easier to slip and fall. Check Chapter 9 for basic medical practices, but make sure you always have adhesive bandages and antiseptic when you're out fishing. If it's cold out (and some of the best fishing days you'll have will be freezing), make sure you've got a hot beverage and a set of dry clothes on hand. If you fall in cold water, try to get to shore, but if you can't, don't waste your energy thrashing around—you'll just lose body heat. Bring your knees up toward your chin and bend your legs as though you are sitting—this is known as the Heat Escape Lessening Position, or H.E.L.P.—and stay like that until help comes.

REMOVING A HOOK FROM YOUR SKIN

If the hook is on the face, near the eyes, in the back of the hand, or anywhere near ligaments, tendons, or blood vessels, leave it be and get to the emergency room so the professionals can handle it. Otherwise, here's what you can do:

STEP 1: First, cut the hook away from the rest of the fishing lure. Then, put a loop of heavy twine or fishing line around the bend of the hook.

STEP 2: Next, hold down the eye and shank of the hook, pressing it lightly to the skin.

STEP 3: Finally, grasp the loop in the line and, with a sharp jerk, pull the hook free.

STOCKING YOUR OWN POND

If you've got the space for it, stocking a pond with fish you want to eat is surprisingly easy. You'll want to make sure your pond is big enough to hold a useful number of fish (at least a quarter acre) and deep enough so they can live happily. You'll want some part of it to be at least ten feet deep so the water stays cool in the summer. If your soil doesn't contain a high percentage of clay, you can cover the bottom of the pond in plastic sheeting to ensure it doesn't drain out. Choose a location where rainwater will naturally collect, i.e., some sort of depression on your property. You may need to invest in an aerator system to make sure oxygen levels remain high.

A properly stocked pond will control algae growth, making it easier to maintain, and if you balance your fish with a good

A. Ice Chest
B. Auger
C. Ice 5" thick
D. Line with bobber
E. Bait

predator-to-prey ratio, the population will remain steady and sustainable. You'll want three prey fish (perch, trout, or bluegill) for every predator (bass). Catfish are great, but won't have much of an impact on the overall population. When you're first getting started, toss some minnows in there so the predators don't eat all your prey before they have a chance to establish themselves.

Stock your pond when temperatures are mild and oxygen levels are high, so ideally in the spring or fall. Acclimate the fish by placing them in a shaded area of the pond and letting them float in their transportation bag for fifteen minutes or so, allowing them to adjust to the temperature shift. At this point, you can let the fish swim on out. Try to release the predators at one end and the prey at the other to give them a chance to find some protection. You'll want to make sure that there are some logs and weeds to provide them with some shelter, or you might think about investing in a fish attractor that won't decompose.

ICE FISHING

If you're feeding your family from the land and water, then you're going to want to be able to do that all year round. Ice fishing requires even more patience than fishing in the warmer months, but it can also be quite fun and satisfying, with a great deal of camaraderie out on the ice.

1. Check the ice levels. You want to make sure that the ice is at minimum five inches thick—and that's just for walking on. If you're planning on bringing a truck out, there needs to be between 12 and 15 inches of solid ice. And remember, different bodies of water will freeze at different rates. Just because the cranberry bog is frozen doesn't mean the town reservoir will be. Talk to the locals, and go out as a group. It'll help alleviate boredom, and it's safer.

2. Drill your hole with an auger until you've reached the water below. Scoop out the ice until you have a nice clean hole (you'll need to do this several times over the course of the day).

3. Determine the depth by attaching a sinker to the end of a hook and dropping it in. Once it hits bottom, reel it in a few feet and then place a bobber on the surface of the water.

4. Place your bait on the hook, drop it back in, then relax. Have a chair, a book, a cup of hot tea, and some handwarmers handy. Since this can take awhile, a lot of ice fishermen will use a tip-up, a kind of flag system that will alert you when you've got a bite.

> **"Most of the luxuries, and many of the so-called comforts of life, are not only not indispensable, but positive hindrances to the elevation of mankind."**
>
> **—Henry David Thoreau**

During the winter months you're not going to want to be outside more than you need to—frankly, you'll just be burning extra calories and that just means you'll need to have more food on hand. That said, there's plenty to do inside, even in the warmer months. Much of homestead life is spent outdoors, hard at work, and to be honest you're going to be pretty tired at the end of the day. But you may want to while away some time before you go to sleep, and if you're trying to conserve energy, chilling in front of the TV isn't going to be an option. The reality is, there are still plenty of chores to be done, including making household supplies, mending torn clothing, even spinning wool from your sheep.

Self-sufficiency isn't just about making sure you have enough to eat and drink (though that's definitely a lot of it). It's also about knowing how to do *everything* you need to do, including creating a comfortable and efficient home. That includes making your own supplies—after all, it doesn't make sense to go to the store for fancy shampoos and not for eggs. And fact of the matter is, if you're stuck on your own, nobody's going to be cutting your hair. Maybe you won't mind so much if you're alone on your homestead and have visions of yourself as a beard-wearing mountain man, but your wife may object. And remember, somebody's going to have to cut her hair, too, and she's probably a little more picky about it than you are.

Fashion aside, hygiene matters. It keeps you from getting sick, and it also keeps you from getting sick of yourself. Those quarantine days of sitting around in sweatpants and skipping shaving were fun at first, but eventually most of us started feeling kind of bad about ourselves. Feeling good about your self-image can actually help you ward off depression, which is something to consider when we're talking about living on a homestead.

Even if you have access to a barber, this is just another one of those skills that's handy to learn. Why plunk down $20 (or for women, $80 and up) for something you can do just as well yourself? Why buy that expensive shampoo that's not even good for your hair, when you can make your own? This chapter offers DIY hygiene from head to toe.

You'll want to invest in a bunch of those brown- or blue-tinted glass jars. They'll protect your concoctions from UV light, extending their longevity.

Hair Maintenance

HOW TO CUT HAIR: MEN

Keep the hair dry. Put your clippers on the shortest setting, and working from the base of the head, trim around the edges and up toward the earlobes, including the side-burns. Switch to a slightly longer setting, and trim up the next inch or so. Adjust to the next longest and so on until you reach the top of the head. Repeat along the left side and the right side being careful around the ears.

Take a spray bottle and lightly spritz the top of the head. Comb the hair forward. From the center of the head, take

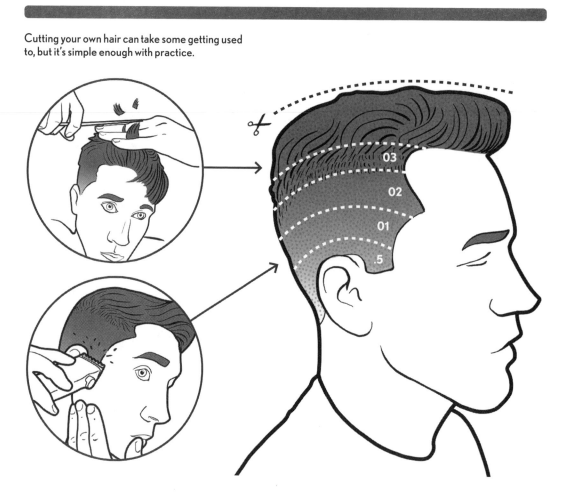

Cutting your own hair can take some getting used to, but it's simple enough with practice.

a half-inch section of hair, and hold it between two fingers of your nondominant hand. Snip off the hair above your fingers, using a sharp pair of scissors specifically for cutting hair. Keep going, cutting the left and right side of the head in the same fashion until all the hair on top has been trimmed.

When you get to the front, comb the bangs forward. Holding the scissors with the tips pointing up, cut just a little at a time until you reach the length you want. Have him scuff his hands through his hair and style it as he normally would. Check for any strays and blend any odd bits.

HOW TO CUT HAIR: WOMEN

If her hair is wavy or curly, it's best to cut it when it's dry and styled as she normally wears it. Take a pair of sharp scissors specifically for cutting hair, and work slowly, making sure the cut is even. Basically, this method just involves cutting and checking to make sure you're doing it right. Take just a little at a time; otherwise you'll end up cutting way more than you need to.

If she has straight hair, you can wet her hair and comb it out, trimming along the bottom slowly and carefully to make sure it's even. If she wants layers, have her pull her hair into a ponytail at the very front of her head, like a unicorn's horn. Snip off the ends at an angle with your scissors pointing up, or even back toward her face for more dramatic layers. (This is a good method if you're not confident, so you can give her a straight trim.)

CUTTING CURLY HAIR

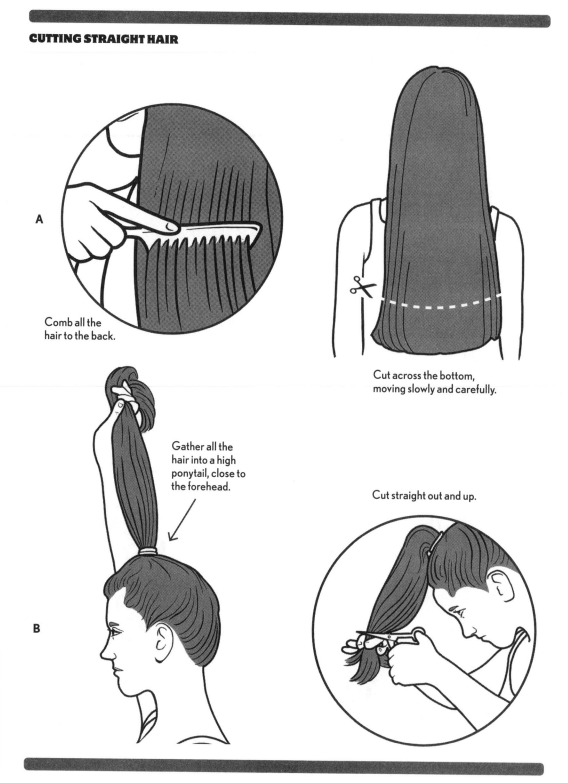

A

Comb all the
hair to the back.

Cut across the bottom,
moving slowly and carefully.

Gather all the
hair into a high
ponytail, close to
the forehead.

Cut straight out and up.

B

Health and Beauty Supplies

Shampoo. First off, get a bottle of Dr. Bronner's castile soap. That stuff is just incredibly useful—you can use it to clean your whole house, including the dishes, and it's still gentle enough to use on yourself, as long as you dilute it. This recipe dilutes it with some oils that'll be good for your hair, and will make it smell good. It will be runnier than you are used to and won't suds up as much, but it is a gentler and greener shampoo. Use your fingers and really scrub at your scalp. If you do want the shampoo to thicken and soap up more, you can add an emulsifier developed from grapeseed oil called BTMS. Otherwise, mix the following ingredients:

1 cup castile soap

1 cup water

2 tablespoons vegetable glycerin

2 teaspoons argan oil

1 tablespoon aloe vera gel (the store-bought, shelf-stable kind)

80 drops of essential oils (see Note)

Note: If you have dry hair, you'll want to use chamomile, peppermint, or rose essential oils. If your hair is on the oily side, try rosemary, ginger, or lemon essential oils. Add them to an empty shampoo bottle.

Hair Oil. If your hair is getting tangled and dry, the best thing to do is bring some coconut oil just to the melting point and rub it into the ends (not the roots). Clip it up and let it sit for half an hour or so, and then shampoo as usual. Do this every other week or once a month as needed, and it'll keep your hair healthy and help you push back a haircut for as long as possible.

Coconut Oil. Yeah, coconut oil is expensive. The production process is laborious and it takes a ton of coconuts to make a batch of oil, which is part of the reason why the price is so high. But those of you with access to coconuts can actually make your own coconut oil (see page 172), though be warned, it's a pain in the neck.

Pomade. Hair pomade or gel may not seem essential, since you don't exactly need to get all dressed up for your livestock, but again, it's nice to feel good about yourself sometimes.

½ cup beeswax

½ cup coconut oil

30 drops essential oil (optional, and just choose a scent you like)

Grate your beeswax and put it in a pot to melt. If you have a double boiler, use that; otherwise just keep the heat really low. Add the coconut oil. Bring the temp up to around 280°F, which will allow your ingredients to bond together at the molecular level. Remove it from the heat. Add your essential oils to a small jar, and then pour the mixture over them—they'll mix together on their own. Screw on the lid. If you're making more than

HOW TO
MAKE COCONUT OIL

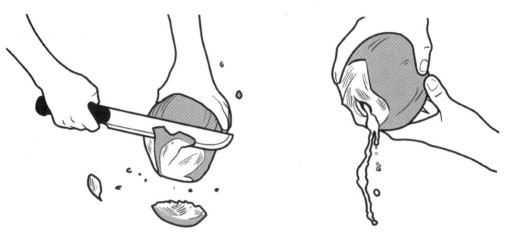

STEP 1

Husk a ripe coconut by bashing it with a machete or a sharp rock. Crack it in half with your machete, saving the water for drinking, as it's full of electrolytes.

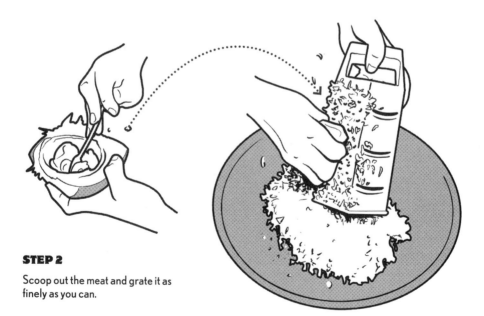

STEP 2

Scoop out the meat and grate it as finely as you can.

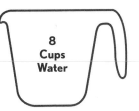

8 Cups Water

STEP 3

Mix the grated coconut with 8 cups of water and mush it with your hands over a bowl. Squeeze out the water a handful at a time and set the rinsed coconut aside in a strainer to drain further. This is the coconut milk. Repeat this process once more, putting the coconut through another round of massaging and squeezing. You should end up with around 12 cups of coconut milk.

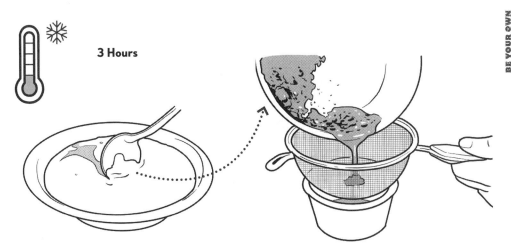

3 Hours

Step 4

Place it in the fridge for 3 hours, which will allow the fat to rise to the top. Skim off that top layer and place it in a saucepan, tossing the thinner layer underneath. Put the heat on medium-high and simmer it, stirring often. You're burning off all the liquid from the fat until just the oil remains, a process that will take around 2 hours.

At the end of the 2 hours, strain out the oil and simmer it again for 10 minutes or so to make sure you've burned off all the water. Let it cool, and then strain into sterilized jars for storage.

one jar, group your jars together so they retain each other's heat. This will slow down the cooling process. As tempting as it is to simply pop your jar in the fridge to make it set faster, you actually want it to cool as slowly as possible. That'll keep the pomade smoother. Once it's set, it's ready to use. Store at room temperature out of direct sunlight.

Shaving Soap. This will give you a gentle, light lather—not like the shaving cream you get at the grocery store, but it'll be enough that you can get a good glide.

2 tablespoons liquid castile soap
2 tablespoons aloe vera gel
1 tablespoon olive oil
¼ cup water
10 drops essential oils

Whisk everything together and pour it into an empty foaming soap dispenser.

HOT TIP

If you don't want to be running to the store all the time to replace your blades (or pay the exorbitant cost), you can get the job done with a straight razor. But it does need to be kept sharp.

Lip Balm. There's that coconut oil again. It's just really useful—I don't know what else to tell you. In a small saucepan over low heat, melt down:

1 to 2 teaspoons beeswax (use more if you want a firmer lip balm, less if you like it on the gooier side)
2 teaspoons coconut oil
2 teaspoons shea butter or cocoa butter

Once everything is melted, you can add a flavoring if you like, like some vanilla extract, mint extract, or cocoa powder. Pour it into a tin and let it cool overnight.

Toothpaste. Honestly, you'll do just fine sprinkling some baking soda on a toothbrush and going from there. But if you want to make it more of a paste, mix the baking soda with some coconut oil until you get the consistency you want—the coconut oil will help prevent gingivitis and tooth decay. Add some mint extract to taste, and some xylitol powder if you're trying to make it palatable for kids.

Toothbrush and Floss. Making a plastic toothbrush with all those bristles is more trouble than it is worth. But you can take a twig from the *Salvadora persica* tree (nicknamed the "toothbrush tree") and according to the *North American Journal of Medical Sciences*, you'll do just as good a job. Using a pocketknife, strip off the bark and then chew on the stick until the fibers become brush-like, at which point you're good to go. You can also just take the corner of a washcloth and use that, making sure to scrub around the gums.

Organic, natural cotton thread works well as dental floss, and if you're really desperate, you can just unravel a cotton shirt, though the gauge might be a little fine. Horsehair from the mane and tail also works remarkably well.

Body Wash. The simplest thing to do is to dilute your castile soap by half, but if you want to get a little fancier, you can add some other ingredients that are good for your skin and will make you smell good.

¼ cup coconut oil
2 tablespoons honey
¼ cup castile soap
1 teaspoon vitamin E or jojoba oil (optional)
30 drops essential oil of choice

DIY TOOTHBRUSH

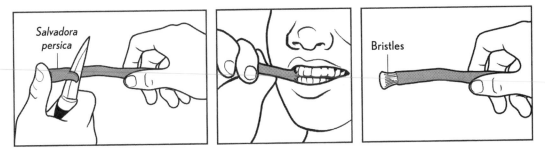

DIY DENTAL FLOSS

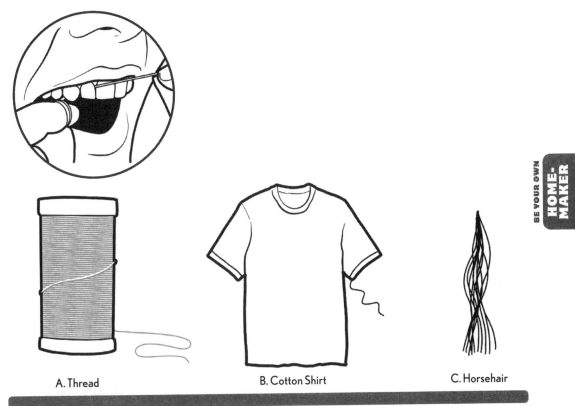

A. Thread

B. Cotton Shirt

C. Horsehair

Melt the coconut oil in a small saucepan over low heat, then remove it from the heat and stir in the honey and castile soap. You can add a teaspoon of vitamin E oil or jojoba oil for an extra treat. Mix in the essential oil (or oils) in a scent you like, and pour the mixture into a leftover plastic bottle.

Hand Soap. This is that nice, prefoamed hand soap, so you'll want to use a leftover dispenser. Add ¼ cup castile soap, top it off with water, and mix in 30 drops of your chosen essential oils. That's it.

HOW TO
STRAIGHT RAZOR SHAVE

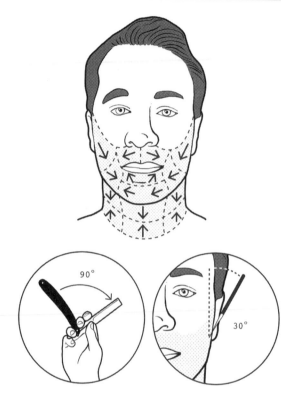

Step 1

Take your time. Get your skin ready with a hot shower or hot cloth, and put a little face oil on before you even lather up.

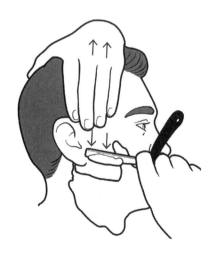

STEP 2

Hold your razor at a 30-degree angle from your face, keeping a firm grip. Pull the skin taut with your other hand, and apply gentle pressure at first, increasing the pressure as needed, but be careful—this thing is sharp. Move with a short, even stroke, working with the grain of the hair. Never begin a fresh stroke on your jawbone, chin, knee, or ankle, but work your way there from the cheek, neck, or calf. After each short stroke, rinse the blade with hot water.

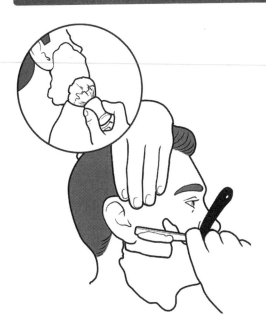

Step 3

Relather and take a second pass, this time going against the grain, catching anything you missed the first time around.

Step 4

Rinse with cold water to close your pores back up, and pat in a moisturizer or post-shave balm.

Step 5

Rinse your blade and wipe it with a soft cloth. Rub it with a blade oil and keep it out of the bathroom, away from the steam so it doesn't rust. If it does get rusty, replace it.

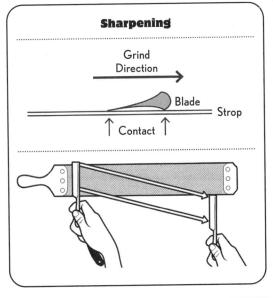

Sharpening

Grind Direction →

Blade

Strop

↑ Contact ↑

HOW TO
MAKE SOAP FROM LARD

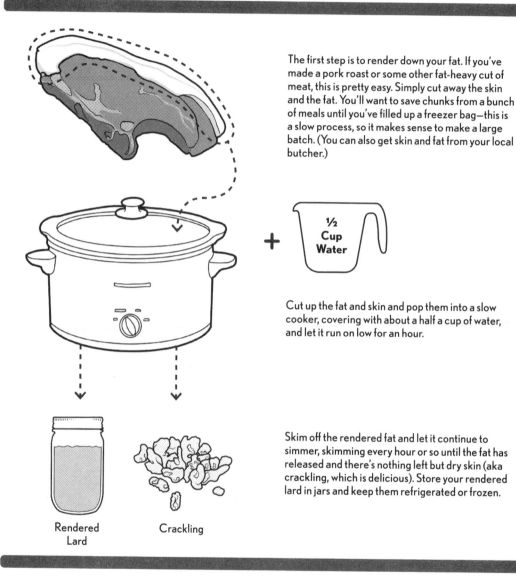

The first step is to render down your fat. If you've made a pork roast or some other fat-heavy cut of meat, this is pretty easy. Simply cut away the skin and the fat. You'll want to save chunks from a bunch of meals until you've filled up a freezer bag—this is a slow process, so it makes sense to make a large batch. (You can also get skin and fat from your local butcher.)

+ ½ Cup Water

Cut up the fat and skin and pop them into a slow cooker, covering with about a half a cup of water, and let it run on low for an hour.

Skim off the rendered fat and let it continue to simmer, skimming every hour or so until the fat has released and there's nothing left but dry skin (aka crackling, which is delicious). Store your rendered lard in jars and keep them refrigerated or frozen.

Rendered Lard

Crackling

Soap from Lye and Lard. Lard retains its glycerin, which is a moisturizing product, and soap made from lard is very gentle while still being quite effective. You can purchase lye (sodium hydroxide) from a hardware or home improvement store, where it is sometimes called caustic soda.

Different fats require different amounts of lye and water to produce the chemical reaction required to turn them into soap. You'll need to carefully weigh the amount of lard you'll be using and then use a soap calculator to get the exact measurements of lye and water you'll need. SoapCalc.net is a good one, as is Brambleberry.com. Cut off the top of a milk carton and rub the inside with a little lard to prep it—this will be your soap mold. Heat your measured lard in a saucepan over low heat until it reaches 100°F, not going over 120°F. Meanwhile, measure your lye and water outside, wearing a mask, gloves, and goggles. *Always add the lye to the water, not the other way around*—the opposite will cause an aggressive chemical reaction. The lye will naturally raise the temperature of the water, so check until it, too, settles somewhere between 100° and 120°F. Once your lard and your lye mixture are at approximately the same temperature, take the lard off the heat and pour the lye carefully into the melted lard. Use an immersion blender (one that you use strictly for soap-making; you don't want to accidentally get some lye into your soup) to mix your soap until it reaches *trace*.

Achieving trace means that the fat, water, and lye have emulsified. When you first start mixing, your soap will look like sweetened condensed milk, with some oily separation. Once all the oils have mixed in and the consistency is that of a thin cake batter, it's time to add any coloring, fragrance, or essential oils you want to use. Keep mixing until the consistency is more like that of a thick pudding and retains its shape when poured. This is full trace. Pour your soap into the prepared mold and cover it with a towel, letting it sit for two to three days. Remove it from the mold and slice it into bars. Let them sit in a cool, dark place for a few weeks, turning them occasionally, as they cure and harden.

Hand Sanitizer. Post-COVID, we all probably know this one, but here's a recipe for you to keep handy. Remember, according to the CDC, in order to be effective, it has to be at least 60 percent alcohol. Mix together the following ingredients:

1 cup isopropyl alcohol 91% or higher
½ cup aloe vera gel
20 to 30 drops essential oils

Note: You can also make hand sanitizer with a lower-proof rubbing alcohol, but in that case you'll use only ½ tablespoon of aloe vera gel, making it better for a spray bottle.

Moisturizer. Moisturizer is essentially oils you apply to your skin. Coconut oil on its own honestly works great for this and you don't need much more than that (just don't put it on your face). But if you want to get a little more fancy, you can experiment with mixing various kinds of oils, like shea butter, olive oil, and vegetable glycerin. This is a basic recipe that you can play with:

½ cup shea butter
½ cup olive oil
2 tablespoons vegetable glycerin
30 drops essential oils (chamomile, rose, frankincense, and tea tree are all good for the skin)

Melt the shea butter on your stove over low heat, then stir in the olive oil. Remove from the heat and stir in the glycerin and essential oils. Pour into a wide-mouthed jar and place into your refrigerator to help it set overnight.

Face Oil. This is perhaps the one place where you don't want to put any coconut oil, as it'll clog your pores. Grapeseed oil, olive oil, or sweet almond oil will work better for you. Add 5 to 10 drops of essential oils for each ounce of carrier oil, and shake well to emulsify. You'll want to store your face oil in a dark glass bottle with a dropper. Rub a little bit into your face after cleansing, and make sure to apply sunscreen.

I'd suggest rose, clary sage, tea tree, chamomile, or frankincense essential oils, or any combination of these. It's mostly about what you want to smell like.

HOW TO ZAP A ZIT

You've got a few options here. The quickest and easiest is simply to dab the spot with a little tea tree oil, diluting it with a little water before putting it on your skin. But if you've got a larger area or particularly set-in acne, you may want a little apple cider vinegar wash.

Mix 1 part raw apple cider vinegar with 3 parts water. Moisten a cloth and dab it all over your face. Let it sit for a few minutes, then rinse. Repeat one or two times a week.

Similarly, a strong cup of green tea may have a cleansing effect on the surface of the skin, and it helps to drink it, too.

MENSTRUATION SUPPLIES

First off, I'm a guy, so I'm definitely not going to be able to anticipate everything women are going to need or want. And I also figure you're probably going to want to go with whatever is most comfortable and easy when dealing with already uncomfortable parts of life like menstruation. But these are some alternatives for when commercial products are unavailable. You can make your own pads out of cloth. Cotton flannel is both soft and absorbent, and you can use as many layers as you like, and put a layer of waterproof canvas in there to prevent leaks. That said, it may make more sense to just buy several pairs of reusable "period panties." Similarly, you can use sterile gauze as an emergency tampon, but you're better off investing in a silicone menstrual cup—they serve the same function and last for years.

TOILET PAPER

In the Great Toilet Paper Shortage of 2020, we all had to contemplate what life would be like without this modern convenience. Honestly, most cultures around the world don't bother—they splash water instead, then wash their hands afterward (which of course we should all be doing anyway). You can do similarly by simply keeping a little spray bottle or cup of water nearby; each member of your household could have their own personal, portable bidet. Or, for a little more spray action, you could just keep a garden sprayer next to the toilet.

But if that doesn't work for you, you can always use newspaper, which while not sterile, is reasonably clean (your toilet paper isn't sterile either). For a longer-lasting solution, you can sew reusable toilet paper. After all, we often turn to reusable cloth diapers, and this is way less grody than that. Get some flannel and just cut it up with pinking shears to prevent fraying. The more squares you make, the less often you'll have to wash—but you don't exactly want used squares piling up, either. Rather than flushing them down the toilet, put them in a bucket with a lid that contains a white vinegar and water solution, then wash them like regular laundry.

Products for the Home

CLEANING PRODUCTS

If coconut oil is the go-to skin care product, white vinegar is your housecleaning hero. Put some in a spray bottle and you're basically good to go. If you don't love the smell, you can water it down using a 50/50 ratio and add some essential oils (tea tree and lemon are both antibacterial and antifungal). You can wash your windows, your counters, your bathroom, and your floors with the stuff. To get a good scrub going, sprinkle some baking soda and then spritz with the vinegar solution—that'll clean up just about anything.

To make a disinfectant spray, you don't have to turn to bleach (although it is the most effective, to be honest). Mix 1 part white vinegar to 3 parts 99 percent isopropyl alcohol and you'll be able to clear away any potential salmonella from your kitchen counter.

BUG SPRAY

Bugs are always an issue, but if you're trying to live a more organic lifestyle, DEET, while effective, isn't all that great. Any combination of these essential oils are natural insect repellents, and you can simply add all these ingredients to a spray bottle, shake it up, and spritz liberally.

➔ Citronella, lavender, rosemary, tea tree, lemongrass, and cedar essential oils

➔ ½ cup witch hazel

➔ ½ cup water

MENDING AND PATCHING

You're going to tear your jeans. A lot. So knowing how to patch them yourself is a useful skill.

Get some pieces of denim, from either an old pair of jeans or a craft store. Start by trimming the hole, making the edges even and cutting the frays down. Flip your jeans inside out and smooth out the tear on a flat surface. Trim your patch down so that it's around half an inch larger than your tear on all sides. Place it right-side down on your hole.

Trim the thread with your scissors to make sure there aren't any frayed edges, then pull it through the eye of the needle until it's about 16 to 20 inches long. Measure your thread from the spool until it's the same length and cut, tying the two ends together with a knot. Insert your needle into a corner of the patch, make a small stitch, and pull the thread through. To secure, place a few small stitches in the exact same place, twisting the thread under itself. Be careful not to sew the other side of the pant leg!

Begin stitching along the side of the patch. Work in a zigzag motion, twisting the thread under itself from time to time to make sure it stays secure. When you run out of thread, knot it in place several times, then use the same method to begin again. Work your way around the entire patch in this way, at least three times.

To mend a smaller tear, trim the edges in the same way as above. Stitching from

HOW TO
SEW A PATCH

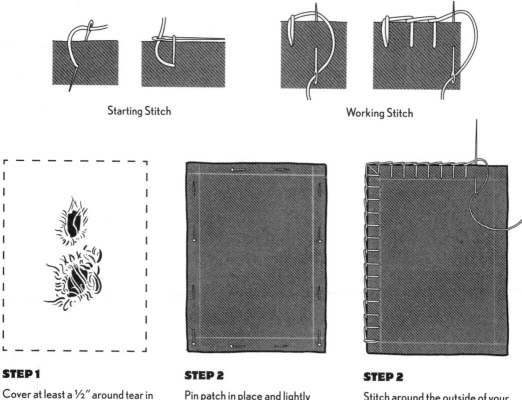

Starting Stitch   Working Stitch

STEP 1

Cover at least a ½″ around tear in fabric and trim any frayed edges.

STEP 2

Pin patch in place and lightly pencil in your stitch line.

STEP 2

Stitch around the outside of your patch, following your pencil line.

the inside out, insert your needle on one side of the tear, then bring it back through on the other side, attaching both sides of the tear together. Repeat all the way across the tear, knotting occasionally, and work your way back and forth a couple of times to set the repair in place.

MAKING YARN FROM WOOL

You'll want to start with clean, skirted fleece—definitely don't bring any of that foul-smelling stuff into the house. To prep,

you'll need a set of wool hand carders. Separate a few locks of wool at a time and load them onto one of the cards, trying to keep the locks all going in the same direction. Don't put too much on at a time. Rest one of the cards on your lap and use the other to tug at the wool, transferring it all to the second card. Switch and work back and forth like this a couple more times, aligning the fibers and letting any bits of grass or short cuts (smaller cuts of wool) fall to the floor.

1. Sheep

2. Shear

3. Separate Wool

4. Clean Wool

5. Card Wool

6. Spin Wool to Yarn

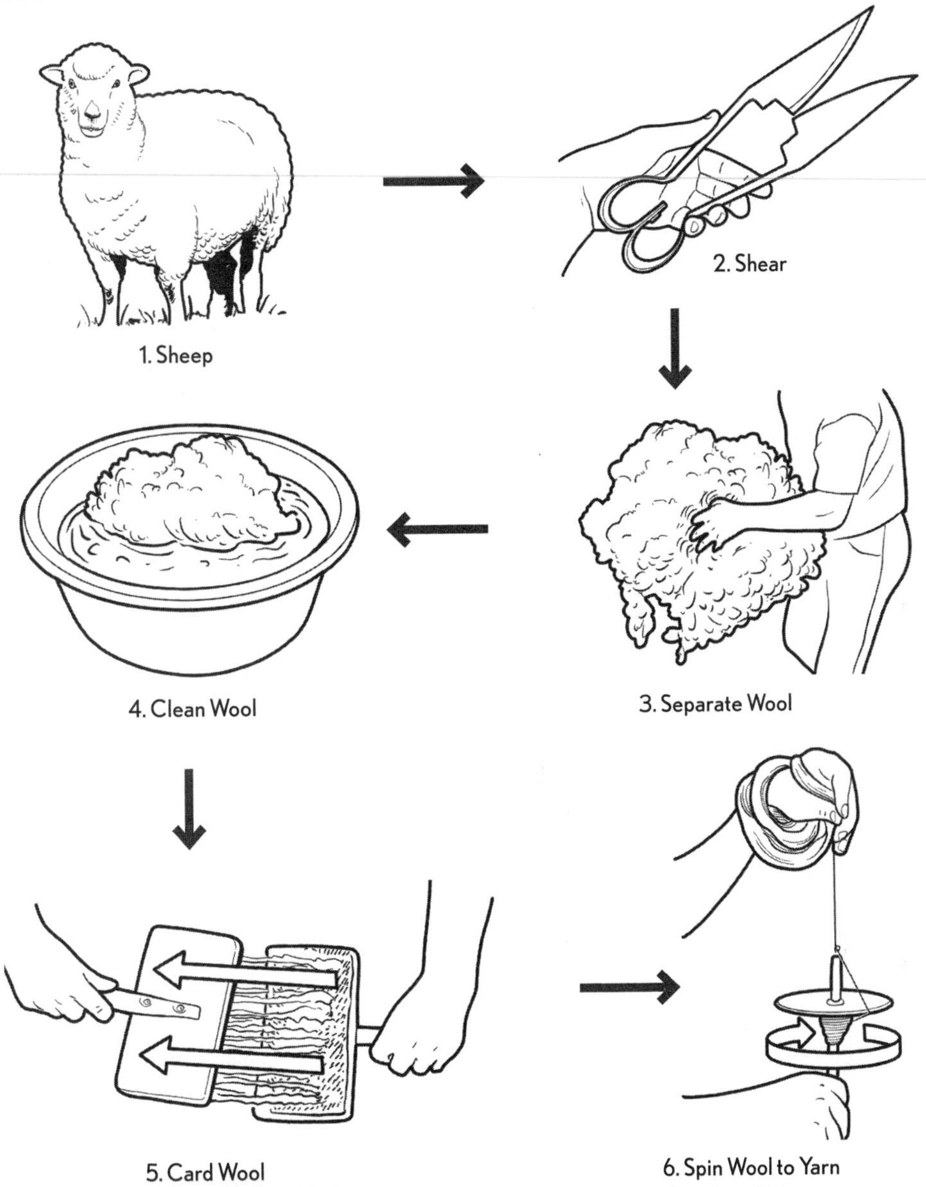

BE YOUR OWN **HOME-MAKER**

Remove the fiber from the card by pushing one card against the other, sliding the top card over the bottom, and gathering the fiber up into a little tube called a rolag. Set it aside, and start again.

When you've got a good supply of rolags, it's time to start spinning. You can make a drop spindle with a couple of old CDs or DVD, a wooden dowel, and a small eye hook. Tie an 18-inch leader of commercial yarn on to the hook and make a slipknot at the end. Pull a bit of fiber from the top of your rolag and insert it into the slipknot. Stand up and let your spindle drop down toward the ground, with the hook pointing up. Give it a twist to start it spinning, paying attention to which direction it's going; you'll want to be consistent.

As it twists together, your fiber will stick together and grow stronger, creating yarn. As you're spinning, be careful not to let the twist go past your fingers and up into your rolag. Feed more fiber from your rolag until the spindle reaches the floor. Pause, release it from the eye hook, and wind it around the spindle (the length of dowel beneath the CDs). Repeat until the spindle is full, then wind off the yarn by wrapping it around the top of a chair, creating a skein.

Dip your skein in warm (but not hot) water mixed with a little Dr. Bronner's. Don't mess with it or the yarn will felt together. This warm water sets the twist, helping your wool stay yarn. Let it sit for several minutes, then give it another bath in water that is the same temperature—again, temperature shock may cause it to felt. Let it hang to dry.

Once you get comfortable with spinning, you can invest in a spinning wheel, practice plying yarn singles together, and certainly take up knitting or crocheting if you don't do them already. Whatever yarn you don't want to use yourself, you can always sell—good-quality handspun yarn goes for a pretty penny.

MAKING CANDLES FROM BEESWAX

The first step involves processing the beeswax, as even the cleanest of hives has some impurities. Melt your beeswax over very low heat in a double boiler (you can make your own by setting a metal mixing bowl in a pan filled with water). Line a bowl with an old T-shirt or a couple layers of cheesecloth, then pour in the melted beeswax. Hold the cloth over the bowl and allow the wax to drip through completely. It'll leave any propolis and debris behind—but don't throw away that propolis! This sticky, brownish green residue is made from sap collected from evergreens, and it's high in antioxidants as well as being antimicrobial and antibacterial.

Unless you're ready to make candles immediately, simply pour your melted beeswax into smaller molds for later use—you can make them out of cut-up milk cartons and the like. To make your beeswax

BEESWAX CANDLE

A clothespin will help keep the wick straight while the wax cools and hardens.

candle, attach a premade, purchased wick to the bottom of a glass jar. Add any essential oils or fragrance oils you like to your beeswax, stirring well, then pour it into the jar. Help the wick stay upright by threading it through the center of a clothespin and resting the clothespin atop the jar. Let it harden completely for at least two days, then trim the wick to ¼ inch.

Cleanup can be a little tricky, as the wax will have adhered to everything it touches. Pop everything in the oven and heat it to 200°F, lining the oven rack with foil to catch any drips. Once the wax is all melted down again, wipe it out as best you can, then wash everything with soap and hot water.

ITEMS TO HAVE IN YOUR CUPBOARD

Right Now
- ☐ Pots and pans
- ☐ Coffeemaker
- ☐ Cast-iron skillet
- ☐ Chef's knife
- ☐ Bread knife
- ☐ Plenty of mason jars
- ☐ Dark glass bottles and jars
- ☐ Cheesecloth
- ☐ Needle and thread
- ☐ Deck of cards

Soon Enough
- ☐ Coffee grinder
- ☐ Slow cooker
- ☐ Knife sharpener
- ☐ Double boiler
- ☐ Dutch oven
- ☐ Games

Someday
- ☐ Pressure cooker
- ☐ Juicer
- ☐ Ice cream maker

BE YOUR OWN HOME-MAKER

Have Some Fun

This might seem obvious, but don't work *all* the time. Yeah, homesteading means putting in a lot of effort, but it also means enjoying each other's company. And you may end up spending time together in a way you didn't otherwise—after all, without TV and phones, what is there to do?

The answer is: plenty. Reading of course, but also playing cards, charades, board games. If someone plays the guitar or a ukulele, others can sing along. Storytelling is also an age-old way to spend time, particularly if you can share the story with a group of people. Kids love playing "And then . . ." One person starts a story with a sentence or two, and then the next person takes it and adds to it, then the next person, and so on.

"Man is timid and apologetic; he is no longer upright; he dares not say 'I think,' 'I am,' but quotes some saint or sage. He is ashamed before the blades of grass or the blowing rose. Those roses under my window make no reference to former roses or to better ones; they are for what they are."

—Ralph Waldo Emerson

Lots of things can go wrong when you're out on your own. You might have issues with predators such as bears or wolves. There might be a storm, like a hurricane or a tornado. There might be a fire. There might be an earthquake. You need to know how to minimize these threats, and how to respond if and when something does happen.

Know Your Land

First, know what you're walking into. Before you set up your homestead, consider what threats you're willing to deal with. Hate snakes? Don't move to rattler country. Do you want to deal with drought, hurricanes, tornadoes, blizzards? Every single place has its issues, and you have to decide what you're willing to cope with and manage.

Once you've moved onto your homestead, the best thing you can do to protect yourself is to be fully aware of your surroundings. Walk your boundary lines often, and make sure they are well marked—most states require you to post "No Trespassing" signs every 25 to 50 feet and at all entries, but consult your local regulations to make sure. Also, if you own a great swath of land, you should make sure to check out all parts of it at least every couple years to ward off squatters. That's right, many states still have Squatter's Rights/Adverse Possession. So if someone builds a cabin on your land and stays there for a certain amount of years continuously while you don't notice or ask them to leave, they may be able to formally come to own that portion of your land.

As you walk your property, consider the terrain. Are there any areas that could camouflage an intruder? Make sure you have a clear line of sight for your home, and if you have livestock, make sure you can see or at least hear them from your house—they will alert you if something is wrong. Keeping predators away means letting them know you're dominant. You have to be the alpha. Put your tracks everywhere and leave your scent. Pee on trees. And make sure to make some noise regularly, whether that means target practice or having a dance party out in the yard. Make your presence known, and dangerous wildlife will stay away.

And make friends with your neighbors! They are your best line of defense, as they will watch your property for you when you aren't there, and can always serve as a place to retreat to if necessary. This is an easy—and important—exchange, so make sure they know that you will do the same for them.

Natural Disasters

The first step is making sure you've prevented as much damage as possible. If you're in a flash flood area, put your house on stilts and carefully choose the locations of your chicken coops, pigpens, etc., keeping them on high ground.

If you live in an area where forest fires are an issue, make sure you've got a firebreak around all of your structures. You'll want a minimum of 50 feet between the structure and the nearest tree, but the bigger the break, the safer you are. If you're surrounded by a particularly flammable tree such as spruce, push that break back to 200 feet. And don't burn brush. Just don't.

For hurricanes or tornadoes, you want to make sure you've locked your things down. Have plywood boards sized to fit your windows that you can screw in place (taping your windows does jack, don't even bother). Store as much as you can indoors, but for larger equipment that you worry might blow around, create a rock dead man by digging a hole and putting a boulder down in there. Wrap a metal cable several times around the boulder, bury it, then bring the lines up to attach to your solar panels or whatever else you want to make sure stays in place.

SHELTERING IN PLACE

It's a good idea to have some sort of safe place you can get to in the event of a storm such as a hurricane or a tornado, a visit from a bear, an attack by someone intent on violence, or some kind of local or global catastrophe. We're talking about a standby safe room, something that can provide protection for a limited period of time, rather than something that can last for months or years—though with some planning, you can easily create that with the information you have here.

There are two types of shelters to choose from: standalone or internal. A standalone shelter is a separate building designed and constructed to withstand a range of either natural or manmade hazards. An internal shelter provides the same protection, but is located within a larger structure, like your house or your barn. When it comes to choosing your site, start by considering an internal shelter. If you do not have a site that will provide sufficient protection, you may have to create a standalone, but ideally that won't be necessary.

An internal shelter must be somewhere everyone in your household can get to easily, and can enter and exit easily—without making it also easy for a threat to enter, so a strong lock on a metal door is a good idea. It must have enough space to comfortably hold your entire household for the necessary period of time—depending on the hazard, that may be up to a few days. You can consider basements, bathrooms, closets, small storage rooms, or anyplace else that has one door and no more than one window. (A bathroom has the added benefit of water supply and a toilet.) The walls and ceiling of the internal shelter must be strong enough so they will remain standing if the rest of the house is damaged by extreme winds.

To see if your site will provide adequate protection, you can reference the Building Vulnerability Assessment Checklist included in *FEMA 426, Reference Manual to Mitigate Potential Terrorist Attacks Against Buildings*; *FEMA 452, A How-To Guide to Mitigate Potential Terrorist Attacks Against Buildings* for the assessment of CBRE (chemical, biological, radiological, and explosive) events; and *FEMA 433, Using HAZUS-MH for Risk Assessment* for the assessment of major natural hazards. If your site is not totally safe, you can determine if all you need to do is retrofit it with additional structural protections . . . or you can shift to a standalone shelter. In the case of a standalone shelter, you are constructing a building that is strictly for emergency use, so comfort is less of an issue. It can be an underground bunker, or it can be aboveground, but built in such a way that it can withstand all potential hazards.

Your root cellar will work, as will a buried shipping container. You could put a concrete storm drain into a hillside, attaching a plywood door on it. None of these are a waste of time or money—they can serve as storage, particularly for food, and you'll have them when you need them.

You'll want to make sure everyone in your household knows how to get to the shelter and when to get to the shelter (i.e., you have a comms system worked out in case of emergency). The shelter should be stocked with food and water for the minimum amount of time you think is necessary, depending on likely hazards.

Predators

Predators might be animals or they might be humans. If you're off in the middle of nowhere, nobody's going to hear you call for help. 911 is a long way away and you need to be able to protect yourself. You also have to worry about predators that maybe don't have claws or fangs, but just want to drop by and eat your food. Snakes, venomous or otherwise, feral pigs, rodents, groundhogs—you're not going to be able to keep all predators away entirely, particularly if you've got a garden or livestock that will attract them. But you can minimize their visits with some basic hygiene. Don't leave food or trash out. Store your food in a freezer or refrigerator so it doesn't give off a scent, and keep your canned goods and root vegetables in a root cellar or other rodent- and bear-proof shelter. A bear, wolf, or coyote can smell your food from miles away, and they will want to come get an easy meal. Same with your trash—you can't just leave it lying around. If you're way out where there's no trash pickup, you need to take your garbage to the town dump or waste transfer station; between visits, you'll need to keep it in secure metal containers. Rats can bite through plastic.

But dealing with any kind of predator begins and ends with the five Ds: Deter, Detect, Deny, Delay, and Defend. You want to work from the perimeter of your property all the way in to your shelter, making sure that you have intentional and effective security measures in place.

Deter. The best option is to get any would-be threats to change their mind and go away, never bothering you at all. This can be done with a mix of physical infrastructure like fencing. For human surveillance, you can also set up a security camera, but in this case the point is to make the intruder reconsider whether it's even worth attempting a

5 D's

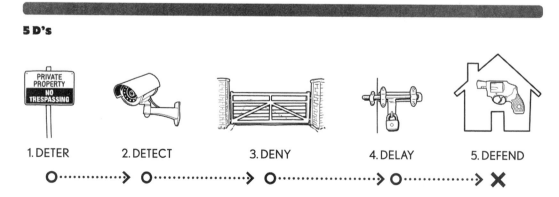

1. DETER 2. DETECT 3. DENY 4. DELAY 5. DEFEND

DETECT WITH TRAIL CAMERAS

22:35:50 11/09/21 48°F

breach. Put up signs saying "Area Under Surveillance," "Beware of Dog," and "No Trespassing" to make your deterrent message clear.

The general rule is that the farther away from your home, the more expensive the security measures, no matter what they are. So the trouble with fencing, of course, is that it can be prohibitively expensive, particularly if your property is quite large. In that case, you may want to fence a smaller area within your property, closer to your house and any outbuildings. Fencing will keep out most pests and predators you don't want getting into your crops or livestock, so there is an additional benefit there that may make the investment worth the expense.

If you want to predator-proof your livestock, you've got to build a really good fence. The posts need to go 2 feet down, with a trench in between. You can fill that trench with barbed wire, and any canine predator who wants to dig its way in will find an unpleasant surprise. The fence line comes straight up 6 to 8 feet from there. If you want to keep bears and mountain lions away, add in a $100 12-volt electric fence kit. It's solar-powered and it'll give just enough of a zap to make an animal change its mind about dropping by for a snack. An electric fence doesn't have to be secured in place like a regular fence, so you can move it as needed to protect crops or pastures during rotation periods. Electric fencing does require maintenance, as a fallen limb or fast-growing grass can cause it to short out. And you do need to make sure everyone in your household knows how to approach an electric fence safely.

For the low-tech, all-natural approach, consider a living fence! Like Sleeping Beauty's castle, you can create a thorny hedge that will keep out even the most determined visitors. The following are

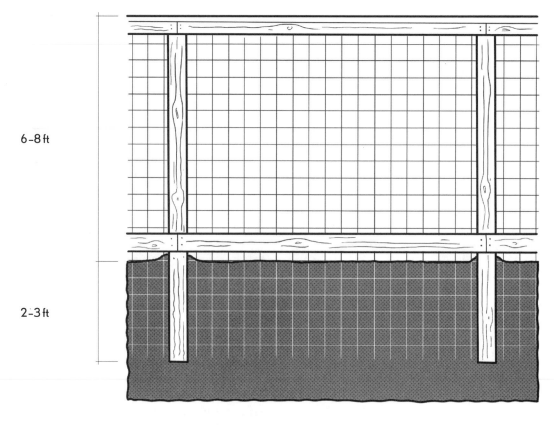

6–8 ft

2–3 ft

TYPICAL MEDIUM-SIZED LIVESTOCK FENCE

some good options for living fences in a variety of climates:

→ **Berries.** Raspberries, gooseberries, blackberries—all of these bushes produce delicious fruit, grow quickly, and provide an extremely effective barrier.

→ **Century plants.** This lovely plant will look like incredible landscaping, but try getting through a thick bush of them and you'll understand why they are sometimes referred to as sentry plants. This large succulent grows long, firm,

three to five feet long leaves armed with sharp, heavy spikes. They are easy to grow in warm, dry climates and spread quickly with little to no maintenance.

→ **Honey locust.** This is a tall tree with thick branches that are loaded with thorns—and those thorns can grow up to four inches long. It spreads easily, so you will want to watch that it grows only where you want it.

→ **Citrus trees.** Most citrus trees, including lemon and lime trees, have surprisingly sharp thorns. If you plant them at a range of sizes, they will form a formidable barrier, and again, you get some fruit, to boot. They prefer warmer climates, generally speaking, though some varieties are more cold-tolerant.

→ **Juniper.** This hardy and drought-resistant shrub makes an excellent hedge because of its density and grows quickly.

→ **Roses.** Every rose does indeed have its thorn, and your decorative hedge will keep out trespassers and many predators as well. You can plant these thorny bushes beneath your window—the howls of pain you hear will serve as your alarm system.

A dog, of course, is the best security system you can buy. The right dog will bond with you and your livestock and will take his or her job extremely seriously, patrolling the boundaries and protecting your territory from any potential threats, including both predators and intruders. Ideally you want a few dogs, so they can keep each other company, cover more territory, and serve to assist you in all of the five Ds.

Other animals also make excellent protectors and alarm systems: Geese are shockingly intimidating when they're riled up. Mules, donkeys, and alpacas are also very protective and will defend your livestock, to the death if need be. But your best bet is probably a flock of guinea hens. These are the meanest of birds and they travel in packs. They can scare off coyotes, they're so intense and loud. Build their coop up in a tree and drape some netting down so they have free-range capability, and they will wander around your property eating fleas and ticks during the day and keeping an eye and nose out for predators at night.

Detect. Going hand-in-hand with Deter is Detect—you want to *know* if someone is out there, and you want them to know you know. Surveillance cameras, particularly those with megapixel cameras, are extremely effective, particularly since they allow you to zoom in and get more detail on the intruder.

Of course, in order for detection to have a deterrent effect, you have to be able to recognize the threat in real time, which means those security cameras have to be monitored. Most of us don't have full-time security personnel, so surveillance cameras are most useful for identifying the culprit after the crime has been committed. And if you're living off-grid, they can be a major power draw that your system can't handle. That said, you can get battery-operated alarms and put them on entryways, including exterior gates and all the doors and windows of your home. If the batteries are rechargeable, they shouldn't be too much of a draw on your system. If the batteries need to be replaced, you'll need to monitor them and make sure you have spares on hand at all times. You may also want infrared lights and motion sensors in place of cameras, or in addition to them.

It can also be useful to build a bear stand. It will serve as a lookout, and if you end up with a bear, mountain lion, or wolf on your property, you can get up there and get a shot off. Mind you, most bears and mountain lions can climb, but trying to get up there will slow them down enough so you can take the shot. Make sure you've got a retractable ladder, like a rope ladder you can climb up quickly, and pull up just as quickly.

There's also nothing like the old tin-can alarm system. It really does work. Figure out the perimeter of the area you want to secure and set aside enough empty cans so that you can string them a foot or two apart. Cut an entrance and exit hole in the can, just wide enough to slide your string through—you'll want something stiff and strong like nylon, but nothing too thick that will make it more noticeable. Fill the cans with marbles or rocks to make them even louder. You'll want to string them about two to three feet off the ground— that height will make them less easy to spot, and they'll still be tripped by anything bigger than a cat.

Deny. A Deny objective is something like a security gate. In office buildings or other secure locations, it can also include key cards or biometric security systems (like the face scans you see in the movies).

DIY TREE STAND

HOT TIP

Building a tree stand with a retractable ladder will give you a safe place, free of predators, to get a view of your land.

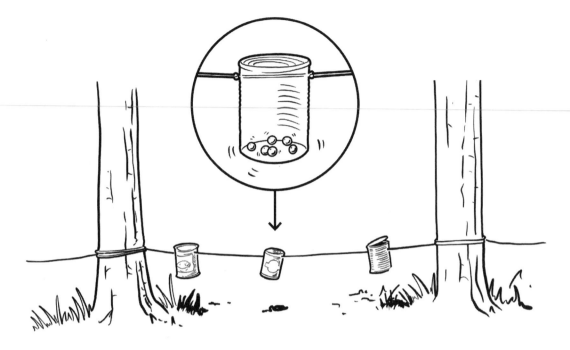

TIN CAN ALARM

A sturdy gate at all entrances to your property is essential, but make sure it's something you and your invited guests can get through easily, as you don't want to accidentally strand yourself. A tried-and-true method of blocking the path of bears into your home is a bed of raised nails hammered into plywood and placed in front of each of your doors and windows, like an "unwelcome mat." This is especially recommended if you live way out in an area like Alaska and are leaving your home for a good amount of time.

Delay. By the time you get to Delay, the intruder is inside your perimeter, is definitely a threat, and should be treated accordingly. That can mean multiple entryways, like a series of gates they have to get through, or locks or other barriers to entry that will slow them down. Multiple fence lines that someone has to scale, solar-powered motion detection lights that they have to avoid, and thick vegetation they have to get through will all help to cause delays.

If they do reach the house, you can slow them down further by installing storm doors or screen doors—even that one additional barrier could give you enough time to ready yourself.

Similarly, tinting your windows can help them be more shatterproof; someone can still get in, but it will take them a minute longer.

Defend. Ideally, this step is never reached and never becomes necessary, but it is always important to be able to defend yourself in case it does. Every single member of your household should know what to do if they encounter a predator. If there's a wolf on the property, what do you do? You should have a predator plan in place, just as you have a plan in case of fire.

If you encounter a bear or wolf, stand your ground. They really do like it when you run. Wave your arms and make yourself appear as large as possible. Make a lot of noise. If you've got bear spray on you—and you should, if you live near bears—use it. Your shotgun is your next line of defense.

What about if we're talking human predators? This list is formatted in terms of distance-from-your-predator. Basically, you never want to get into close quarters with them. That said, we are moving from most lethal to least lethal, while never crossing into more firepower than you really need for home defense.

→ **Handgun.** Your basic handgun is smaller and therefore something you're more likely to be able to keep somewhere secure but close by and accessible if you need it. It will also hold more ammunition. The Smith & Wesson J-frame is great and allows both .38 and .357 ammo. It's a hammerless compact revolver and will perform without malfunction, but it is limited to six rounds of ammunition. An alternative that would be just as reliable is the Glock 19 9mm, which holds far more rounds. You'll want to use frangible bullets to minimize any

potential ricochet harm to bystanders or family members.

→ **Shotgun.** The 12-gauge pump-action shotgun is the venerable king of home defense weaponry. It's reliable and devastating at close range—and oftentimes just the sound of the pump racking is enough to get your intruder to leave you alone. The Mossberg 500/590 and the Remington 870 are popular and economical choices.

→ **Taser.** Tasers have a reliable range of up to ten feet away.

→ **Stun baton.** If that doesn't feel like enough, get an electrified baton—you'd be surprised how quickly they can drop even the heaviest intruder.

→ **Collapsible baton.** A step up from a bat is a collapsible baton, which has the added benefit of being more compact, something you could keep on an end table or in a kitchen drawer.

→ **Baseball bat.** A good old heavy bat can be handy to keep by the bedside.

→ **Bear spray.** It works like pepper spray, but it's stronger and sprays farther, meaning you can keep your distance from your attacker.

→ **Kubotan.** To step up your punching power, you can hold a kubotan or other keychain weapon, which can also have a sharp point that will make it even more effective. A kubotan will increase your fist density, allowing for a more powerful strike—and those blunt points will make for more destructive hammer strikes and body strikes.

HOW TO MAKE A FIST

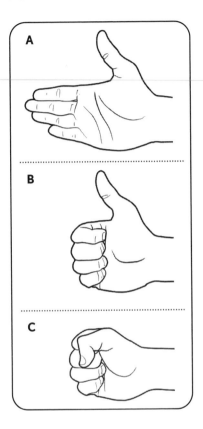

A

B

C

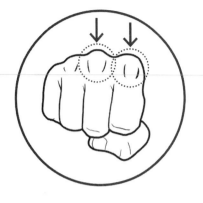

→ **Fists.** There is a right way and a wrong way to throw a punch, and your typical fist punch is out—you're just going to hurt yourself if you do that. Instead, try for a hammer punch: make a fist, keeping the thumb outside, but instead of hitting with the first two knuckles, hit down with your hand like you're striking with a hammer, pounding the pinkie side of your fist down into your attacker. Alternatively, go for a palm strike, hitting the heel of your palm into your attacker, keeping your hand tense and your thumb tucked.

HOT TIP

The Tactical Nightstand. Use your nightstand for more than just a place to charge your phone. It is the easiest place to reach in the middle of the night, and it should always be stocked with items you'll need in an emergency, including your car keys, a heavy flashlight, a first aid kit, and all of the items listed on these pages (except your fist, keep that with you).

BE YOUR OWN PROTECTOR

PALM STRIKE

HAMMER FIST

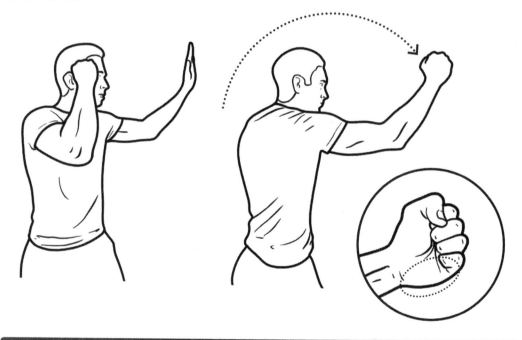

MAKING A KUBOTAN

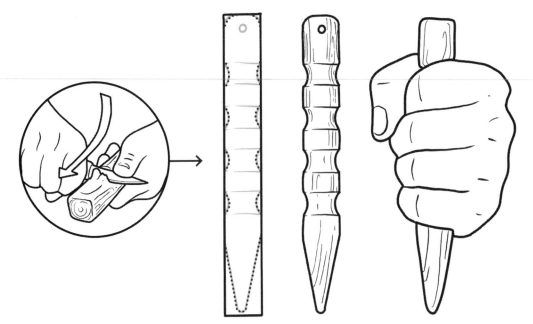

HOT TIP

Make Your Own Kubotan. Your basic kubotan is a sharp cylinder, and a stick of hard wood works great. You'll want to use something like boxwood, dogwood, walnut, oak, hickory, or ash—whatever grows nearby is great. Start with a piece that's a little larger than you want it to be. Ideally you want your finished kubotan to be 15 mm X 100 mm or thereabouts.

Use a simple pocketknife to whittle your stick down to those basic measurements. You can carve in some bulbs to make it easier to grip, and you can sharpen the pointy end a little, though kubotans are meant for serious bruising, not stabbing. When you're whittling, go slow and keep your knife sharp—that will help you avoid injury. Cut with the grain of the wood, and always push the blade away from you, not toward you.

Once you've got your kubotan in the shape you want it, take some sandpaper and sand it smooth. Bare wood will absorb moisture and get stained, so you may want to treat it with linseed oil and a layer or two of shellac to prolong the life of your kubotan.

BE YOUR OWN RTO

> ***"Nothing makes the earth seem so spacious as to have friends at a distance. They make the latitudes and longitudes."***
>
> **—Henry David Thoreau**

As tempting as it may be to turn off the world—believe me, I get it—it's not actually a good idea. Even the most hardcore of off-the-gridders needs to have some way to get information from the outside world, and even more importantly, to send information in case of an emergency. There is literally not a single situation in which you should cut yourself off entirely. In the military, we call the guy in charge of communication our RTO, or Radio Telephone Operator. On your homestead, that person has four main goals for communication:

1. Information. You have to be able to get the information you need. Does that mean you need an Instagram feed to see what all your friends are having for lunch? No. But you do need weather alerts, basic world and nation news, and a headsup about any disasters.

2. Person to person. You want to be able to talk to people. Homesteading can be isolating, and you want to keep those lines of communication open. You want to be able to talk to your friends, your neighbors, and of course the other people on your homestead.

3. Business. You're going to need to earn an income, and most people need some form of digital communication in order to work.

4. Emergency. Shit happens, and you want to be able to call for help.

Communication Plan

Your communication plan can be broken down into three parts. Part one is internal comms, or Near Recognition, meaning on property or within the homestead. It's your primary form of communication with the people you live with. In an apartment or a house in the suburbs, that can be just you shouting at them (which is mostly how I would communicate with my family). But if you've got fifty acres of field and forest, you've got to do better than that. This is where PACE (Primary, Alternate, Contingency, Emergency) planning comes in, so make sure everybody's got a cell phone and/or a handheld radio or walkie-talkie.

Part two is external comms, or Far Recognition, meaning communication outside the homestead. You may think this is primarily in case of emergency, but you'd be surprised. What if you need advice on dealing with your bees? What if you want to see if someone has a hog for sale? What if you want to breed your goats? Yes, you're self-reliant, but that doesn't mean you can't take advantage of what others have to offer, and/or give advice yourself. Thanks to the conveniences of the modern age, a cell phone can let you chat with someone in Australia. But if you're way off-grid, you'll want to have a Ham radio. And know this: the kinds of folks you'll want to talk to, for barter and information? They will absolutely have Ham radios, too. These are your people.

Part three is when you've got an emergency. For most people, that means calling 911. It's also a good idea to be able to contact your nearest neighbors, who are likely to get there a lot faster than an ambulance or a firetruck. But if you're out of range, you'll need another plan.

HOT TIP

Starlink

If you end up living in a rural area where high-speed internet options are limited or nonexistent, Starlink could be a great option. Starlink, which is engineered by Elon Musk's SpaceX, uses a string of low-orbit satellites to provide high-speed, low-latency internet across the globe. All you need is a clear view of the night sky for download speeds between 100 and 200 Mb/s, and you can be sure that Starlink's performance will only improve with time. It will cost a couple hundred dollars and a monthly fee, which would be manageable by most homesteaders that have a part-time job or working farm.

PACE

As with everything, we hope for the best but plan for the worst. That means we need to have various levels of communication, backup plans upon backup plans. What if the cell tower goes down? What if all electricity goes out, so your hard line is down, too? What will you do then?

Primary. This is your most routine and effective method of communication. For most of us, that's a cell phone. You may be thinking about ditching these entirely, which I get but don't actually recommend. Why ditch your most effective form of communication? You don't have to have all the apps, Facebook, and games and all that shit, but keep the phone. It's useful. That said, you may be out of cell range, in which case you may want to put in a hard line. If it's wired by the phone company, it won't go out when your electricity does. On the other hand, if you're way out and a hard line isn't an option, your primary communication is going to be a Ham radio shack. You may also want to look into Starlink, a satellite internet offering being developed by SpaceX. (See Hot Tip on opposite page for more information.)

Alternate. Unless you're way out, your alternate is probably a hard line, as I said above. If that's not available, a handheld radio or a satellite phone is your best bet.

Contingency. So let's say the electrical grid is down. In that case, suburban or city homesteaders can switch to sat phones; if you're farther out, you can make use of a Ham radio.

Emergency. PLB or SEND. If it all goes nuts, this is the backup to your backup. PLBs (Personal Locator Beacons) are registered with NOAA (National Oceanic and Atmospheric Administration), and when activated, they will send a distress signal via satellite relaying your GPS coordinates to local rescue teams. PLB batteries last for years, and there's no need to carry a charger. SEND (Satellite Emergency Notification Device) works much the same way, but has more flexibility. PLB is for emergencies only, while SEND, because it involves a subscription to a satellite (like Garmin or SPOT), allows communication with family members. For example, my friend's dad has a SEND device that he uses when he goes hiking for several days. He can use three preset messages, including "Ok," "Help," and "SOS," plus one custom message of up to 160 characters. If all is well, he just pushes the Ok button and my friend gets a message with his GPS coordinates updating him on his location. So you can see how SEND would be helpful even in nonemergency situations, as a way of keeping track of your loved ones.

Must-Haves

PACE is mostly for emergencies, but communication is an all-day, everyday activity, and something we need to make a priority, even when we're trying to isolate ourselves a bit from the "real world." These are the three absolutes for everyday communication:

Smartphone. Look, you may hate the idea of them, but let's face it, smartphones are pretty much the most handy device ever invented. They can capture incredible photos and videos, they're basically an encyclopedia, and they can summon help—and oh, yeah, it fits in your pocket. It can provide immediate answers to just about any question you might have (like what's that mysterious rash on your rabbits?), it'll help you monitor the weather in real time, and of course it'll keep track of you and the rest of your family. It is a must.

Shortwave radio, receive only. This is the easiest and most reliable way to get information when standard lines of communication go down. If there's a crisis, you'll know about it.

Walkie-talkies. You may not want to shell out for multiple cell phones for the whole family, and if you're far enough out that there's no mobile phone service—well, that's not a problem. Two-way person-to-person communication allows for up to 50 miles of distance as long as you can maintain line of sight—that is, as long as there are no mountains or other obstructions in the way. You can install them in your vehicles, carry them in your pocket, or both. Most are plug-and-play, and they're very affordable. You want to look for range, durability, privacy settings, and user-friendly programming.

Ham Radio

Taking information-gathering and communication a step further from receive-only shortwave, Ham radio (or amateur radio) allows you to communicate to anywhere, from anywhere, without needing either the internet or a cell tower. You can even talk with astronauts in space! You can use talk, text, send images, and even use Morse code. When everything went down with 9/11, the Amateur Radio Service was still up and running, and the same was true during Katrina and various other disasters.

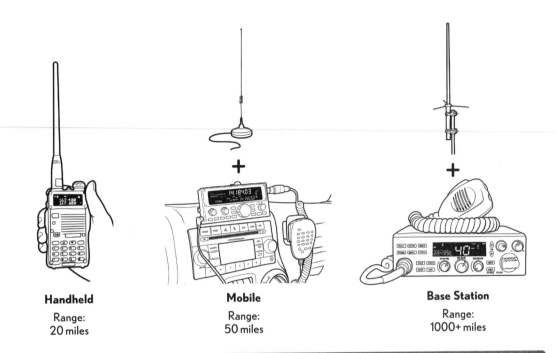

Handheld
Range:
20 miles

Mobile
Range:
50 miles

Base Station
Range:
1000+ miles

MANY (BUT NOT ALL) FREQUENTLY USED BANDS

34.90	Internal National Guard emergency frequency		**156.80**	International maritime distress
39.46	Interdepartmental communication of local and state police forces		**162.40**	NOAA weather broadcasts and bulletins
47.42	Red Cross emergency relief		**163.4875**	National Guard emergencies
52.525	Used by Ham radio operators in FM on their six-meter band. Can be filled with signals from hundreds or even thousands of miles away.		**163.5125**	Armed Forces national disaster preparedness
			164.50	Department of Housing and Urban Development
121.50	International Air Distress		**168.55**	Civilian agencies for federal government emergencies
138.225	FEMA emergency relief		**243.00**	Military aviation emergencies
146.52	Used by Ham radio operators for nonrepeater communications on the two-meter band, it is very busy in many parts of the country.		**259.70**	NASA or other space agency during launch and reentry
			311.00	US Air Force active in-flight
151.625	Traveling sports teams, circuses, and other itinerant businesses		**317.70**	US Coast Guard active in-flight
154.28	Interdepartmental communication by local fire departments		**340.20**	US Navy active in-flight
			409.20	Interstate Commerce Commission emergency
155.160	Used by state and local police forces during search and rescue operations		**409.625**	Department of State
156.75	International maritime and weather alerts		**462.675**	General Mobile Radio Service travel assistance

You do need a license to legally operate a Ham radio; the FCC wants to make sure they can rely upon the people using these airwaves to respond correctly in case of an emergency. There's a lot to learn, but once you dive in, it's both fun and incredibly useful. Ham radio has a strong signal range, allows you to listen to emergency broadcasts and communicate with emergency services as needed, is relatively low cost, and doesn't require an engineering degree to keep it in repair.

There are several different levels of Ham radio:

→ **Handheld.** This may look like a walkie-talkie, but it goes a lot farther, and communicates beyond just the guy on the other side. It uses a rechargeable battery and likely will allow access to the two most popular channels. It's not very flexible, and it doesn't have too much range, but it will get you the information you need and allow you to contact EMS.

→ **Mobile.** A mobile Ham radio can go in your glove box or on the dashboard of your truck, but you can also probably carry it in a backpack. It has a larger antenna and has about twice the range of a handheld, along with access to a wider range of channels.

→ **Base station.** If you're way off grid and Ham is likely to be your primary method of communication with the outside world, you'll want something less portable but more flexible. You can get on to bands that can reach thousands of miles away and that allow for plenty of experimentation.

If you're not sure which you'll need, consider the following: a handheld will basically function like a walkie-talkie, letting you talk one-on-one, taking turns, and with emergency services. Your range is also likely to be quite small—you'll see them advertising ranges like 36 miles, but that'll only work if you're on a mountaintop and the person you're talking to is also on a mountaintop. In a forested area, you'll be lucky to get a range past a couple of miles, which just isn't that far.

Radio range is a function of three things: power, height, and frequency. A general technician license won't give you access to the frequencies that go the farthest. If you're in a suburb, that's probably not a big deal. But if you're way out in the sticks, you'll need some juice, and the license to go with it.

HOT TIP

Military Comms Lingo
Whiskey Tango Foxtrot: What the fuck?
Lima Charlie: Loud and clear.
FUBAR: Fucked up beyond all recognition.
Pop Smoke: Get the fuck out of there.
Zero Dark Thirty: Up before the chickens.
Watch your 6: Watch your back.
Bravo Zulu: Good job!

Zero-Tech PACE Plan

You remember that movie *A Quiet Place?* They couldn't talk yet communication was of the utmost importance. And they had what we in the field would call Far Recognition and Near Recognition—we always need both. Remember the fires that all the families had on top of their towers at night? Those fires let everyone know that they were all out there, and that they'd survived another night. That's Far Recognition. The Christmas lights served as Near Recognition—they were white if everything was copacetic, and red if there was danger.

The good news is we can get a little more detail since we're actually allowed to talk out loud without fear of monsters killing us (but hey, you never know . . .). In the movie it's monsters, but in the real world, it could be a home invasion. Say you're out hunting and you come back and you see that there's something placed in your window, like a designated vase, something only you would know is out of place. This is a secret way of communicating to you that something is wrong. It lets you know how to adjust your approach and consider whether you need to go into rescue mode.

This kind of low-tech communication isn't just about potential violence, of course. It could be as simple as a colored flag hung up to let you know you've got a visitor dropping by, or a ringing cowbell to let you know lunch is ready.

In case of emergency, you need to plan for the worst. If the cell lines go down, the phone lines go down, *and* all electricity goes down, you won't be able to work a sat phone or a Ham radio for long, either. Say NOAA is overwhelmed with a climate catastrophe, and no one is going to be able to respond to your PLB. All your tech is offline. What can you do?

The following are last-resort emergency communication options when all other communications have failed.

BE SEEN

The best method of visual communication is with light. Shoot a flare straight up and make sure it's not going to hit a tree branch or overhanging rock—you want it to be free to go as far as possible. If you have roadside flares, place them a hundred meters apart in a triangle—this is the international distress signal.

If flares aren't available, you can light three distinctly different fires in the same triangle formation. You can also light trees on fire, which will serve as a really big torch—but comes with severe risk of wildfire, so don't do so unless you absolutely have to. But both of those only really work at night. During the day, you need to work with smoke. If you're in the winter or on wide-open terrain, black smoke is the most visible, so burn items made of rubber. But if you're surrounded by green cover or other dark colors, a lighter smoke will be

1. FLARES

2. FIRE

3. MIRRORS

more visible, in which case you should burn dry wood.

If it's a sunny day, you can also work with mirrors or other shiny objects to direct light at any potential help, perhaps an aircraft flying overhead. You can also use a flashlight or a strobe, shining it in the direction of potential help, or setting it to reflect off of other objects in the area. If you have large, brightly colored objects, such as aircraft panels, you can arrange them in a field in a large geometric pattern.

HOT TIP

Be Heard. Stick with the rule of three: if you have a firearm, fire three shots with five seconds in between, which will allow any listeners to identify your direction. Do the same with a whistle or an airhorn, which has the added advantage of not wasting ammo, and both are lightweight and easy to carry if you're venturing off in the woods around your homestead.

X3

Finding Your Way

Part of being in tune with nature means being able to understand what it has to tell you. The world around us offers nature signs that can tell us how to predict the weather, how to tell time, how to find water, and how to get ourselves unlost.

GETTING UNLOST

→ Which way is north? This one is pretty easy, as you can usually tell from the direction of the sun which way is east or west, and then roughly work out

north from there. It won't be as precise as a compass, but you'll get the general direction. To get more precise, find a stick that's around a foot tall and place it in the ground so it's standing straight up. Where is its shadow? Place a rock at the end of the shadow, and wait about 15 minutes. Put another stone at the end of the shadow (it will have moved). Stand at the stick, and place your left foot at the first rock, and your right foot at the second. You are now facing north.

BE YOUR OWN RTO

FINDING NORTH (DAY)

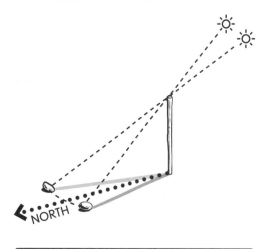

FINDING NORTH (NIGHT)

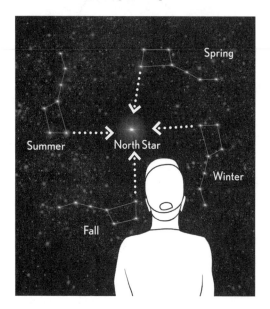

READING CLOUDS

→ At night, of course, it's a little more complicated. If you can see the stars, start by looking for the Big Dipper. Find the two stars at the outer edge of the Dipper's bowl—these two will point to the North Star. If you can't find the Big Dipper, try fixing your gaze on a single star, using a tree or branch to help fix a location. After a few minutes, the star will have moved. If it has moved up, you are facing east. If it has moved down, you are facing west. If it has moved right, you are facing south, and if it has moved left, you are facing north.

→ If it's cloudy and you can't see anything at all, use these nature signs: in the forest, moss will tend to grow on the northern sides of trees, avoiding the sun. In the desert, giant barrel cacti lean toward the south. And on the prairie, the leaves of the pilot weed always grow in a line pointing north-south.

HOW TO TELL TIME

➜ At its most basic, we need to know if it's morning or afternoon. If the sun is rising, it's morning, and if it's going down, it's afternoon. But you can get way more specific than that. Find a spot where you can see the horizon, and extend your arm so that the edge of your hand, pinkie-finger down, lines up with the horizon. Four finger-widths equals one hour. So if you've determined that the sun is going down, use your hands, laying them one over the other, to count the remaining hours in the day. Eight finger-widths equals two hours, and so forth.

HOW TO FIND WATER

➜ Start by listening. Do you hear running water? Then look for animal tracks—animals always have to get to water, and they can lead you there. Keep an eye on birds overhead, as they are also excellent guides. And as you're watching, head downhill. Water obeys gravity, and searching gullies and valleys will help you find it.

HOW TO PREDICT THE WEATHER

➜ Barometric pressure is something we can all feel. If the air feels heavy and you're tired, there's likely a storm front on the way. On the other hand, if you feel light and energetic, the day will probably remain clear. If you're unsure whether your sluggishness is due to a poor night's sleep, watch the ants—if they move slowly, then the barometric pressure is dropping. Spiders will abandon their webs in anticipation of bad weather, and swallows or martins will fly lower to the ground. On the other hand, if the locusts are singing, you're likely to have a few days of good weather.

➜ Watch the plants. Clover will close up when rain is coming, while deciduous trees will flip their leaves over when heavy rains are about to fall. If there's dew or fog in the morning, the rest of the day will likely be dry.

➜ Watch the sky. A halo around the moon signals a coming warm front and likely some rainfall. The expression "Red sky in the morning, sailors take warning. Red sky at night, sailors delight" can work for you, too—a bright red dawn will often mean clear weather has passed, with poor weather on the way. But a bright red sunset means that the clear weather has yet to arrive.

➜ Watch the wind. Winds coming from the east and northeast are often storm winds, while south winds are warmer, with a gentler rain. The best winds, weather-wise, come from the west and northwest—cool, crisp, and dry.

"Insist on yourself; never imitate. Your own gift you can present every moment with the cumulative force of a whole life's cultivation; but of the adopted talent of another, you have only an extemporaneous, half possession."

—Ralph Waldo Emerson

In this chapter, we're going to talk about what to do when things go wrong. When you're setting up your homestead, obviously you're going to do your best to anticipate all eventualities and create a safe haven for yourself, but accidents will happen. As with everything, it's best to be prepared and capable of handling those situations when they inevitably arise.

The beauty of emergency medicine is that it's the same regardless of your environment. If you follow the practices of EMT Basic, those skills will give you the foundation you need, no matter where you are. The human body is the same whether it's on the floor of the kitchen or down in a ravine, and the methods you use to assess and treat it are the same, too. Depending on how rural you are, you may need to improvise certain technology and equipment, but I'll give you some tips on how to improvise when necessary. And even if you've got a hospital right down the road, you want to be able to help yourself and others in the time before the ambulance arrives.

First things first: call that ambulance. Self-reliant doesn't mean being stupid. If someone is badly hurt, get them to the hospital. Period.

That said, if 911 is delayed or unavailable, here's how to prepare for an emergency medical situation.

Prep

Have a plan for what to do in case of an emergency. At a minimum, your medical plan should be a 9-Line, which is a standard military medevac request. We've already talked about the importance of having working comms, and a medical emergency is absolutely one of those situations where comms are essential.

→ **Line 1:** Location of pickup site. If you're in an urban or suburban environment, that'll just be your address. But if you're way off-grid, you'll need to scout a location where an ambulance or helicopter can meet you, and get those coordinates.

→ **Line 2:** Contact information. This could be your phone number, or it could be your radio frequency.

→ **Line 3:** Number of patients by preference. You may find yourself in a situation where multiple people are hurt. In that case, you'll need to assess and rank them in order of need: A. Urgent, B. Urgent Surgical, C. Priority, D. Routine, E. Convenience.

→ **Line 4:** Special equipment. Be able to let responders know what they'll need to bring with them, whether that's a ventilator, extraction equipment, or anything else they might not necessarily have on hand.

→ **Line 5:** Number of patients by mobility. Who can walk? Who will need a stretcher?

→ **Line 6:** Security at pickup site. In the military, this mostly applies to combat situations—are there enemy combatants in the area?—but it can also refer to the surroundings. In case of a fire or a cave-in, what is the scene like? What do responders need to know before they get there?

→ **Line 7:** Method of marking the pickup site. If you're sending responders to a pickup site that isn't marked by an address or anything else obvious, how are you going to let them know where you are? Will there be flares or something else?

→ **Line 8:** Allergies of everyone in the family and their blood types.

→ **Line 9:** Terrain. What's the ground like at pickup? Can a helicopter land? Can an ambulance drive, or will the responders need to send something with four-wheel drive?

Fill out as much as you can of your 9-Line in advance and put it up by your refrigerator, next to your phone or radio, in your backpack, and in every location you have, including your barn, your shed, your greenhouse, and so forth. That way, it'll be accessible and easily read and understood even in the most stressful of situations.

In times when you can't call for help, or when you know that a one-way trip will be faster than an ambulance going back and forth, know your own routes. Where is the closest medical facility/trauma center? What is the fastest way to get there? Map it, and then drive it so you're familiar with it. This isn't a time when you want to get lost or have to rely on Waze.

GEAR

You'll need two types of medical kits: one larger kit to be stored on-site, whether that's in your home, barn, or workshop—ideally all of the above; and one for each member of the household, an individualized personal medical kit that they take with them whenever they leave any of the above locations. It should be tailored to the specific person, so that if you have someone with asthma, it includes an inhaler, or if they are diabetic, it includes a glucagon autoinjector.

You will need to figure out the needs of everyone in your household, but the basics of each individual kit should include the following:

→ EpiPen. You never know what you may turn out to be allergic to.

→ 2 tourniquets (I recommend Black CAT7 TQ and SAM XT TQ OR)

→ 2 pairs large nitrile gloves

→ 1 BurnTec dressing set, 5″ by 5″

→ 2 sets Emergency Trauma Dressing— 6″ Flat

→ 2 vented chest seals (I recommend a two-pack of Hyfins)

→ 2 triangle bandages

→ 1 roll of surgical tape

→ 20 flexible fabric bandages

→ 2 tubes of antibiotic ointment

→ 20 antiseptic towelettes

→ 2 nasophryngeal airway kits

→ 1 roll of combat gauze with hemostatic bandage

→ 2 packs NAR Wound-Packing Gauze

→ 1 polycarbonate eye shield

→ Trauma shears

→ Splinter forceps

→ Emergency survival blanket

→ Permanent marker

→ Pocket penlight with working batteries

→ Luminous ID Patch

→ One roll of 2-inch duct tape

Your more robust, on-location kit should include all of the above as well as these items:

→ Sterile sodium chloride irrigation

BE YOUR OWN FIRST RESPONDER

- Tissue adhesive
- Steri-Strips (small)
- Steri-Strips (large)
- Benzoin swabs for applying Steri Strips
- Sting-eze wipes
- Benzalkonium chloride antiseptic wipes
- Triple antibiotic ointment
- 5x9 abd pads
- 4x4 gauze pads
- 3x4 non-adherent dressing
- 3x9 petrolatum gauze
- Triangle bandages
- Antiseptic spray
- Disposable razor
- QuikClot hemostatic gauze
- NAR 4-inch emergency trauma dressing
- NAR Hyfin vent chest seals
- Nasopharyngeal airway tubes 28fr
- Oval eye pads
- Surgical tape
- Eye wash
- Nitrile gloves
- Surgical face mask
- Trauma shears
- Lidocaine burn gel packets
- Oral glucose gel
- Electrolyte powder packets

- 1 bottle acetaminophen
- 1 bottle aspirin
- 1 bottle ibuprofen
- 1 box bisacodyl laxative
- 1 box cetirizine antihistamine medication
- 1 tube clotrimazole antifungal cream
- 1 bottle diphenhydramine anti-allergy medication
- 1 bottle guaifenesin cough medicine
- 1 tube hydrocortisone cream
- 1 box anti-diarrheal medication
- ACE wrap
- Athletic tape
- Cold packs
- HotHands handwarmers
- SAM Splint (18 inches)
- SAM Splint (36 inches)
- Duct tape
- EMS bag with shoulder strap
- First-aid guide
- SAM splint guide

MEDICINE FROM THE EARTH

One of the best things about the Rugged Life is the ability to work with what you have. Your homestead is teeming with all-natural remedies you can just pluck out of the ground, and you'll find some of them right in your backyard. Depending on where you live, you'll likely have regionally

MEDICINAL PLANTS

Yarrow

Burdock

Dandelion

Stinging Nettle

Blackberry

Plantain

Willow

Echinacea

specific medicinal plants growing in your area, so do some of your own research, but here are the eight most common (and most useful) medicinal plants in North America:

Dandelion. All parts of this "weed" can be eaten; the leaves can be added to a salad or made into a pesto. Dandelion root is also known as chicory and is a tasty coffee replacement. Dandelion helps with digestion, helping the body absorb nutrients and supporting the liver.

Plantain. You'll recognize this as the plant you're always trying to get out of your yard. When crushed, the leaves can provide relief for sunburns, stings, and bug bites, reducing both itching and inflammation.

Stinging nettle. Although this is among poisonous plants, it's also very helpful. Handle the leaves carefully, but if you make them into a tea, they can treat anemia, menstrual pain, and pollen allergies.

Burdock. The leaves and roots can be eaten and will help with digestion; they also can be made into a salve that will treat dry skin and eczema.

Yarrow. All parts of this plant can be used, and if it is made into a tea, it may bring down a high fever. It can also lower blood pressure, works as an anti-inflammatory, and can help stop diarrhea.

Blackberry. The berries are delicious, but the leaves and roots can be used to calm a sore throat or canker sores.

Willow. The same active ingredient that is found in aspirin—salicin—is in willow bark. Use it in a tea to calm a headache, relieve menstrual pain, reduce a fever, or reduce inflammation.

Echinacea. The flowers, leaves, roots, and seeds of this lovely plant boost the immune system, helping to fight both viral and bacterial infections.

Remember that it's always possible to have an unexpected side effect when consuming any plant; some people are allergic to even gentle herbs like peppermint or chamomile. See pages 86–88 for more information on foraging for wild plants and testing them for adverse reactions.

What to Do: The Modern Homesteader

It doesn't make you any less rugged to rely on 911. The intent behind a medical plan is that you'll never have to wonder when to call for help, and you know exactly what to do. That said, we're planning for worst-case scenarios, so here's a brief overview of what you can do if, for whatever reason, 911 is not available.

STEP 1: Always ensure the scene is safe before approaching the injured. If you get injured, too, you won't be able to help them. Although your instincts will tell you to run up to them immediately, you have to stop long enough to see what the situation is. Assess by using as many of your senses as you can; look, listen, and smell. Did this injury happen because of an animal attack? An electrocution? A fire? A fall? You're going to experience tunnel vision, seeing only that someone is hurting. Force yourself to look around and pay attention.

Step 2: Once you've determined that the scene is safe and you are safe, you can approach. If someone else is with you—someone who also is uninjured—have them call for help, or if you're out of range of a cell phone or radio, send them running. Then begin your primary assessment by beginning your MARCH algorithm:

Massive hemorrhage: If you notice massive bleeding, stop blood loss by applying direct pressure, using a tourniquet, pressure bandages, or by packing the wound.

Airway: Ensure the airway is clear by placing your ear next to their mouth and looking at their chest. You are listening for breaths, and seeing if the chest rises and falls. Check for obstructions in the airway by tilting the jaw and looking down the throat. Perform the Heimlich maneuver if necessary.

Respirations: If the airway is clear but the person is not breathing, check for any other causes. Are there any punctures to the torso?

Circulation: Perform a full-body sweep with your hands, checking for any bleeding. Check the pulse by placing your fingers on the carotid artery. If the pulse is weak, elevate the chest 12 inches. If there's no pulse and no breathing, begin CPR.

Hypothermia: In cases of extreme cold, prevent loss of body heat by using heat reflective or dry blankets, moving the person off the cold ground and out of any wet clothing.

STEP 3: Once the injured person is stable, it's time to think about transport. If they can't move on their own, you'll need to make a stretcher. You can grab a board out of the barn or quickly put

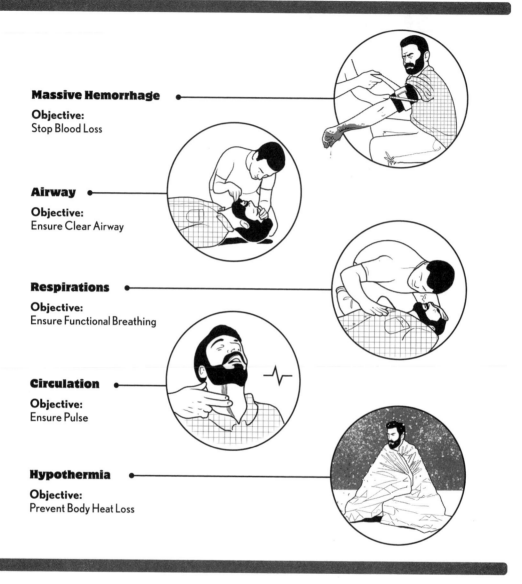

Massive Hemorrhage

Objective:
Stop Blood Loss

Airway

Objective:
Ensure Clear Airway

Respirations

Objective:
Ensure Functional Breathing

Circulation

Objective:
Ensure Pulse

Hypothermia

Objective:
Prevent Body Heat Loss

something together. Get them to where they need to go, whether that's your car, your house, or your designated pickup location.

STEP 4: Once you're there, it's time to keep them stable—or even improve their condition, if you can—while you wait for help. The rest of this chapter will fill in as many of those blanks as possible,

listing out the most common potential injuries or dangers and offering a loose plan for how to handle each of them. That said, you're going to have more knowledge of what potential pitfalls may await you—it's your homestead, after all, and you know it best. Scan through this list, and if I've left something out, add it to your own list and do your own research on how to address it.

SEASONAL INJURIES

Hypothermia. Hypothermia is defined as a dangerously low body temperature; our bodies fluctuate, of course, but anything below 95°F is considered hypothermic. If you don't have a thermometer with you, you can easily guess whether the person is hypothermic; as ever, it is always best to operate on the assumption that they are rather than risk not treating them. Signs and symptoms of hypothermia include

→ Shivering

→ Slurred speech or mumbling

→ Slow, shallow breathing

→ Weak pulse

→ Lack of coordination

→ Lack of energy, sleepiness

→ Mental confusion

→ Loss of consciousness

It's likely that the person won't be aware that they have hypothermia, as it sets in very gradually. Someone with severe hypothermia will often become disoriented and put themselves in even more danger. Always approach a hypothermic person gently and calmly. Limit their movements as much as possible, and resist the temptation to massage or rub them to boost their circulation as this could trigger cardiac arrest. Get them indoors if you can, but if that isn't possible, shield them from the cold as much as possible, keeping them in a horizontal position. Remove any wet clothing, cutting it away to reduce unnecessary movement, then cover them with blankets or coats, including the head, though make sure they can breathe. Use warm compresses to bring up their body temperature, but apply them only to the neck, chest, and groin area; do not warm the arms and legs, as this can actually cause the core temperature to drop. Do not use direct heat, but instead work slowly so you don't cause their heart to race and induce additional stress. Monitor their breathing and be prepared to perform CPR. If the person has improved enough to sit up and move a little, provide warm, sweet, nonalcoholic, noncaffeinated beverages to warm them from the inside out.

Frostbite. Frostbite occurs when the skin becomes overly cold and exposed. It happens most often on the extremities, including fingers, toes, ears, cheeks, and chin. It's an advanced form of frostnip, and can cause permanent damage. Frostnip can be treated simply by going indoors, but frostbite requires more intentional rewarming. Place the affected area in a warm (not hot) water bath for 15 to 30 minutes. The skin may turn soft and turn red or purple. Encourage the person to gently move, even if it causes pain. If you have ibuprofen or acetaminophen on hand, that will help. Once the skin thaws, loosely wrap the affected area with sterile bandages, keep it elevated, and get to a hospital as soon as possible.

Heatstroke. On the other end of the temperature spectrum is heatstroke, which happens when the body overheats due to prolonged exposure to high temperatures, often during physical exertion. Symptoms include flushed skin, rapid, shallow breathing, a racing heart, headache, and mental confusion. At worst, heatstroke can cause seizures or induce a coma. If you diagnose someone with heatstroke, get them to a hospital immediately. While you're waiting, work to bring down their temperature by getting them out of the sun; removing excess clothing; and cooling them with a garden hose, a cool shower or bath, ice packs, or cold, wet towels placed at the person's head, neck, armpits, and groin.

Severe sunburn. First off, wear sunscreen. It's the most basic protection you can give yourself, particularly if you're working out in the sun all day. A painful sunburn can slow you down, and skin cancer is no joke. But if you do get a sunburn, most of the time it'll heal on its own with aloe and a cool bath with some baking soda. But more severe sunburns can cause blistering and severe swelling. When that happens, drink lots of water to prevent dehydration and resist the urge to break the blisters. If they burst on their own, clean them with mild soap and water, apply an antibiotic ointment, and cover with gauze. It'll take several days for your skin to heal, and it will be very sensitive to the sun for a while. Treat your skin gently, and feel free to use pain relievers as necessary.

ALLERGIC REACTIONS

If you know you have an allergy, take precautions. Even if you don't, you may encounter a new allergen or develop a new reaction, so it's always best to be prepared. Carry Benadryl or another antihistamine to treat allergic reactions, as well as an EpiPen, even if you've never had an anaphylactic-level reaction, for some allergies get worse with exposure, rather than better. If someone does go into anaphylactic shock, get help immediately, even if you're able

to administer epinephrine. Loosen their clothing and cover them with a blanket. Don't give them anything to drink, and lay them on their side to prevent choking if they should vomit. If they stop breathing, begin CPR. And don't decide to become a beekeeper if you have a deathly allergy to bee venom.

TRAUMATIC INJURIES

Sprain. A sprain is a stretching or tearing of the ligaments around a joint, usually around the ankles or wrists. It hurts, but not nearly as much as a broken bone. There will be swelling and bruising as well as limited movement, and the person may have heard or felt a "pop." Immediate care involves R.I.C.E.:

→ **Rest:** For the first day or two, stay off the injury. Avoid any activities that cause pain, swelling, or discomfort. Give your body time to heal.

→ **Ice:** Immediately ice the area to reduce swelling. Apply an ice pack for 15 to 20 minutes, and then repeat every two or three hours (except when you're sleeping) for two to three days after the injury.

→ **Compression:** Wrapping an elastic bandage around the injury will also help reduce swelling. Don't wrap so tightly that you cut off circulation, and begin your wrap at the area farthest from the heart. If the wrap causes increased pain or if the area becomes numb, loosen or remove it.

→ **Elevation:** Keeping the injured area above your heart will allow gravity to assist in reducing swelling. Try to do this while you are sleeping for the first few nights after the injury.

Take pain medication such as ibuprofen or acetaminophen as necessary, and begin to gently move the injured part after the first few days. It can take weeks or months to fully recover from a sprain, so be patient, but with careful use it will improve. If you suspect a torn ligament, seek medical attention.

Concussion. A concussion can be difficult to diagnose, considering we bang our heads all the time, and oftentimes the symptoms don't show themselves for days after the initial injury. If there's a loss of consciousness, mental confusion, dizziness, nausea, weakness in the extremities, dilation of one or both pupils, or clear fluids draining from the nose and ears, assume that this is a severe concussion and seek medical help immediately. While you wait, keep their neck immobilized and be ready to perform CPR if necessary.

If none of those symptoms are in evidence, apply ice packs to reduce swelling and internal bleeding and make sure the injured person gets plenty of rest and avoids screen time before going to bed—but watch them closely over the next few days, and if they experience a persistent headache, excessive fatigue, unusual behavior, or slurred speech, assume that the condition is worse than you thought and get them to a hospital.

Massive hemorrhage. Sweep the body front and back and look at your hands. Are they bloody? Is there a pool of blood anywhere? If so, you have a hemorrhage.

Locate the source of the bleeding and then place a tourniquet as far up the limb as you can. Go high or die.

Tourniquets were once considered a last resort, as it was believed they led to amputation—but that's not true anymore. After years of treating combat injuries, tourniquets have been proven to be the best first option. They can be left in place in combat for days without any injury to the limb and with zero amputation required.

"Go high or die" means that regardless of the location of the bleeder, you want to go as high on the limb as possible and tighten the tourniquet, cranking it down until the bleeding stops.

Unless the wound is actually gushing and you're concerned the injured person is going to bleed out, take a moment to wash your hands or douse them with hand sanitizer. Yes, you want to move quickly, but you also want to ensure that you don't introduce an infection, which in the case of most wounds is the true danger. Once your hands are clean, apply gentle pressure to the wound with a clean bandage or cloth, and keep the wound elevated until the bleeding stops.

Once the bleeding has stopped, run tap water over the wound for a few minutes to reduce the risk of infection. If you see dirt or debris in the wound after running tap water, use sterilized tweezers to remove it. Wash the area around the wound with soap, but don't let soap get in there. Avoid hydrogen peroxide or iodine, which just cause unnecessary pain and irritation. Finally, apply a thin layer of antibiotic ointment—this will not only reduce risk of infection but also keep the surface moist and help prevent scarring.

Cover the wound with a bandage or gauze, and change the dressing at least once a day, more often if it gets wet or dirty.

If the wound is deep or dirty, get a tetanus shot if you haven't had one in the past five years. If you see signs of infection, such as redness, increasing pain, pus, warmth, or swelling, go to a doctor.

Abradement. If you do get a severe infection and antibiotics don't work, either because they aren't strong enough, you haven't hit the right one, or you're simply dealing with a MRSA (Methicillin-resistant *Staphylococcus aureus*) bacteria that doesn't care how much you throw at it, then there is still a way to fight the infection. It's just not very much fun. Abradement is the best way of defeating a stubborn infection, but it's incredibly painful.

Lance open the wound and squeeze it, getting all of the pus and nastiness out of there until it bleeds clean, then scrub it vigorously. If there's necrotic tissue underneath, scrub even harder to get rid of that dead tissue. If you don't, the infection will only get worse. Infections from brown recluse spider bites are likely to require this kind of treatment.

Bone fracture. If someone has fallen and you suspect a broken bone, operate on the assumption that it *is* broken. Move the person as little as possible to avoid causing them further pain. If there is any bleeding, apply pressure with a sterile bandage or clean cloth. If it's a compound fracture (i.e., if you can see a bone sticking out), don't try to stick it back in. Likewise, don't try to realign any broken bones—leave that to an orthopedic surgeon. Do try to immobilize the injury by applying a splint above and below, adding padding to reduce discomfort. Apply ice packs to reduce swelling. If the person goes into shock, have them lie down with their head lower than their heart and their legs elevated.

Since they are so common, it's a really good idea to know how to splint a broken bone. A splint will reduce pain and immobilize the injured limb, hopefully preventing the jagged edge of bone from shredding muscle tissue or blood vessels.

Do not put pressure on the break. Instead, carefully tape the length of the limb to a rigid, stabilizing object like a stick, a folded-up newspaper, a hiking pole, or anything else you can find. Keep the limb straight and splint the bone above and below the joints—for example, for a broken shin, you want to extend the splint from the ankle and over past the knee. Once you've splinted the limb straight, immobilize it even further by taping it to the body—arms wrapped around the torso, and legs wrapped together. For hip fractures, tape the legs together at the thighs, and for broken ribs, gently tape the arm on the injured side to the body, and be extremely careful to avoid movement, as a broken rib can puncture a lung.

Amputations. No one wants to have to do this. No matter how far off-grid you are, get yourself to a hospital long before this becomes necessary. But if that's impossible, then you have to ask yourself, if the choice is life over limb, what do you choose? If you have to get rid of that limb, do it and know how to do it right.

Burns. As I'm sure you know, there are three levels of burns:

→ **First degree.** This causes redness and pain, but affects only the outer layer of skin.

→ **Second degree.** This goes down to the second layer of skin and may cause swelling and red, white, or splotchy skin. Blisters may develop and pain can be severe. May cause scarring.

→ **Third degree.** This goes all the way to the fat layer beneath the skin, and the

burn appears black, brown, or white. This kind of burn can destroy nerve endings, causing numbness.

To treat a first-degree burn, run cool water over it for several minutes. If there is still discomfort, apply a cool, wet cloth until the pain eases. Do not use ice. Keep it clean, and it should heal on its own. Put some lotion or aloe vera gel on it to speed the healing process.

For a second-degree burn, immediately run cool water. Don't break any blisters that appear, but if they break on their own, clean the area with water and apply antibiotic ointment. Bandage the burn loosely with sterile gauze and take pain reliever as necessary.

For a third-degree burn, run cool water while seeking emergency medical attention. Administer pain reliever and make sure the person drinks plenty of fluids.

Poison. Even if you only suspect the person has been poisoned, call Poison Control at (800) 222-1222. Symptoms can include vomiting, stomach pains, confusion, difficulty breathing, heart palpitations, or loss of consciousness. If the person is conscious, try to get them to spit out anything that may be remaining in their mouth. If a harmful substance was splashed onto their skin or clothes, remove the clothing and wash the affected area, being careful not to get anything on yourself. If the eyes are affected, flush them with lukewarm water. If you believe the substance was inhaled, first check to make sure you aren't in any danger, then get them to fresh air. Don't try to make them vomit, but if they do vomit, wipe it away from their mouth and keep their head

BURNS

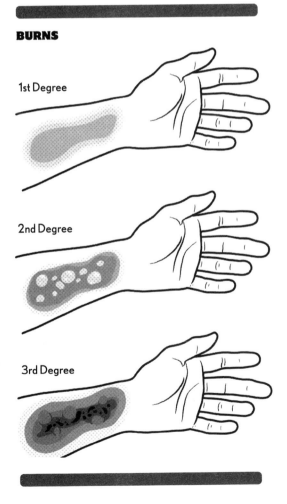

1st Degree

2nd Degree

3rd Degree

pointing down to prevent them from choking. Don't give them anything to eat or drink. While you're waiting for medical help, place them in the recovery position—have them lie their side (it doesn't matter which side) and extend their bottom arm out, palm facing up. Bend their top arm so that they can rest their cheek on the back of their hand.

Be prepared to begin CPR.

When EMTs arrive, or when you get to the hospital, do your best to have the following information ready:

What substance was taken

How long ago

If it was an accident

How was it taken (swallowed, inhaled, contact)

How much was taken

The person's age and weight

Any existing medical conditions

Any medications they are currently taking

GENERAL ILLNESS

Sometimes we just get sick. We can catch a cold, or a virus, or even the flu. It's not fun, but it happens. When it does, there isn't much you can do except wait it out. Drink plenty of liquids, including water, juice, and soup to prevent dehydration. Rest as much as you need to, whether that's napping, sleeping for longer at night, or simply taking it easy for a while. Give your body a chance to recuperate. If you're in pain because of body aches, or if your fever has spiked, take a pain reliever/fever reducer like acetaminophen or ibuprofen, but resist the urge to take medicines such as DayQuil that simply suppress your symptoms and may actually prolong the illness. If you're having trouble sleeping, a cough suppressant or a sleep aid may help. As always, if you get really sick (i.e., if your fever won't go down, or if your illness lasts more than a week), consult your doctor.

HOT TIP

Practice your plan. Know how to do everything, including practicing giving your 9-Line. Treat it like a drill, something you do over and over again so you know you'll get it right when it matters. Trust me, you don't want your first time suturing to be on a person.

Evil Insects, Animals, and Plants,

Spiders. Although most bug bites are annoying but essentially harmless, certain spider bites can be dangerous, even life-threatening. Brown recluse and black widow spiders are the ones to be concerned about in North America. A black widow spider bite can cause severe abdominal cramping, along with pain, swelling, and chills. Brown recluse spider bites feel like a sharp pain, like a beesting, and the pain increases over time. The skin turns brown or purple or becomes an open sore, and with severe bites, the surrounding skin may die within a few hours.

Clean the bite with mild soap and water, then apply an antibiotic ointment. Reduce pain and swelling by applying a cool, damp cloth, and elevating the affected area. Take pain medication as necessary and watch for signs of infection.

Ticks. Most tick bites are harmless, but we do always need to worry about Lyme disease and Rocky Mountain spotted fever. If the tick has latched on, remove it immediately, but be careful not to break it. Use sterile tweezers to grab the tick as close to the skin as possible, and pull it out using a slow and steady upward motion. Don't use a match, petroleum jelly, fingernail polish, or any other suggested home remedies that are likely to cause more harm than good. Seal the tick in a container and keep it in the freezer in

POISONOUS SPIDERS (Common to North America)

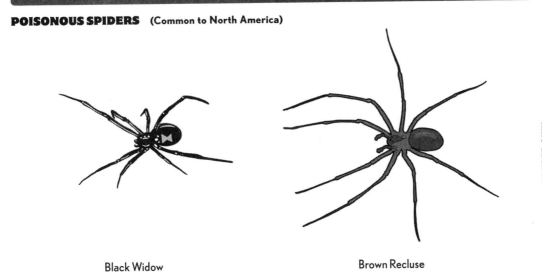

Black Widow

Brown Recluse

BE YOUR OWN FIRST RESPONDER

227

case you begin to show symptoms—your doctor will want to test it. Wash the bite site with soap and water. Watch the bite site for the next 3 to 14 days. If a rash appears, or if the bite begins to look like a bull's-eye, go to the doctor.

Snakes. Only 20 percent of snakes in North America are venomous, so most of the time a snakebite won't cause you serious harm. But if you aren't sure whether or not the snake was venomous, assume that it was and act accordingly. Get away from the snake—don't try to capture it or anything, but try to remember what it looks like. Remain as still and calm as possible—increased heart rate will speed the spread

of the venom. Avoid caffeine or alcohol for the same reason. Remove any jewelry or tight clothing in case of swelling, and try to keep the bitten area elevated. Clean the wound with soap and water and cover it with a sterile bandage. Don't use a tourniquet or ice, and obviously don't try to suck out the venom.

If the snake was venomous, the bite will likely cause severe, burning pain within 15 or 30 minutes, progressing to swelling and bruising around the wound. Other symptoms include nausea, labored breathing, a strange taste in the mouth, and weakness. If any of this is present, seek medical attention.

DEER TICK

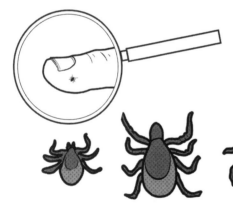

Larva   Nymph   Adult Male   Adult Female

POISONOUS SNAKES (Common to North America)

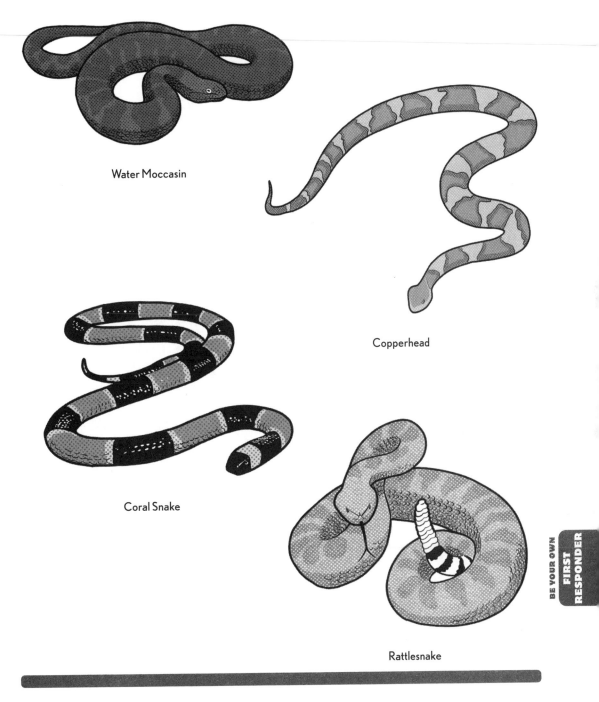

Water Moccasin

Copperhead

Coral Snake

Rattlesnake

Wild Parsnip

Giant Hogweed

Stinging Nettle

Poison Sumac

Poison Ivy

Poison Oak

Animal bites. You can basically treat an animal bite the same way you would any other wound. Watch out for infection, as always, but in this case you have the additional concern of rabies. *Old Yeller* aside, the animal you are most likely to get rabies from is a bat. If you get one caught in your attic, give it a wide berth. If you do come in contact with a bat, assume you've been exposed, even if you weren't aware of being bitten. You'll also want to steer clear of coyotes, foxes, raccoons, and skunks. Rabies appears to be the flu at first, but if you get it and it isn't treated, it *always* results in death. If you've been exposed to an animal you suspect may have rabies, see a doctor.

Poisonous plants. While I'm certain you know better than to eat a plant you don't recognize, there are some plants that can harm you even if all you do is brush up against them. The plants listed on the opposite page are the ones you'll most want to avoid.

Luckily, it's usually not that big a deal. You can treat poison ivy, poison oak, and poison sumac the same way: give the blisters a good scrubbing with Tecnu or Fels-Naptha laundry soap. They'll itch and drive you crazy, but that's about it. Don't scratch, though, or they may become infected. That said, if you've accidentally inhaled some smoke from burning one of these plants, you may have trouble breathing. Get to fresh air right away, and use an inhaler if necessary.

Stinging nettle hurts. Spit on it and see if your saliva eases the pain; when you get back home, try some baking soda with water. The rash should ease up in less than a day.

Wild parsnip often feels most like a sunburn, though blisters can develop. Wash with soap and water as soon as you think you may have been exposed—symptoms often don't show up for a day or two. Cover the area with a cool, wet cloth and try not to pop those blisters.

Giant hogweed is probably the worst of these, as it can leave scars that last for up to six years and leave the affected area with a long-term sensitivity to sunlight. The blisters are dark red and painful. If you think you've been exposed, wash with soap and cold water as soon as possible, and keep the affected area out of the sun for 48 hours. You can use a topical steroid to alleviate discomfort.

10 | BE YOUR OWN HANDYMAN

> *"Aim above morality.*
> *Be not simply good; be*
> *good for something."*

—**Henry David Thoreau**

What exactly does it mean to be "handy"? Really, it's a matter of degrees. Depending on where you live, being handy could mean knowing how to use a drill properly—or it could mean knowing how to build a wall. Both of those are skills you're going to want to know how to do. Those . . . and a lot more. You will have noticed this symbol ⊤ throughout the book directing you to this chapter to learn how to do a certain handyman skill. What's here is hopefully helpful, but in reality this is just the tip of the iceberg. You're going to have to figure out how to do *a lot* more to live independently than we could possibly cover in these pages, and at the beginning you're probably going to do it wrong.

So often, we're afraid to tackle something we don't really know how to do because we think we're going to do it wrong. And we're right—we are. But that's okay! Remember, nobody gets it right the first time. You only really know how to do something by doing it wrong and then doing it wrong again, but maybe a little bit closer to right, and then again and again—until you actually become adept at it. But that's OK—and part and parcel of living a Rugged Life.

The biggest challenge with being self-reliant is not knowing how to do something. But you get over that by doing it anyway, even if you're doing it badly. Nobody's going to yell at you. Do it badly, and then do it again.

The Basics

These are the things everyone should probably know how to do. They are your rudimentary household skills, the kind of handy you need to be even if you live in a city and your homestead is your tiny backyard.

HAMMERS AND NAILS

It might seem like all you need to do is place a nail and bang on it, and that's pretty much true, but if you go a little deeper, you'll make things a lot easier on yourself. First off, there are a lot of different kinds of hammers, and they all do different things. A claw hammer is good for most household projects—it weighs about a pound, and that claw on the back is good for pulling out nails or prying up boards. You may also want a framing hammer, which is similar but heftier, allowing you to bang in nails faster and with less effort. And, depending on what you'll be doing, you'll want a sledgehammer for demolition work and a trim hammer for smaller, more delicate projects, like hanging a picture frame.

If you think that sounds like a lot of different hammers, well, there are exponentially more nails. Hardware stores have rows of buckets full of all different kinds of nails, all with their own specific job. When you're starting a project, choose your nail first, and then choose the hammer that suits the nail.

HAMMERING THE NAIL

You have to hold a nail in place to hammer it, and of course there is the risk of smashing your finger. It just goes with the territory. If you're scared of the hammer, you're actually more likely to miss the nail and hit your finger—it's all about confidence (but not arrogance).

Hold the nail with the thumb and forefinger of your nondominant hand. Use the nail to make a little notch against the surface, which will help keep the nail in place. Try to keep the nail at a right angle to the wood.

HOT TIP You may want to drill a pilot hole partway into the wood to prevent cracking—this will also help keep the nail in place when you start hammering. This isn't necessary with plywood or medium-density fiberboard.

Next, locate the nail with your hammer using the two-tap method: one light tap to know where it is and a second, harder tap in the same place to drive the nail in. Once you've done a couple of those, the nail will be in far enough so you can let it go and carry on hammering. As you hammer it in, shift your grip so that you're holding farther back on the hammer, which will allow you to let the hammer do the work, using its weight to drive in the nail. Keep the hammer at a 90° angle to the nail head. The more you do this, the easier it gets, as muscle memory will help you know how to hammer. You'll also learn to hear when a nail has been struck wrong and is bending or going in crookedly.

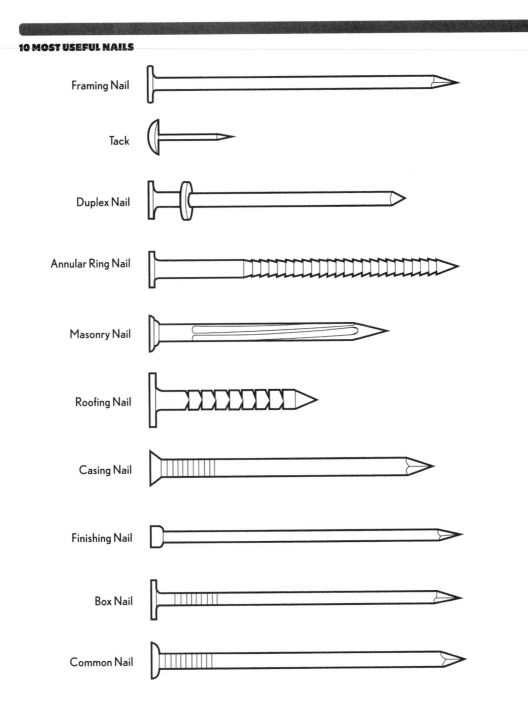

Framing Nail

Tack

Duplex Nail

Annular Ring Nail

Masonry Nail

Roofing Nail

Casing Nail

Finishing Nail

Box Nail

Common Nail

BE YOUR OWN
HANDY-MAN

HOW TO FIND A STUD

Once your wall is up and covered in dry wall, it can be hard to tell where those framing panels are—and you need to know if you're going to, say, hang a picture or secure a shelf. There are electronic stud finders that use magnets to detect nails or screws holding the supports in place, or electricity to detect the current running through the wires. But they're not incredibly reliable or consistent, and you can find a stud without them. There's the old knock-and-see-if-it-sounds-hollow test, though that's not particularly reliable, either.

But with some basic information, you can do a little math and measuring to find your stud. Baseboards are always nailed to studs, so if you can see where they're attached, you can follow the vertical line up, and then once you find one, you can measure 16 inches to the next one, and so forth across the wall (typical stud spacing is 16 inches on center, though on some older houses it may be up to 24 inches on center). Similarly, there are always studs on either side of a window, and you can work your way toward your preferred location from there. Once you've got a general sense of where the stud is, the knock test will help you be certain before you start drilling holes or hammering nails.

HOW TO FIND THE STUD

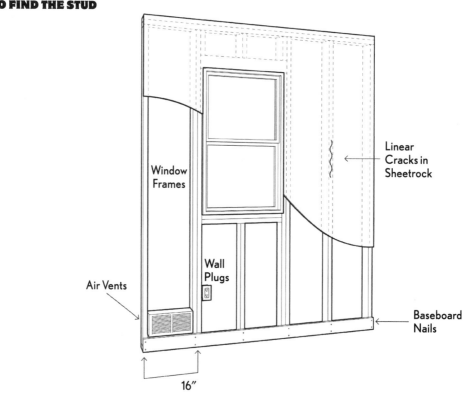

Linear Cracks in Sheetrock

Window Frames

Wall Plugs

Air Vents

Baseboard Nails

16"

DRILLING AND SCREWING

Although a screw takes longer to prep and put in, sometimes a screw works better than a nail. Screws are stronger and can hold more weight. However, if you're joining two pieces at an angle, as in when you're framing a wall, a nail works better since it has more give and will be able to sway a little with torque. So really, you need to know how to use both.

You'll need to know how to drill a hole to drive in a screw, and you can get a combo drill/screwdriver that will help you do both, saving on storage space (believe me, as you get into this, you'll just end up wanting more nifty tools, and space *will* become an issue). If you get a cordless drill, make sure you get one that is powerful enough and has a long-lasting battery. An electric drill-driver may come with a set of drill bits of various sizes (these are what you will use to drill the hole) or you can buy them separately. There are bits for drilling wood, metal, concrete—you name it. An electric drill-driver will likely also come with different kinds of screwdriver bits for different kinds of screws, including Phillips, square head, flat head, etc.

Choosing a Screw. There are just about as many types of screws as there are nails, so choosing the right screw for your project can be tricky. There are several different types of screw heads, but basically the

TYPES OF SCREW HEADS

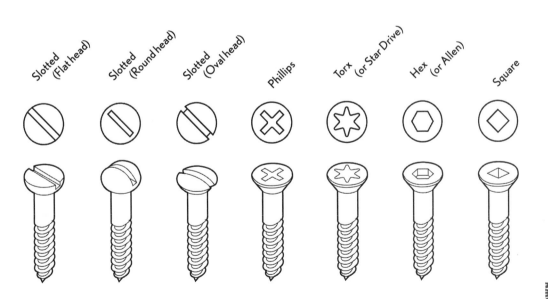

Slotted (Flat head) Slotted (Round head) Slotted (Oval head) Phillips Torx (or Star Drive) Hex (or Allen) Square

more sides or angles in the shape of the screw head, the more surface area the screwdriver has to work with—which means greater torque. You may not always need a ton of torque, but when you do, you'll want something like a Torx (or star drive) head.

Next you'll want to consider whether the screw needs to be flush with the material (countersunk) or if the head can rest above the surface. What kind of metal does the screw need to be? If it's for outdoor use, you'll probably want silicon-coated bronze or stainless steel, but you can get away with a more attractive or cheaper metal for indoor use.

Finally, there's size. For length, you want your screw to reach approximately three quarters of the way into your material, i.e., ¾ inches into a two-by-four. When it comes to diameter, the thinner the screw, the weaker it is, so for something really thick and heavy, you'll want a 12 to 14 gauge, but most of the time an 8-gauge screw will do the trick.

Unless your wood is very soft, you'll need to drill a hole for your screw before driving it in (and as mentioned above, you may need to do this for nails occasionally, as well). Your hole shouldn't go the full length of the screw, but should get it going partway so that the screw can secure itself into place.

ANATOMY OF A CORDLESS DRILL

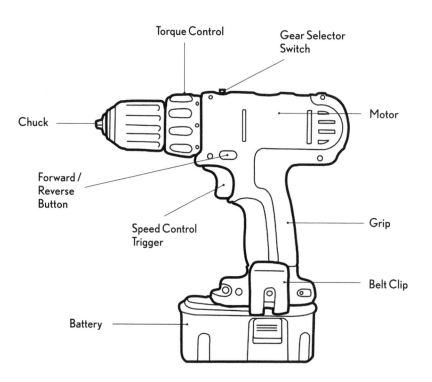

Torque Control

Gear Selector Switch

Chuck

Motor

Forward / Reverse Button

Speed Control Trigger

Grip

Belt Clip

Battery

Start by measuring the width of the piece of wood you're drilling into, to make sure your bit is long enough but not too long. Mark the spot where you want to drill, either by scratching it with the screw or using a pencil. If the wood is soft enough, you can press the screw in slightly to notch it and create a place for the drill to start, or you can create a small indentation with a hammer and nail. Fit the drill bit into the indentation, and start drilling at a low speed, increasing the speed slowly. Reduce the speed of the drill when your hole is complete, then slowly pull the bit out, then turn off the drill.

Change to the screwdriver setting, selecting the right bit for your chosen screw. Insert the screw, making sure it's resting firmly on the bit. Holding the screw gently, place it against your marked spot. Begin screwing slowly, applying force from your arms and shoulders if needed to help the bit stay in the screw head. When the screw is almost but not yet flush with the surface, ease off on your speed and finish slowly so you don't overdo it and create an indentation.

BEST PRACTICES WHEN USING A CORDLESS SCREWDRIVER OR DRILL

→ Wear the appropriate safety gear, whether that's glasses, hearing protection, etc.

→ Clamp your work in place to keep it from shifting, and put it on top of a scrap of plywood that you can drill into without damaging the bits—and you don't want to drill into your work table or any other surface you like.

→ If you need to drill a hole that's a specific depth, you can wrap your bit with painter's tape at the desired depth point on the bit. That way you'll know when to stop.

→ Always hold your drill perpendicular to your work surface to keep everything straight. You can use a square to help you stay at a 90° angle.

→ For every ¼ inch of drilling depth, back the bit out slightly from the wood to clear any debris.

→ When driving a screw into a hardwood such as oak or maple, apply a bit of finishing wax or soap to the threads to reduce friction, making it easier to drive in the screw.

HOT TIP

Magnetic screwdriver bits are a wonderful invention that will save the skin of your fingers. Instead of holding the screw as you start the screwdriver, you can simply let it be secured by the weak magnet within the bit itself.

Basic Household Electrical Work

However electricity enters your home, whether it's through the grid, through a propane tank, or through a battery charged by solar panels, it needs to enter a circuit breaker, and then the fuse box. From there, it's spread over numerous circuits, moving through breaker after breaker (those things you can shut off in the fuse box), divvying up all that electricity to keep the system from getting overloaded.

Electrical wiring comes in different gauges, and the heavier the gauge (meaning the thicker the copper wire), the more current it can carry without overheating. Electrical wire is gauged like ammunition, so the smaller the number, the heavier the gauge. There are two standard wire gauges: 12/2 and 14/2. 12/2 is rated up to a maximum of 20 amps, while 14/2 gauge electrical wire is rated to 15 amps, and shouldn't be used with a circuit breaker that's larger than those 15 amps. If you don't match them up properly, you can get a malfunction, or worse, a fire. There are some heavier gauges meant for heavier appliances, like your washer/dryer. Always consult your local and state building codes before doing any electrical work.

Before you do any electrical work, turn off the appropriate breaker. If you're not sure, or you just want to double-check (never a bad idea), you can use a volt detector, which is an inexpensive tool that indicates if there's any electricity running through the wires. No matter the gauge, standard household electrical wire actually contains three wires: black, white, and copper. The black wire is the one that carries the electrical current, and so is usually referred to as the "hot" wire. The white wire is neutral, and the copper wire is the ground. When you're joining electrical wires, strip the insulated sleeve with wire stripping pliers, then twist the black wire together with the other black wire, the white wire with the white wire, and the copper wire with the copper wire. Remember, always matchy matchy.

If you require an additional hot wire, you can purchase three-conductor wiring, which, confusingly, actually contains four wires: a copper ground wire, a white

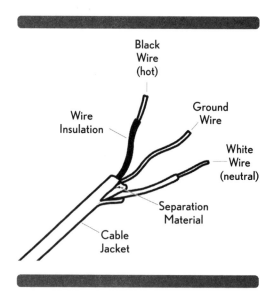

Black Wire (hot)

Ground Wire

Wire Insulation

White Wire (neutral)

Separation Material

Cable Jacket

TYPICAL WIRE CONNECTIONS

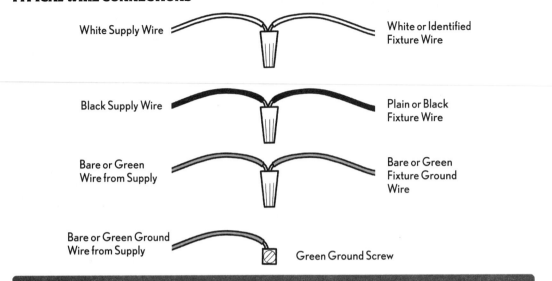

White Supply Wire — White or Identified Fixture Wire

Black Supply Wire — Plain or Black Fixture Wire

Bare or Green Wire from Supply — Bare or Green Fixture Ground Wire

Bare or Green Ground Wire from Supply — Green Ground Screw

neutral wire, a black hot wire, and a red secondary hot wire.

Wires are generally connected with wire nuts, which will match the gauge of your wire. So if you're going to wire a light fixture, join the wires of the fixture to the electrical supply wire by first stripping both wires, twisting like wires together, and then securing them in place with a wire nut. Always make sure the breaker is off when working with electricity.

If your light fixture doesn't have black or white wires, look for a rib on the wire sheathing—that will tell you which is the neutral wire.

To connect a light switch or a wall outlet, you'll be working with electrical screws. In this case, green screws represent the ground wires, silver screws are neutral wires, and brass screws are hot. A switch serves to break the current or to join it, depending on whether the switch is on or off. An outlet provides access to the

current (which is why you don't want to stick anything up in there).

To connect a switch box, route the ends of the two wires into the box, then strip them and connect the white wires together, securing them with a wire nut. Connect the copper wires to the green screw on the bottom of the switch by bending the wire into a hook shape, wrapping it around the screw. Connect each black wire to its own brass screw using the same method.

To connect a wall outlet (also known as a receptacle), you're joining up with the current running from the circuit breaker throughout the house—think of each outlet as a bulb on a string of twinkle lights. Most outlets these days have two entry points, and so are called duplex receptacles. You can add your outlet to that string by joining the white wires together, wrapping the copper wire around the green screw at the bottom, and connecting each black wire to its brass screw.

Cutting Things

A big part of building is cutting stuff up. You'll need to cut two-by-fours, plywood, maybe even planks if you're going to build a shed or a house. You'll need to cut metal for the roof or to make a smoker. And you will definitely need to be able to cut PVC.

WOOD

The first rule is this: *measure twice, cut once.* It seems simple and obvious, but the majority of rookie mistakes in carpentry come from not being careful enough when you're making your measurements. Use a straightedge to make sure you've got your lines correct, and then use a tape measure to get the length. Mark the place with a sharp-tipped pencil. The better your accuracy, the better your build. And then,

do it again. If you end up marking the same place, you're ready to cut.

A second rule is: *secure your wood.* If you've got someone to hold it in place for you, great, but best of all is to use clamps when you can. Saws make the wood wiggle around, and it's hard to cut straight if your material is moving.

If you're cutting a two-by-four or a plank, you'll want to use a circular saw. Line up the guide so that it's just outside your line, cutting a little bit larger, because the blade will take off more wood than the width of the line. If you've overestimated, you can always cut down, but you can't make the piece bigger after you've cut it. Keep your cut straight until it's finished.

HOW TO MAKE CLEAN, PRECISE CUTS

→ **Know your saw.** There are lots of different brands and styles; while the basic designs are the same, there are some small differences and you should familiarize yourself with how your saw works before you start. Typically you'll grip the tool by both its front and rear handles, using the trigger on the rear handle to control the blade.

→ **Use the correct blade for the job.** Circular saw blades come in several different sizes: 6.5-inch blades are good for nominal lumber construction, as

with plywood; 7.25-inch blades are the standard for lumber up to 2.25 inches thick. Beyond that, you're looking at 8- to 10-inch saw blades, common in industrial work.

→ **Always wear work gloves and eye protection.** If you're going to be sawing for a while, grab some earplugs or muffs, too. You will likely be inhaling some sawdust, so you may want to consider a dust mask. Make sure all clothing and hair is secure and out of the way.

ESSENTIAL WOODWORKING CUTS

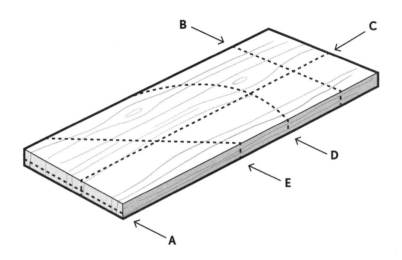

A. Resawing.
This cut moves along the edges of boards to make them thinner in width. You can use a finely tuned band saw, and then smooth the edges with a sander.

B. Crosscut.
This cut slices across the grain of the wood. For best results, use a miter saw.

C. Rip cut.
This cut follows the direction of the grain. Just about any saw will work, including a miter or table saw. Never use your hands to push the board through a table saw, unless you don't think you'll need all your fingers.

D. Curved.
Most of the time we try to cut straight, but sometimes we need to make a curve. When you're doing this, make sure to cut outside your mark—remember, you can always make it smaller. For thin wood like plywood, you can use a jigsaw; otherwise you'll want a band saw.

E. Miter.
A miter cut is anything that is at an angle other than 90°. This could mean a 45° cut to make a frame or boxes, and obviously is best done with a miter saw.

- **Measure, measure, and measure again.** Use a straightedge and a carpenter's pencil to draw a line for your blade to follow.

- **Sawhorses are useful.** Rest your material between two sawhorses, making sure it's supported and free of obstructions below. That way you won't have to worry about cutting through anything underneath.

- **Set the blade to the desired cutting depth.** Pull the shoe lever between the two handles all the way down to disengage the baseplate, then place the baseplate against your material, adjusting it until it stops just below the bottom of the material you're cutting—no more than ⅛ or ¼ inches below the bottom. Setting it too deep will make the saw work harder than it needs to, and it can be dangerous. So if you're cutting a 1-inch-thick piece of lumber, set your depth to 1.125 to 1.25 inches.

- **Getting fancy.** To make a beveled or contoured cut, twist the small knot on the front end of the saw counterclockwise to unlock the pivoting scale that sits around the blade. Slide the scale to a preset angle or to an angle of your choosing, then lock it in place.

- **Place your saw.** On the front edge of the baseplate you'll find a small notch. Position the line on the baseplate labeled "0" right over your cut line (note that this is for normal, 90° cuts. For a beveled cut at a 45° angle, for instance, you would place your saw at the line labeled "45" on the right-hand side of the notch).

- **Pull the trigger.** There may be a blade guard near the top of the saw that you'll need to flip over in order to pull the handle trigger. Once both are engaged, the blade will spin. Once it reaches full speed, begin your cut.

- **Push the saw.** Move it slowly and smoothly along the surface of the material, using both hands to keep going straight down the cut line. Don't move too quickly or jar it, as this can cause mistakes or jam the saw.

- **Keep away from the blade.** Keep your hands away from the blade whenever the saw is in operation. Don't make any adjustments without taking your finger off the trigger, and if you're not ready to cut, keep your finger away from the trigger so as to avoid starting the saw accidentally.

- **Complete the cut.** Release the trigger and wait for the blade to come to a complete stop.

- **Store your saw.** Make sure the blade guard is locked down, then unplug your saw and either store it in its case or on a flat, stable surface inaccessible to small children.

METAL

Fair warning, sawing metal makes a terrible noise. You'll probably want to wear earplugs or other protection. And there's a real risk of metal dust and fragments, so be sure to wear goggles and a dust mask, and always wear a long-sleeved shirt, long pants, and boots. Most of the time, you're going to be cutting corrugated metal for roofing, so that's what I'm going to talk about here, but the same skills are used to cut any sort of metal. The same principles apply.

Start by calculating what you need—remember, always measure first, and do so twice. How many panels do you need? How big do they need to be? Measure your roof by first calculating the external area of the building. Next, figure out the roof's pitch (slant) by climbing up on a ladder and setting your level at the edge of the roof, making sure the bubble is centered. The math here is X-in-12, so if you're using a 1-foot level, this is nice and easy. All you have to do is measure the distance between the top of the level and the roof. Say it's 3 inches—that means you have a pitch of 3-in-12. Run that through a pitch multiplier table (there are lots of websites that offer this online), and you'll get the factor you need. For 3-in-12, it would be 1.031. Multiply your area by the pitch multiplier, and you'll get a fairly accurate estimate of the square footage of your roof.

Let's say you're roofing a 12 × 12 shed. 12 × 12 × 1.031 = 148.5 square feet of roofing. Roofing materials come in panels, so if you divide this by 100, you're probably going to need 1.5 panels—so, two panels,

MEASURING ROOF PITCH

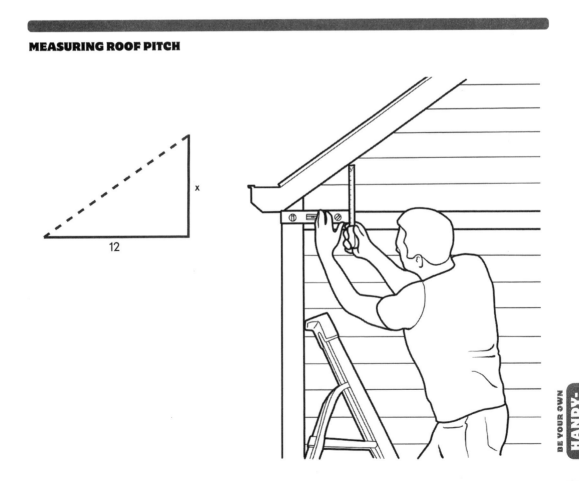

and you'll have some roofing left over. This is a good thing. You always want to order more than you'll need, in case of mistakes in either measurements or cutting—and remember, the edges need to overlap a little.

Plan out your roof—what piece will go where and how big it needs to be. If you're making something simple like a shed, this is pretty straightforward. When you're ready to cut, lay your sheet of corrugated metal on a flat surface upside down—the underside is flatter than the top edge, making it easier to cut. Look for deep valleys instead of ridges. Clamp it in place. Use a tape measure to mark where you will cut—in this case, you'll need to use a permanent marker, as pencil won't show. Use a combination square (basically a big ruler that can attach to the thing it's measuring) to help you draw a straight guideline to follow as you cut. Be as precise as possible; you don't want your roof to leak.

HOT TIP If you're just doing a small job, use tin snips, which are basically scissors for metal. It's a fast and easy method. Follow your guideline, working slowly, and wear gloves in case of jagged edges. For longer cuts, you can use power shears.

If you need to begin your cut in the middle of a solid piece of metal (say if you're making room for a chimney), make a pilot hole with a drill, using a metal-cutting drill bit. If you're starting at the end of the sheet, you're good to go without the drill. A circular saw fitted with a metal-cutting blade (i.e., steel-tooth or carbide-tooth) can slice through multiple sheets of roofing at once, so if you want to make sure they're all the same, take advantage of that. Just watch to make sure the saw blade isn't getting too hot, or it will damage the roofing. Move slowly and carefully, following your guideline.

CUTTING PIPES AND PLASTIC TUBING

As with any kind of metal cutting, there's a risk of flying fragments when cutting pipes and tubes, so be sure to wear goggles and a dust mask.

→ **Copper pipe.** Use a standard tubing cutter. Tighten the cutter so the blade just scores the pipe, then rotate the cutter around the pipe. Tighten it a little more, and go around again. Repeat until the blade severs the pipe.

→ **Steel pipe.** You'll need a steel-pipe tubing cutter, or you can use a hacksaw or reciprocating saw if you don't need quite as much precision.

→ **PVC.** Use a ratcheting PVC cutter by moving the top handle up and down until the blade slices through the pipe.

Chainsawing

If my house was on fire and I could take only one tool with me, it would be my chainsaw. (In reality, I'd let it burn, but you get what I'm saying.) These are so useful, particularly when you're out on the homestead and using the materials the land provides.

That said, they're a bit awkward to use, and if you get it wrong, you can lose a limb. So let's talk a little about how to do it right.

SAFETY FIRST

Know your chainsaw. Know its parts and controls and safety features. Wear protective clothing including long pants and long sleeves, steel-toed boots, gloves, ear protection and eye protection, and if you're really smart, chaps and a helmet.

MAINTENANCE

This isn't just to make sure your chainsaw works well—it'll also keep you safe. Always check the chain tension before use, and regularly inspect the bar and the air filter, making sure they're clean. Some chainsaws require a very specific mix of fuel, so follow the manufacturer's directions.

You'll need to sharpen your chainsaw regularly. Depending on the saw, you may need to have this done professionally, or you can buy a kit that contains a round file, a flat file, a file guide, and a depth gauge. You'll probably also need to replace the chain from time to time.

SHARPENING YOUR CHAIN

➜ Wear gloves and eye protection. This is sharp metal.

➜ Secure the saw using a vise to make sure it's held in place. Activate the brake to lock the chain.

➜ Place the file guide with the arrows pointing away from the engine. Using a round file, sharpen every other tooth at a 30-degree angle to the rollers with a pushing stroke. Repeat 20 times or so. Do this on all the teeth, on both sides of the chain, unlocking the brake and advancing the chain when necessary—but be sure to lock it again.

➜ File the depth gauges at 90 degrees using a flat file, continuing until the file contacts the depth guide.

BE YOUR OWN HANDY-MAN

HOW TO
USE A CHAINSAW

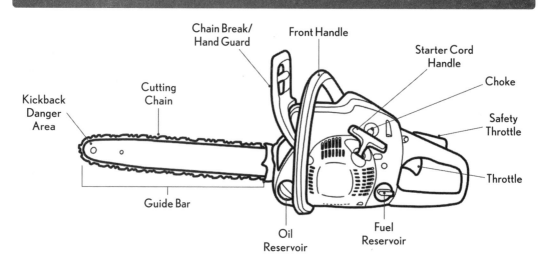

Chain Break/
Hand Guard

Front Handle

Starter Cord
Handle

Choke

Cutting
Chain

Kickback
Danger
Area

Safety
Throttle

Throttle

Guide Bar

Oil
Reservoir

Fuel
Reservoir

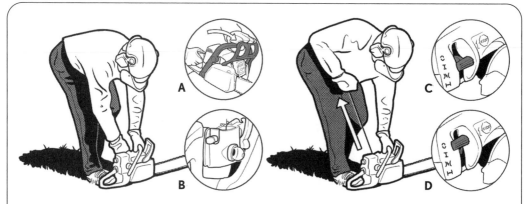

A

B

C

D

STARTING YOUR CHAINSAW

Step 1
Engage the chain brake. Place your chainsaw on flat ground and push the chain brake forward until it engages (A).

Step 2
Set the choke (C) and prime the gas engine (B). This won't be necessary if you're restarting a hot chainsaw.

Step 3
Brace the saw and pull the starter handle. Pull it a couple of times to get gas into the engine.

Step 4
Shift switch into start position (D), and pull again. This might take a couple of times, but then the chainsaw will start roaring.

MAKING A CUT

Step 1
Stand with your legs apart for stability and pull back the chain brake to disengage it. Hold the front handle with your nondominant hand and grab the rear handle with the other.

Step 2
Start your cut using the middle of the saw, away from the tip—this can cause kickback, which could engage the chain brake. Cut at waist level, and never above shoulder height. Try to stand to the side of the saw.

Step 3
Avoid cutting too close to the ground—if the blade digs in, it may kick back.

Working with Concrete

You'll need to be familiar with mixing concrete for a variety of jobs, whether that's laying fence posts, setting a foundation, or making a walkway. Concrete is reasonably easy to work with, fairly inexpensive, and incredibly durable.

MIXING CONCRETE

You can buy a big paper bag of the stuff, and the package will indicate its yield in cubic feet—and it's probably less than you'd think. If you're laying a slab, you're going to need *a lot*. You can go online and find a concrete calculator to help you determine how much you'll need.

Only mix as much as you can use in a day; otherwise it'll dry out and go to waste. (That said, if you're laying a slab, that's not something you can do in shifts, so plan your day carefully.) Cut open the bag and carefully empty what you need into a wheelbarrow. If it's windy out, you may want to do this under shelter. Using a hose or watering can, add a little water into the center of the mounded concrete mix. Add water little by little until you've reached the suggested ratio printed on the bag. Go slowly—you can always add more water if needed, but you can't take it out once it's in.

Using a shovel or garden hoe, stir up the mixture, working in a back-and-forth motion. If the mixture stiffens and crumbles, you can add a little more water, doing so until you've got a relatively smooth, moldable consistency, with no puddles.

Once your mixture is ready, leave any tools you won't be using in water to keep the concrete on them from setting—and use the concrete quickly so it doesn't set in your wheelbarrow.

HOT TIP

To check your mixture, do a "slump" test by cutting off the bottom of a paper cup and shaping it into a cone. Fill that cone with concrete, then empty it onto a flat surface. If it slumps to about half the height of the cone, it's perfect. If it doesn't slump at all, you need more water. If it slumps too far, you'll need to add more concrete mix.

LAYING A SLAB

STEP 1: The first thing you need to do is frame it out. You can use 2x4s to create the shape, hammering or screwing them into place—it's only temporary so it doesn't need to be pretty, but it does need to be measured perfectly. Set landscaping stakes at the corners.

STEP 2: Remove the frame, leaving the stakes in place, and dig it out, keeping the corners as sharp as possible. If you're not way out in the boonies, you'll want to call 811 before beginning any excavation to check for any underground utilities. Make sure your depth is at least four inches.

STEP 3: Fill the hole with a gravel base, likely in base course; otherwise, the slab will crack. Level it out as best you can, and compact it with a hand tamper. Repeat until those 4 inches are filled.

HOT TIP Check the weather forecast before laying your slab, making sure it isn't going to rain that day.

STEP 4: Now it's time to mix your concrete. Once it's ready, put the frame back in place atop the gravel and between the stakes, and hose down both the frame and your gravel bed, getting them nice and wet. Pour the mixed concrete into the frame atop the gravel.

STEP 5: Screed, or smooth, the concrete by passing a board across the surface— a 2x4 that reaches all the way across the bed will do. This will help it set flat.

STEP 6: After screeding, the concrete will begin to set and lose its sheen. Smooth it again with a concrete float, basically a flat sheet of metal with a handle. The smoother your concrete is, the better. Once you've done that, you can scrape it up just a little with a stiff, straight-edged broom to make it non-slip. Use a concrete edger (similar to a float) to finish the edges, and spray the whole thing down with concrete cure and seal. Let it cure completely according to the manufacturer's instructions, then remove the frame. It'll be dry after 48 hours or so, but it won't harden fully for about a month.

HOW TO
POUR A CONCRETE SLAB

Step 1

The first thing you need to do is frame it out. You can use 2x4s to create the shape, hammering or screwing them into place—it's only temporary so it doesn't need to be pretty, but it does need to be measured perfectly. Set landscaping stakes at the corners.

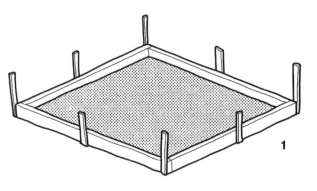

Step 2

Remove the frame, leaving the stakes in place, and dig it out, keeping the corners as sharp as possible. If you're not way out in the boonies, you'll want to call 811 before beginning any excavation to check for any underground utilities. Make your depth at least 4 inches.

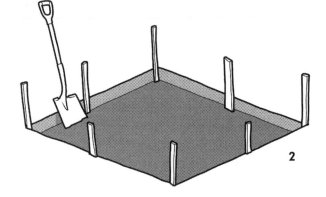

Step 3

Fill the hole with a gravel base, likely in base course; otherwise, the slab will crack. Level it out as best you can, and compact it with a hand tamper. Repeat until those 4 inches are filled.

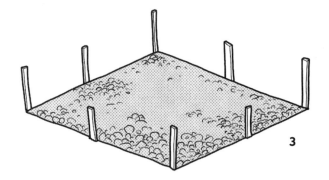

Step 4

Now it's time to mix your concrete. Once it's ready, put the frame back in place atop the gravel and between the stakes, and hose down both the frame and the gravel bed, getting them nice and wet. Pour the mixed concrete into the frame atop the gravel.

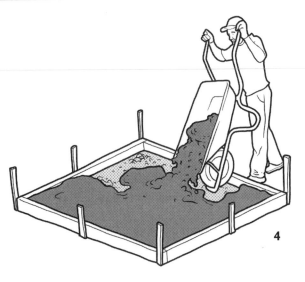

4

Step 5

Screed, or smooth, the concrete by passing a board across the surface—a 2x4 that reaches all the way across the bed will do. This will help it set flat.

5

Step 6

After screeding, the concrete will begin to set and lose its sheen. Smooth it again with a concrete float, basically a flat sheet of metal with a handle. The smoother your concrete is, the better. Once you've done that, you can scrape it up just a little with a stiff, straight-edged broom to make it non-slip. Use a concrete edger (similar to a float) to finish the edges, then spray the whole thing down with concrete cure and seal. Let it cure completely according to the manufacturer's instructions, then remove the frame. It'll be dry after 48 hours or so, but it won't harden fully for about a month.

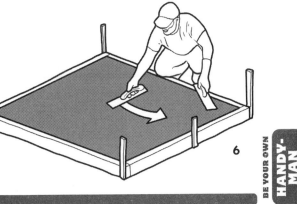

6

Fencing

A homestead is only as secure as its fence, so you need to know how to do it right. Simply stringing hog wire from metal post to metal post is not going to get it done. You can use a mixture of metal and wooden posts, but you'll want at least one big wooden post every twenty feet, with metal posts every five to six feet in between.

Knowing all that, you can figure out what materials you're going to need, including how many posts of each type, and how many yards of hog wire. If you want to keep out predators that like to dig, consider some barbed wire that you can string underground. Walk your lines and plan out exactly where your wooden posts are going to go—they will be set first.

STEP 1: Plan. Lay out your perimeter using string, extending your lines several feet at each end so they cross at the corners. The math used to square the corners is the Pythagorean theorem: measure 3 feet from the point where the lines intersect, and make a mark along a string. Measure 4 feet and place a mark along the line that runs perpendicular to the first line you marked. Measure between these two marks and adjust your place-ment until they are exactly 5 feet apart. That's a squared corner. Repeat with all four corners. Use spray paint to mark

HOT TIP You can make the corners extra sturdy by creating two H-braces at a right angle to each other, and put H-braces around each of the gates.

the location of each corner post, and spray paint to mark the place for your first perim-eter post, 8 feet away from corner posts. Carry on marking the location of each wooden post, remembering to place them no more than 20 feet apart. Install wooden posts around each planned gated entry.

STEP 2: Dig a hole for your post. If you're making a relatively small fence, you can get away with a manual post-holer, but if your property is large, you're going to want to rent an auger. Remember to call 811 to check for underground utilities. Make your hole a third as deep as the post's height, plus 6 inches for gravel. You'll want it to be wide enough to fill with concrete—the minimum recommended diameter is three times the diameter of the post. So if you've got a 4-inch diameter treated wood post, your hole will need to be 12 inches in diameter.

If you're in a cold climate, make sure to dig below the frost line.

STEP 3: Dig a trench just outside the perimeter of your planned fence. It should be about a foot deep. If you're building a large fence, you can save time and effort by renting a trencher.

STEP 4: Set your posts. Pour about 6 inches of gravel into the hole, then tamp it down—you can just ram the post down onto it a few times. Set the post upright and have one person hold it in place while

TYPICAL FENCE CONSTRUCTION

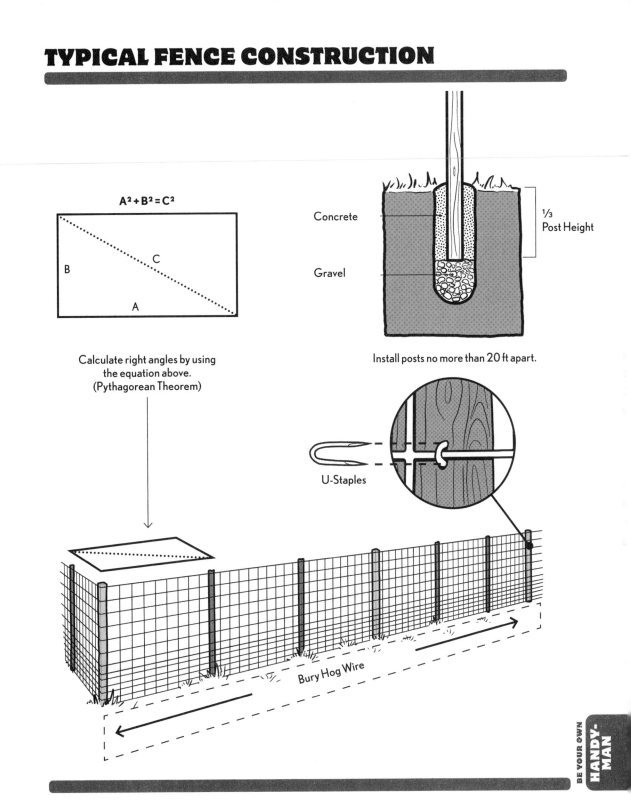

$$A^2 + B^2 = C^2$$

C

B

A

Calculate right angles by using
the equation above.
(Pythagorean Theorem)

Concrete

Gravel

1/3
Post Height

Install posts no more than 20 ft apart.

U-Staples

Bury Hog Wire

the other person sets the concrete—but don't let them lift or move the post. You can just shovel it from a wheelbarrow. Check carefully to make sure your post is level, then press concrete around the base (a stick works fine) to help it set. Repeat with all your planned wooden posts.

STEP 5: Set your metal posts. Spray paint to show where they need to go, spacing them as evenly as possible between the wooden posts. Again, the depth here should be around a third of the height of your post. It wouldn't hurt to use concrete for these, but it's not absolutely necessary—you can just dig the hole and pound them in.

STEP 6: Unwind your hog wire. Lay it level with the ground, and as you reach each post, help it reach tension by using a "come-along" winch, then use galvanized U-staples to attach it to the post. You can tie it more securely by adding galvanized fence clips. To splice in a new roll, cut the finished roll right at a post, and overlap the second roll over that same post, securing them both in place.

STEP 7: Keep out predators. Down in your trench, unroll galvanized mesh or barbed wire to keep out any predators that could dig their way in.

Operating Heavy Machinery

If you're running a large working farm, you may need to know how to operate a tractor. And if you're digging up a big hole to, say, create a root cellar or storm shelter, you'll want to know how to work a backhoe. That's probably not something you'll need to own, but renting one for a day or two is worth the money—if you know how to use it.

The first step, as with anything, is to get to know your machine. Just as you do with an unfamiliar car, walk around it, getting familiar with its layout. Where are the controls? Backhoes have both forward and rear operations, and you'll want to look at the setup before starting it up—but use your eyes, not your hands. Sometimes parts will move when you move the levers, even if the engine isn't running.

Check the safety equipment to make sure it's in good working order, including the seat belt, fire extinguisher, and roll-over protection system. Is everything in good condition? Are there any oil leaks or

ANATOMY OF A BACKHOE

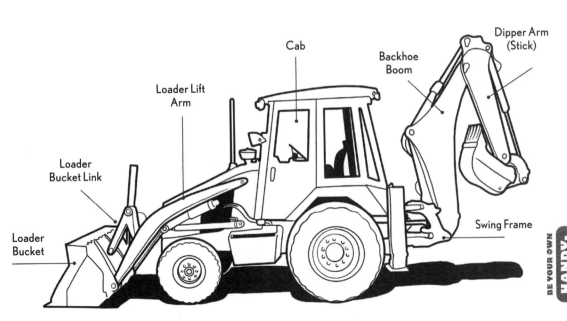

Cab

Loader Lift Arm

Loader Bucket Link

Loader Bucket

Backhoe Boom

Dipper Arm (Stick)

Swing Frame

damaged hoses? Is it fueled and oiled up? Is there sufficient hydraulic fluid?

Nobody likes doing this, but when it comes to using equipment you're not familiar with, it's a really good idea to read the operator's manual. Each backhoe has its own special procedures for how to operate the boom, and you'll want to familiarize yourself with how to work the particular model you're renting (or buying or borrowing).

→ **Forward Facing:** For driving the backhoe (steering wheel, shifter, front-loader control lever, brake pedals with independent left and right brakes, gas pedal, and control switches for lights, horn, emergency brake actuator, ignition switch, gauges).

→ **Rear Facing:** For operating the boom (three-stick that includes foot controls to swing the bucket, joysticks, and two auxiliary controls to raise and lower stabilizers).

Once you feel like you know what you're doing and you're certain the machine is safe and ready to go, turn it on. Let it run for a few minutes, warming up the hydraulic fluid and allowing it to circulate. Before putting the backhoe into motion, make sure all attachments are clear of the ground, including the stabilizers, the front bucket, and the boom. Use all controls delicately until you have a feel for them, as moving slowly is better than causing the machine to shake violently or bang into something.

Release the parking brake and shift in to forward. Drive it around for a bit to get the hang of how to steer and break. You may want to stay in low or second gear the whole time, as that'll make it easier to steer. Backhoes tend to bounce, so you want to move slowly in order to stay in control. Get a feel for how to raise and lower the front end loader bucket—in most models, you pull the control lever toward the rear to raise the bucket, and lower it by pushing the lever straight forward. Pulling the lever toward the center of the machine tells it to scoop, and pushing it outward is how you dump.

PRACTICE DIGGING

Before excavating, find a spot with plenty of clearance to practice how to operate the controls. Remember, the boom swings left to right 180° and has a reach of up to 18 feet, so you'll need a lot of space to work with.

Set the throttle to rev the engine at about 850 rotations per minute, nice and slow while you're getting the hang of it. Lower the stabilizers until they raise the rear of the tractor so that the back wheels no longer touch the ground. Don't raise it too high, though, as the lower you are, the more stability you will have. Next, lower the front bucket to its limit, raising the front wheels. Pay attention to those stabilizers—if you're on a slope, you may have to lower one stabilizer lower than the other to keep the machine level. The idea is to get the machine just a bit off its wheels, so that its weight is resting on the stabilizers and the front bucket.

Unlock the back boom by pulling toward you on the left control lever, and then once it pauses at its highest point, push it back away from you, all while holding the unlocking lever with your foot.

(Depending on your model, there may be a manual unlock lever near the seat, instead.)

After the boom is unlocked, push the left lever farther out to lower the main boom (the top part), then push outward on the right lever to extend the lower half, extending the bucket. Get the bucket in position, and then push the right control stick to open the bucket for scooping. Lower the main boom to get the bucket into the soil, then pull the right lever to drag the bucket through the soil. Roll the bucket forward by moving the right control lever to the left. With a little practice, these actions will come more smoothly and naturally.

Once you've scooped your dirt, raise the boom by pulling the left control arm, keeping the bucket upright by swinging the right control toward your left. Using your left control, swing the bucket over to where you want to dump your soil, then push the right lever to the left to open it.

BACKHOE CONTROLS

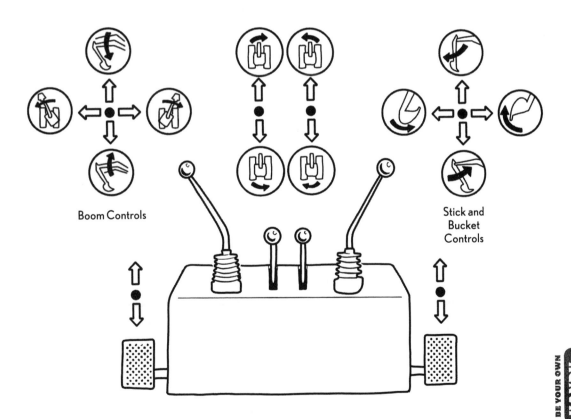

Boom Controls

Stick and Bucket Controls

TYPICAL BACKHOE USES

DIGGING

MOVING

GROUND
CLEARING

Swing the bucket back to the starting position, and repeat until you feel confident that you are digging how and where you want to. When you are finished using the backhoe, even just for a brief time, make sure the front bucket is placed firmly in the ground—you don't want to get off the machine with it up in the air. Keep the back boom in its locked position to keep it from bleeding hydraulic fluid, and set the parking brake.

AFTERWORD

BE YOUR OWN HOME-STEADER

> *"In proportion as he simplifies his life, the laws of the universe will appear less complex, and solitude will not be solitude, nor poverty poverty, nor weakness weakness. If you have built castles in the air, your work need not be lost; that is where they should be. Now put the foundations under them."*
>
> —**Henry David Thoreau**

The kind of Rugged Life you choose is entirely based on you—*you* get to make it exactly what you want it to be. That's the whole point. You can live entirely off-grid, in your own world like the Trayers. You can do it partway, like the Rapiers, whose house is off-grid, but not their barn and outbuildings. You can live like the Norrises, on the grid but almost entirely self-sustaining when it comes to your food.

Either way, it's a lifestyle choice. If all you care about is getting the cheapest egg, you're going to be better off buying a dozen at the store. It isn't less expensive to grow your own food, and it's way more work. On the other hand, eggs from your own chickens are fresher, they taste better, and they are better for you. When you grow your own food, you have much more ability to manage your diet. If you have health issues and need to stay away from certain products, like processed foods, homesteading for health is the way to go.

In the Introduction, we talked about your Why, the thing that will keep you going when shit gets hard. And it *will* get hard. It's a laborious life that requires your commitment, but it also requires your ability to keep going when things go wrong. There are going to be days when nothing goes right. Say a tree drops on your smokehouse—there's nothing you could have done to prevent it, and of course you're going to be frustrated. You've got to cut that tree away, chop it up, and rebuild your smokehouse, and there's always more to it than you think there's going to be. Life in the 9 to 5 has its hiccups, when you get a flat tire or you've got a sudden rush on a project, for instance. But hiccups in the Rugged Life are felt more deeply and require more creativity.

That said, when you fix them, there's a huge sense of satisfaction. You did that. You handled your situation.

You have to *love* this lifestyle to get through times like that. Everyone will have a different Why, and you have to find yours. Maybe it's the satisfaction you get from eating food that you raised. Maybe it's joy in the process, figuring things out, researching, planning ahead, and doing the work.

It takes a leap of faith to do this, especially if you didn't grow up this way. And it's all exciting and great in the beginning, but once that newness wears off, what's going to sustain you? It's the pride and satisfaction. *Look what I did. Look what I can do.*

You're going to work hard, but it's important to rest hard, too. Sleep with the sun, take naps when you want to—after all, you're on no one's schedule but your own. But rest also means recreation, and trust me, this is important. Boredom is destructive, and there is a certain amount of sameness in the Rugged Life. The repetitive nature of your 9 to 5 traffic-heavy commute is replaced by doing the same chores day after day. You have to find a way to make it fun, and to have fun around it.

A lot of that will depend on who is sharing this lifestyle with you. You definitely do not want to do this alone—that's a good way to go crazy. The person who is your partner in life, whether that's your wife, your sister, your boyfriend, your best friend, whatever—that's the person you need to have on board. Make sure that you are on the same page and that you feel the same level of commitment to this life.

Whoever lives on the farm with you, your partner or your kids or whoever, you are going to be together all day every day. Communication and emotional skills are going to be really important, because it's hard to get along all the time. You can love each other a lot, and you can know that you have each other, but when you're *all* the other person has, it's easy to get sick of each other. Be patient with each other, remember to let your people know how much they matter to you, and try to let the little things slide as often as you can.

It's important for everyone on your homestead to work and participate in the Rugged Life. You're a family and you should all have responsibilities—so that you're all equally invested in your life together. Even the smallest child can have a job. Every single person should have a schedule of tasks, some of which are done together as a team, and some that are done individually. This way everyone has personal and communal satisfaction, and that's what's going to keep everyone sane and healthy—not to mention happy and getting along.

And have bonfires! Campfire therapy is amazing for mental health. Just getting people together so they're hanging out and relaxing does wonders. And remember, not everything you grow needs to be for food. Stopping and smelling the roses is real. Plant flowers just because they look nice and smell nice.

You'll also want to make sure you have a trusted group of like-minded friends. Not all your friends are going to get what you're doing—some of them will, but most of us don't like change, especially when it means our pals won't be around to go out for beers when we want to. You have to prepare yourself for some changes in your friendships, as people you've been close to in your old life may no longer have as much in common with you. The good news is that those people will be replaced by fellow homesteaders who not only get it but will be able to give you the advice and support you need. It's always good to have some folks around for a barn raising, and you know you'll be able to repay the favor whenever they need it.

There's a wonderful kind of community that you can create with this lifestyle. No homesteader is an island, and some of these projects will require more hands than you possess. You don't have to do *everything* by yourself. If Joe has goats, maybe he'll trade you some milk for some eggs or some lemons. If you're slaughtering a cow, you want to get everybody over because that's a lot of meat. And parties hosted in the middle of nowhere can be as loud and raucous as you want.

This can be an incredibly satisfying, rewarding life. It's a job, but it's a job well done, with the knowledge that you did it, and that you can pass down a way of life that has just about disappeared—but that we may all need to relearn someday.

ACKNOWLEDGMENTS

Thank you for picking up this book and taking one or one thousand steps down the path of self-reliance. Be curious, be confident, and be more rugged.

I would also like to thank Melissa Norris, the Trayers, and the Rapiers for sharing their homes, lifestyle, and experience with me. All of your real-world knowledge helped shape the book into the Rugged Life philosophy.

And thank you to the entire team at Rodale Books and Penguin Random House—Matthew Benjamin, Kenny Martin, Jessica Heim, Mark McCauslin, Jan Derevjanik, Andrea Lau, Anna Bauer, Irene Ng, Jim Tierney, Odette Flemming, and Lindsey Kennedy—who edited, designed, proofread, and produced this book, and helped get the word out.

Thank you to Nikki Van De Carr for taking my words and making them way better and more poetic. And a final thank you to my illustrator, David Regone, for turning my words into fine pieces of art.

INDEX

A-frame houses, 19, 20

adobe homes, 17

aesthetics, building and, 15

allergic reactions, 222

animals, raising for food. *See also* chickens; fencing; goats; pigs; rabbits

  about: protein and, 93

  cattle, 41, 119–120

  considerations before, 94

  sheep, 41, 110

  smoking meat, 122–123

axe, using, 25

backhoe, operating, 257–261

batons, for defense, 196

batteries, 31, 38, 42–45, 81

beans, growing, 60, 62

bear spray, 196

bears, 124, 134, 190, 191, 193–194, 196

beaver, snaring, 144

beekeeping, 124–129

  about: equipment, 126; overview of, 124

  getting, feeding bees, 124

  harvesting honey, 128–129

  hives for, 124, 125–126

  minimizing bee stings, 127

  types of bees in hive, 124

beeswax candles, 184–185

blackberry, 217, 218

blackwater, 50, 51

body wash, 174

bread, wheat to, 69, 80, 82–83

bug spray, 181

building. *See also* electricity; heating home

  about: self-reliance and, 233; skill importance, 12

backhoe operation, 257–261

basics, 15–16, 234–239

by climate zone, 17–20

concrete work and, 250–253

costs of homesteading, 41

cutting things, 242–249

drilling and screwing, 237–239

factors to consider, 15–16

fences (*See* fencing)

finding studs, 236

hammers, nails/nailing, 234–235

home types and, 17–20

insulation and, 16, 17, 20

styles of homes by zone, illustrated, 19

thermal mass and, 16, 17, 20

tools needed for, 35

van dwelling and, 22–23

where to live while, 33–34

burdock, 217, 218

butchering. *See* chickens; pigs; rabbits

candles, making, 184–185

canning food, 73–78

cattle, 41, 119–120

chainsawing, 21, 27, 247–249

chanterelle mushrooms, 89

cheese (goat), making, 108–109

chicken of the woods, 89, 90

chickens, 95–103

  about: protein and, 93

  basic care, 100

  butchering, 100–103

  coops for, 96–99

  cost per each, 41

  cuts of, 103

  egg collection, 100

  egg-laying breeds, 95–96

  feeding, 99–100

  feeding family with, 121

  free range, 96–99

  roosters and, 96, 100

  smoking meat, 122–123

  turkeys and, 101

chimney, cleaning, 29

cleaning products, 181

climate. *See* zones (climate)

cob homes, 17

coconut oil, 171, 172–173

communication

  about: goals/overview/plan, 201, 202

  Ham (amateur) radio, 204–206

  must-haves, 204

  PACE backup plans, 203–209

  visual, 207–209

  zero-tech plans, 207–209

composite homes, 17–20

composting/compost tea, 57–58

composting toilets, 50–51

concrete, working, 250–253

container gardening, 56, 63

coops, chicken, 96–99

cords of wood, 25, 28

corn, growing, 62, 69

costs of homesteading, 41

coyotes, 144, 190, 193

crops. *See* growing food

cutting things, 242–249

dandelion, 217, 218

deer, field-dressing, 141–142

deer, hunting, 132–133, 139, 144–147

deer tick, 228

defending yourself, 196–201

dental floss, 174, 175

directions, finding your way, 209–211

drilling and screwing, 237–239

earthen homes, 17

earthships, 19, 20

echinacea, 217, 218

eggs

  chickens for, 95–96

  collecting, 100

  daily needs for family, 100

electricity. *See also* power

  amps, 38, 240

  basic work with, 240–241

  circuits, 37–38

  current, 37, 38, 240, 241

  explained, 37–39

  formulas, 38

  resistance, 37, 38

  resistors, 38

  terms defined, 37

  voltage, 37, 38

  wire and connections, 240–241

elk meat, 121

emergency communication, 203–209

emergency medicine, 212–231

  about: overview of, 213

  allergic reactions, 222

  animal/insect/snake bites, 227–231

  first-aid responses, 219

  gear (kits) for, 215–216

  general illness, 226

  MARCH acronym, 219, 220

  medicinal plants, 216–218

  prep (9-line), 214–215

  removing hook from skin, 163

  seasonal injuries (cold/heat), 221–222

  stabilizing/transporting, 219–220

  traumatic injuries, 223–226

fabric, mending/patching, 181–182. *See also* wool

face oil, 179–180

farming, skill importance, 12

feeding

  bees, 124

  chickens, 99–100

  family of four, 121

  goats, 106

  pigs, 116–117

  rabbits, 112

felling trees, 24–28

  chainsaw and, 21, 27, 247–249

  estimate felling zone, 26

  how to use an axe, 25

  step by step, 26–27

fencing, 124, 191–193, 254–256

fermenting, 78, 79

fire, building, 30–31

fireplaces. *See also* felling trees

  building fire in, 30–31

  cleaning chimney, 29

  maintaining, 29

  pellet stoves and, 28

  wood types to burn, 24

first aid. *See* emergency medicine

fish and fishing, 148–165

  about: research for, 148

  bait, 151–152

  casting, 153, 154–155

  cleaning fish, 159, 160

  first aid and, 163

  fly-fishing note, 151

  freshwater fish, 148–149

  hooks, 151, 152, 153, 156, 163

  how to fish, 153–158

  ice fishing, 164, 165

  knots for, 161–163

  line types/selection, 149–151

  making pole and line, 152

  net fishing, 157–158

  reeling in fish, 153

reels, 149, 150

roasting whole fish, 159

rods, 148–149, 150

saltwater fish, 149

setting drag, 153–156

smoking fish, 122–123

stocking your pond, 163–165

terminal tackle (bobbers, weights, etc.), 151

fisherman's knot, 161, 162

fist, making/striking with, 197–198

food. *See* growing food; storing food

foraging, 86–90

frostbite, 221

fun, having, 185

geothermal heat, 32–33

goats, 104–109

  about: protein and, 93

  basic care, 106

  best for milk, 104

  cheese, making, 108–109

  costs per each, 41, 104

  feeding, 106

  feeding family with, 121

  milking, 106–107

  shelters for, 104–105

  smoking meat, 122–123

graywater, 50

greenhouses, 81, 84–85

growing food. *See also* animals, raising for food; maple syrup, tapping; *specific foods/animals*

  buying farm equipment, 55

  clearing land for, 54

  compost(ing) for, 57–58

  container gardening, 56, 63

  cooperative nature of, 53–54, 264–265

  crop rotation and, 59, 87

  farming vs. gardening, 53

foraging and, 86–90
greenhouses for, 81, 84–85
manure for, 59
pest control and, 59
planting crops, 70–72
raised beds for, 60–61
seed saving, 73
soil preparation, 54, 56
3 sisters, 62
victory garden, 55
waffle gardens for, 63–64
watering and, 65
when/what to plant by zones, 60, 66–69
winter and, 81–86
guns and game. *See also* hunting
action types, 138
bullet types/sizes/
components, 136, 137, 138
guns for defense, 196
rifle parts illustrated, 137
rules for handling guns, 135
safety precautions, 134–135
sighting rifle, 138–139

hair maintenance, 168–170
hair products, 171–174
hammers and nails/nailing, 234–235
hand sanitizer, 179
hand soap, 175
hangman's knot, 161–163
health and beauty. *See also*
emergency medicine
about: overview of, 167; self-
sufficiency and, 167
hair maintenance, 168–170
menstruation supplies, 180
supplies, 171–180
toilet paper, 180
zapping a zit, 180
heating home, 24–33
about: overview of, 24
felling trees for fuel, 24–28

fireplaces for, 29–31
geothermal heat, 32–33
heatstroke, 221–222
herbs, growing, 60
hives. *See* beekeeping
honey, harvesting, 128–129. *See
also* beekeeping
hoop coops, 96, 98
household products, 181–185
hunting, 131–147. *See also* fish
and fishing; guns and game
about: overview of, 131; skill
importance, 12
attire for, 139
cameras helping with, 132, 133
checklist, 140
field-dressing your game
(and deer example),
141–142
finding game, 132–133
old-school style, 133
safety precautions, 134–135
shot placement for kill, 139,
141
snares for, 143–144
tanning hides, 144–147
tree stand for, 133, 194
weight classes of game, 134,
136
where to go, 131–132
hypothermia, 221

ice fishing, 164, 165
injury. *See* emergency medicine
insects/spiders, 227–228. *See
also* bug spray
insulation, 16, 17, 20

knots, common, 161–163
kubotans, 196, 199

land, clearing, 54
land, costs, 41

lard, making soap from,
178–179
lion's mane mushrooms, 89, 90
lip balm, 174
livestock, 41. *See also* animals,
raising for food; *specific
animals*
lonzino, curing pork and,
118–119
lost, finding your way, 209–211

manure, 59
maple syrup, tapping, 90–91
medicinal plants, 216–218. *See
also* emergency medicine
menstruation supplies, 180
metal, cutting, 244–246
microhydro electricity, 45–47
milking goats, 106–107
mobile coops, 96
moisturizer, 179
mushrooms, 89–90

net fishing, 157–158
nightstand, tactical, 197
Norrises' story, 10, 77, 95, 101,
119, 263

oil, face, 179–180
oils, hair, 171–174
outbuilding, costs, 41
oyster mushrooms, 89–90

PACE communication, 203–209
Palomar knot, 161, 162
pellet stoves, 28
pest control, 59
pickling and fermenting, 75,
78, 79
pigs, 116–119
about: overview of, 116;
protein and, 93
basic care, 117–118
breeding, 117

pigs (*continued*)
  butchering, 118
  cost per each, 41
  curing meat and lonzino
    recipe, 118–119
  cuts of pork, 118
  dealing with hogs, 117
  feeding, 116–117
  feeding family with, 121
  making soap from lard,
    178–179
  shelter for, 116
  smoking meat, 122–123
  starter breeds, 116
  using meat from, 118–119
pipes, cutting, 246
plantain, 217, 218
plants, medicinal, 216–218. *See
    also* emergency medicine
plants, poisonous, 230, 231
poison test, 88
poisonous bites/plants, 227–231
poisons, 225–226
pomade, 171–174
porcini mushrooms, 89, 90
potatoes, growing, 60
power. *See also* electricity
  about: off-grid options
    overview, 37; propane
    and, 37
  costs of homesteading and, 41
  heaviest demands on, 40
  microhydro, 45–47
  needs, determining, 40–41
  options for, 42–47
  reducing requirements, 40–41
  solar, 42–45
  spring box for, 46, 47, 49
  wind, 45
propane power, about, 37
protection/security, 186–199
  about: 5 D's for, 190
  alarm options, 193, 194, 195
  defending yourself, 196–201

delaying intruders, 194–195
denying access, 194–195
detecting threats, 193–194
deterring threats, 190–193
dogs/other animals for, 193
fencing, 124, 191–193,
    254–256
gates/entrances and, 194–195
knowing your land, 187–188
natural disasters, 188–189
predator protection/defense,
    190–199
security cameras and, 191,
    193
sheltering in place, 189
tree stand for, 194
protein, 93, 94
puffballs, giant, 89

rabbits, 111–115
  about: protein and, 93;
    usefulness of, 111
  basic care, 113
  breeding, 113
  butchering, 113–115
  cost per each, 41
  feeding, 112
  feeding family of four with,
    121
  hutches/areas for, 111–112
  meat rabbit breeds, 111
radios, shortwave, 204–206
raised beds, 60–61
rammed earth homes, 17
Rapala knot, 161, 162
Rapiers' story, 10, 40, 41, 93, 96,
    104, 107, 110, 116, 119, 263
razor, shaving with, 176–177
roofing calculations, 245–246
root cellar, 34, 73, 74, 190
rotating crops, 59, 87
Rugged Life
  about: this book and, 9–10
  basic skills, 12

choosing your adventure, 13
deciding what you are ready
    for, 10–11
questions to answer, 11
self-sufficiency and, 9, 13, 167
your choice, 263–265

sanitizer, 179
screwing, drilling and, 237–239
seeds, planting, etc., 70–71, 72
self-sufficiency, 9, 13, 167
septic systems, 51
shampoo, 171
shaving soap, 174
shaving with straight razor,
    176–177
sheep, 41, 110. *See also* smoking
    meat
sheltering in place, 189
shipping container, building
    with, 33, 34
smartphone, 204
smoking meat, 122–123
snakes, poisonous, 228–229
snares, 143–144
soaps, 174–175, 178–179
soil. *See* composting; growing
    food
solar power, 42–45
soy milk, making, 94
spider bites, 227
spring box, 46, 47, 49
stars, finding your way, 210
stinging nettle, 217, 218
storing food, 73–79
  after butchering, 101
  canning and, 73–78
  chest freezer for, 101
  freeze-drying and, 78
  pickling and fermenting, 75,
    78, 79
  root cellar for, 34, 73, 74, 190
straw homes, 17
streams, power from, 45–47

studs, finding, 236
sunburn, severe, 222
surgeon's loop knot, 162, 163

tanning hides, 144–147
tea, compost, 57–58
thermal batteries, 33, 81
thermal mass, 16, 17, 20
tick bites, 227–228
time, telling, 211
tofu, making, 94
toilets, composting, 50–51
tomatoes, growing, 62, 63, 69
toolbox essentials, 35. *See also specific tools*
toothbrush and floss, 174, 175
toothpaste, 174
traps and snares, 143–144
Trayers' story, 10, 20, 21, 40, 47, 51, 139
tree stand, 133, 194
trees. *See* felling trees; wood
turkeys, 101. *See also* chickens

van dwelling, 22–23
vegetarians, protein for, 94

waffle gardens, 63–64
waste systems, 50–51
water
    blackwater, 50, 51
    calculating needs, 48
    catchment systems, 48–49
    for chickens, 99–100
    composting toilets, 50–51
    filtration, 49–50
    finding, 211
    for gardens, 65
    graywater, 50
    microhydro electricity with, 45–47
    river/spring sources, 49
    septic systems, 51
    source redundancy, 48
    waste systems, 50–51
    wells, 49
weather, predicting, 211

wheat to bread, 69, 80, 82–83
willow, 217, 218
wind power, 45
wood. *See also* felling trees
    chopping and storing, 25, 27, 28
    clearing trees for, 54
    cords of, 25, 28
    cutting, 242–244, 247–249
    cutting planks from trees, 21
    living fences and, 191–193
    pellets, stoves burning, 28
wool, making yarn from, 182–184
wool, sheep and, 110

yarrow, 217, 218
yurts, 19, 20

zits, zapping, 180
zones (climate), 16, 17–20, 66–69

About
the Author

CLINT EMERSON is a retired Navy SEAL with twenty years of service with the Special Operations community. He served as a SEAL operator at SEAL Team Three, the NSA, and SEAL Team Six. He is the founder of Escape the Wolf, which focuses on crisis management for global companies both large and small. He's the bestselling author of the 100 Deadly Skills series. For more about Clint, visit clintemerson.com.